SACRED TEXTS, MODERN QUESTIONS:

Connecting Ethics and History Through a Jewish Lens

FACING
HISTORY
AND
OURSELVES

A FACING HISTORY AND OURSELVES PUBLICATION

Facing History and Ourselves is an international educational and professional development organization whose mission is to engage students of diverse backgrounds in an examination of racism, prejudice, and antisemitism in order to promote the development of a more humane and informed citizenry. By studying the historical development of the Holocaust and other examples of genocide, students make the essential connection between history and the moral choices they confront in their own lives. For more information about Facing History and Ourselves, please visit our website at *www.facinghistory.org*.

Cover art credit: *A Tree of Learning* by Samuel Bak.
Image courtesy of Pucker Gallery, *www.puckergallery.com*.

For more information about this resource,
visit *www.facinghistory.org/sacredtexts*.

ISBN-13: 978-0-9837870-6-8
ISBN-10: 0983787069

FACING
HISTORY
AND
OURSELVES

Facing History and Ourselves Headquarters
16 Hurd Road
Brookline, MA 02445-6919

ABOUT FACING HISTORY AND OURSELVES

Facing History and Ourselves is a nonprofit educational organization whose mission is to engage students of diverse backgrounds in an examination of racism, prejudice, and antisemitism in order to promote a more humane and informed citizenry. As the name Facing History and Ourselves implies, the organization helps teachers and their students make the essential connections between history and the moral choices they confront in their own lives. The organization offers a framework and a vocabulary for analyzing the meaning and responsibilities of citizenship and the tools to recognize bigotry and indifference in the world today. Through a rigorous examination of the failure of democracy in Germany during the 1920s and '30s and the steps leading to the Holocaust, along with other examples of hatred, collective violence, and genocide in the past century, Facing History and Ourselves provides educators with tools for teaching history and ethics, and for helping their students learn to combat prejudice with compassion, indifference with participation, myth and misinformation with knowledge.

Believing that no classroom exists in isolation, Facing History and Ourselves offers programs and materials to a broad audience of students, parents, teachers, civic leaders, and all of those who play a role in the education of young people. Through significant higher education partnerships, Facing History and Ourselves also reaches and impacts teachers before they enter their classrooms.

By studying the choices that led to critical episodes in history, students learn how issues of identity and membership, ethics and judgment have meaning today and in the future. Facing History and Ourselves' resource books provide a meticulously researched yet flexible structure for examining complex events and ideas. Educators can select appropriate readings and draw on additional resources available online or from our comprehensive lending library.

Our primary resource book, *Facing History and Ourselves: Holocaust and Human Behavior,* follows a sequence of study that begins with identity—first individual identity and then group and national identities, with their definitions of membership. From there the program examines the failure of democracy in Germany and the steps leading to the Holocaust—the most documented case of twentieth-century indifference, de-humanization, hatred, racism, antisemitism, and mass murder. The program also explores difficult questions of judgment, memory, and legacy, and the necessity for responsible participation to prevent injustice. Facing History and Ourselves then returns to the theme of civic participation to examine stories of individuals, groups, and nations who have worked to build just and inclusive communities and whose stories illuminate the courage, compassion, and political will that are needed to protect democracy today and in generations to come.

Facing History and Ourselves has offices or resource centers in the United States, Canada, and the United Kingdom as well as in-depth partnerships in Rwanda, South Africa, and Northern Ireland. Facing History and Ourselves' outreach is global, with educators trained in more than 80 countries and delivery of our resources through a website accessed worldwide with online content delivery, a program for international fellows, and a set of NGO partnerships. By convening conferences of scholars, theologians, educators, and journalists, Facing History and Ourselves' materials are kept timely, relevant, and responsive to salient issues of global citizenship in the twenty-first century.

For more than 35 years, Facing History and Ourselves has challenged students and educators to connect the complexities of the past to the moral and ethical issues of today. They explore democratic values and consider what it means to exercise one's rights and responsibilities in the service of a more humane and compassionate world. They become aware that "little things are big"—seemingly minor decisions can have a major impact and change the course of history.

For more about Facing History and Ourselves, visit our website at *www.facinghistory.org*.

ACKNOWLEDGMENTS

Facing History and Ourselves is grateful to all those who supported and nourished *Sacred Texts, Modern Questions: Connecting Ethics and History Through a Jewish Lens*. The organization appreciates the extraordinary assistance it received from the Covenant Foundation. Its trust in our work and its valued advice throughout the writing and editing process have been remarkable. Facing History also wishes to thank the Conference on Jewish Material Claims Against Germany for its continued support and its important contribution to the funding of this project.

Sacred Texts, Modern Questions is the work of the Facing History staff, many of whom served as writers, readers, and editors under the leadership of Margot Stern Strom and Marc Skvirsky. A very special thank-you goes to Jan Darsa, whose vision inspired the creation of this resource. Shira Deener played an crucial role as a team member and believed in this project's potential, and Phyllis Goldstein's talent as a writer and researcher made the final product possible. Facing History also values the suggestions, criticisms, concerns, and guidance provided by Beth Cohen, Amanda Hadad, Doc Miller, Leora Schaefer, Marty Sleeper, Adam Strom, Gabrielle Thal-Pruzan, and Tzipora Weinberg. Their efforts enriched the final product in many ways. In addition, this resource has benefited from the management and production support provided by Anika Bachhuber, Nancy Englander, Victoria Frothingham, Brooke Harvey, April Lambert, Catherine O'Keefe, and Chris Stokes. Anne Burt, Dan Merrick, Liz Kelleher, Julia Rappaport, and Emily Blackie contributed their talents by spreading the word about this invaluable resource.

Much appreciation also goes to Rabbi Geoff Mitelman, whose ideas sparked the initial stages of *Sacred Texts, Modern Questions*; Felisa Tibbitts, who worked on the evaluation; Michelle Kwitkin-Close, who served as copyeditor; Celene Clark, who designed the materials; and Joni Sue Blinderman, who shared her wisdom and offered her guidance. Facing History is also grateful to the teachers who piloted lessons and offered valuable suggestions—particularly to Dr. Jack Lipinsky, who worked closely with the Facing History team in creating and testing lessons.

And last but by no means least, Facing History and Ourselves would like to express its gratitude to Samuel Bak for the thought-provoking paintings that appear in this resource, to Bernie Pucker for his help in selecting and interpreting those paintings, and to both of them for allowing us to include these incredible works in *Sacred Texts, Modern Questions*.

TABLE OF CONTENTS

INTRODUCTION

By Jan Darsa, Director of Jewish Education, Facing History and Ourselves

"In no other course was my daughter exposed to real dilemmas as complex and challenging. In no other course has she been inspired to use the whole of her spiritual, moral, and intellectual resources to solve a problem. In no other course has she been so sure that the task mattered seriously for her development as a responsible person."

—The parent of a student in a Facing History and Ourselves course

The parent's comments reveal the power of the Facing History and Ourselves program. That power comes from the ways we link history to the moral questions of our time. These comments also reveal why many teachers in Jewish educational settings have long been attracted to Facing History. In no other course have their students been so inspired to connect their Judaic studies not only to our collective history but also to the choices they face in the world today.

Over the years, Facing History has supported those teachers in a variety of ways. In 1990, we established the Jewish Education Program to provide them with professional development that uses Facing History's content and methodology to enrich their teaching. In 1998, we published *Facing History and Ourselves: The Jews of Poland*—our first resource specifically designed for Jewish educational settings. *Sacred Texts, Modern Questions: Connecting Ethics and History Through a Jewish Lens* is our latest endeavor and the first to integrate the resources of Facing History and Ourselves with biblical, rabbinic, and contemporary Jewish texts. This new resource links selected sacred texts to both historic and current events.

Sacred Texts, Modern Questions is divided into five units, each with suggested readings and activities that align Jewish texts with the major themes of a Facing History and Ourselves course. These lessons

provide opportunities for teachers of both Judaic and general studies to integrate learning and encourage interdisciplinary conversations. These lessons can be used independently or in conjunction with a Facing History course based on *Holocaust and Human Behavior* or *The Jews of Poland*.

Every unit in *Sacred Texts, Modern Questions* focuses on a key Facing History concept or set of related concepts. Unit 1 examines the relationship between the individual and society. It offers responses to questions of "Who am I?" and "What does it mean to be a Jew in today's world?" Those questions are explored through readings, discussions, and other activities. Students will deepen and reinforce their understanding of these crucial questions in later units.

Unit 2 introduces the concept of membership by examining two related ideas: *areyvut* (personal responsibility for another) and *universe of obligation* (the circle of individuals and groups for whom a society has obligations, for whom its rules apply, and in whose name justice is sought). Both concepts are explored through biblical texts, scholarly interpretations, and an examination of the laws and key events in Germany's treatment of Jews over a period of 900 years.

Unit 3 builds on the concept of *areyvut* and universe of obligation by examining the consequences of the ways individuals define their obligations to one another in Pharaoh's Egypt and Hitler's Europe. The unit focuses on issues of conscience and courage by asking students to consider such questions as: How do we decide when to obey an unjust law and when to resist? How can we stand up to powerful authorities when we believe that what is being asked of us is wrong?

Unit 4 examines the way Jews in two cities—Warsaw and Kovno—responded in religious terms to the Holocaust as it unfolded. The lessons consider complicated questions of faith and moral courage. They also reveal why many of the choices open to Jews and other victims of the Nazis are known as "choice-less choices"—decisions made in the absence of meaningful alternatives. And some of the lessons examine the determination of Jews in both cities to document the injustices they experienced in the hope that publicizing those crimes would eventually result in some measure of justice.

In Unit 5, students return to questions of identity and membership in the context of the history of the events that led to the Holocaust. Their reflections focus on the power of memory not only to shape choices today but also to repair and build a better world.

Reflection is important to the success of Facing History and Ourselves in the classroom. As one teacher recently noted, "Students are encouraged to be mindful, to reflect, and to gain a deeper appreciation of the life in us and in others. And in doing all of this, Facing History and Ourselves empowers students to act, to see how each of us can make a difference to help create a more just, more compassionate society." Those goals are reflected in every aspect of this resource. Every lesson contains Activity Ideas (suggested teaching strategies). The first is always "Getting Started"—an activity that introduces key ideas by relating them to previous learning, the world today, or the student's own life. The final activity in every lesson is a strategy for assessment. This approach to learning is in keeping with traditional Jewish education. Many Jewish

schools encourage *chavruta* learning—that is, a one-on-one ongoing discussion between two students. Together they thoughtfully read a particular text, reflect on its meaning, and explore the broader questions that it raises. Partners do not have to agree on an interpretation, but they do have to listen to one another's ideas with respect and challenge one another's thinking. It is a style of learning that engages both "head and heart." It also gives every student a voice and an opportunity to be heard.

Like all Facing History resources, *Sacred Texts, Modern Questions* has been piloted by many teachers in our network. Their comments, suggestions, and additions have been extremely helpful in revising and expanding the resource. Some of these teachers have not only incorporated the lessons into their own classrooms but also added to them or created new ones based on their curriculum. It is a process we value and encourage.

Our hope is that many more teachers will use this important resource in their classrooms. We believe it is more than a valuable way of examining the past; it is also a way of building the skills and instilling the values students need in order to play a positive role in the present and future. It is a process that honors both students and teachers. In that spirit, I would like to pay special tribute to my own teacher, Nechama Leibowitz—may her memory be blessed (ז״ל). She enhanced my love of Torah, and her teachings deepened my understanding of how the universal messages in sacred texts relate to our history and to our lives today.

Identity from a Jewish Perspective

Teaching Focus

Facing History and Ourselves journeys almost always begin with an exploration of identity. Such an examination has great meaning for adolescents at a time when many of them are just beginning to establish their own unique sense of self. The three lessons in Unit 1 consider how a Jewish identity shapes the way we see ourselves as well as the ways we are perceived by others. Like many other parts of this resource, Unit 1 contains a biblical passage that illuminates a key concept—in this case, identity.

Lesson 1: Who Am I? A Biblical Echo of a Modern Question
Lesson 2: What Does It Mean to Be a Jew in Today's World?
Lesson 3: "Us" and "Them"

Essential Questions

- What does it mean to have a Jewish identity?
- How does being a Jew affect other parts of our identity?
- How does a Jewish identity shape the way we see ourselves and others?
- How does a Jewish identity influence the choices we make?

Student Outcomes

Students will . . .

- build an understanding of the complexities of a Jewish identity.
- recognize the ways that a Jewish identity influences perception of oneself and others.
- examine the relationship between the way we define ourselves and the ways that we are defined by others.
- develop strategies for interpreting texts.
- create a working knowledge and understanding of such key concepts as *identity* and *stereotyping*.
- defend their own point of view.

These lessons may be used to extend, reinforce, and enhance concepts developed in:

- Chapter 1 in *Facing History and Ourselves: Holocaust and Human Behavior*
- Chapter 1 in *Facing History and Ourselves: The Jews of Poland*

Who Am I? A Biblical Echo of a Modern Question

Until modern times, few Jews experienced identity conflicts or crises. Historian Michael Meyer explains, "Parents implanted in children the same values that they had absorbed in growing up, values sanctioned by a spiritually self-sufficient Jewish society. Continuity prevailed across the generations." Meyer goes on to note that within the Jewish community, "clear models of Jewish identity were instilled in the home, in the school, in the community. There were no significant discontinuities, no occasions for severe crises of identity."[1]

Life, however, does not always go as expected, now or then. And a number of scholars have pointed out that some Jews did experience identity crises well before modern times. Britain's chief rabbi, Jonathan Sacks, reminds us that by upbringing, Moses was an Egyptian, and yet by birth he was a an Israelite (in today's world, he would be considered a Jew.) This resulted in certain doubts that Moses had about his personal identity.

In this lesson, students analyze Exodus 3, which biblical scholar James L. Kugel describes as an incident that took Moses from "ordinary reality" to "the midst of the extraordinary"—his first encounter with God. They will then consider the impact of that encounter on Moses's identity. They will also read two interpretations of that event, one by Kugel and the other by Rabbi Jonathan Sacks.

Essential Questions
- How did Moses answer the question, "Who am I?"
- What were the consequences of his response?

Recommended Resources
- Reading 1.1: Exodus 3
- Reading 1.2: A Commentary by James L. Kugel
- Reading 1.3: A Commentary by Jonathan Sacks

---

1   Michael A. Meyer, *Jewish Identity in the Modern World* (Seattle: University of Washington Press, 1990), 6.

Activity Ideas

For more information on specific teaching strategies that relate to activities included in this lesson, see the Appendix.

GETTING STARTED

We have all been asked at one time or another to introduce ourselves. In doing so, we often try to distinguish ourselves from others. Ask students how they would introduce themselves to a stranger. How does the situation in which the meeting takes place affect what you reveal to someone new? For example, how would you introduce yourself to a new classmate? How would you introduce yourself to members of a group you've recently joined? What might they learn about you from the way you look or dress? How do you feel when you meet someone new? Are you excited? Eager to get acquainted? Anxious?

Explain that in this lesson, students will be reading the biblical description of Moses's first encounter with God. It was an encounter, as James Kugel points out in Reading 1.2, that "in a twinkling" took Moses from "ordinary reality" to "the midst of the extraordinary."

CREATING A TIMELINE

Before students read Exodus 3 (Reading 1.1), ask them to list what they know about Moses and his life and how they acquired this information. Post their ideas on the board or have students list them in their journals. To help organize their thinking, create a rough timeline beginning with the birth of Moses and ending with his death. As students read the chapter, have them add key events or decisions to that timeline. Ask students: What makes an event "key"? What are the key events in your life?

ANALYZING A BIBLICAL TEXT

Ask students to do a close reading of the entire chapter or a particular passage in the chapter. Explain that when we do a close reading, we study the text in fine detail, as if with a magnifying glass. In a close read, the reader pays attention to *exactly* what is said and how it is said. The reader also takes note of patterns by looking for words or phrases that are repeated, seem to contradict one another, or are similar to other words, ideas, or events. To model a close reading:

- Invite one or more volunteers to read the chapter or passage aloud from start to finish without discussion (or you may want to read it yourself).
- Next, have students reread the text silently, looking for words or phrases that seem important or raise questions about meaning. They might also look for anything that seems to be missing or out of place. Have students record those words, phrases, and questions on sticky notes attached to the text or in their journals.
- Ask students to sum up the plain meaning of the passage in their own words without trying to interpret what they have read.

Once students have completed their close reading of the text, ask them to interpret the passage. What is the main idea of this chapter? For example, if you were to write a title for the passage, what would you call it? Where does this story fit into our timeline of Moses's life? How do the things you already knew about Moses help you understand why he responded to God the way he did? The following questions can be used individually or as a whole to prompt reflection on the passage. Ask students to record their answers in their journals.

- How does Moses see himself at the beginning of this chapter—as an Israelite, an Egyptian, or a Midianite? How does he see himself by the end of the chapter?
- How does God seem to regard Moses? Why do you think God is described to Moses as "the God of your father, the God of Abraham, the God of Isaac, and the God of Jacob"?
- Rabbi Sacks hears a biblical echo of the modern question "Who am I?" in the chapter we read. If you agree, what can we learn from that echo? If you disagree, what do you think is the moral or lesson of the story?

ANALYZING INTERPRETATIONS

Continue the discussion of Exodus 3 by assigning Reading 1.2 and/or Reading 1.3. You may wish to have students work with the text *b'chavruta*—in partnership with another student (or students). Students working *b'chavruta* should be expected to do more than just listen to one another's ideas. They should challenge one another to analyze and explain the passage, point out errors in reasoning, and question ideas. (See "Introduction.") The two might then share what they learned and discuss similarities and differences between their own interpretations and those of James Kugel and Jonathan Sacks.

EXPLORING IDENTITY CHARTS

If students have created identity charts as part of a Facing History and Ourselves unit, you may want to ask them to apply that strategy to this lesson. If they have not yet been introduced to that idea, you may wish to use the IDENTITY CHARTS teaching strategy to explain the process. Then have students create an identity chart for Moses. What seem to be the most important aspects of his identity? How does he see himself? How do others see him? What parts of his identity seem to conflict with one another? How is his dilemma resolved?

As a follow-up to this activity, ask students to think about their own identity: Are there times when various parts of your identity seem to clash? How have you dealt with the dilemma?

ASSESSMENT

Have students use the readings, their notes, and their discussions with their partner and the class as a whole to write an essay in which they interpret Exodus 3. Those essays should reflect their understanding of what the passage is about as well as the insights provided by the two scholars. Look for the use of evidence and reason or logic in support of the opinions expressed in each essay.

3 Now Moses, tending the flock of his father-in-law Jethro, the priest of Midian, drove the flock into the wilderness, and came to Horeb, the mountain of God. 2An angel of the LORD appeared to him in a blazing fire out of a bush. He gazed, and there was a bush all aflame, yet the bush was not consumed. 3Moses said, "I must turn aside to look at this marvelous sight; why doesn't the bush burn up?" 4When the LORD saw that he had turned aside to look, God called to him out of the bush: "Moses! Moses!" He answered, "Here I am." 5And He said, "Do not come closer. Remove your sandals from your feet, for the place on which you stand is holy ground. 6I am," He said, "the God of your father, the God of Abraham, the God of Isaac, and the God of Jacob." And Moses hid his face, for he was afraid to look at God.

7And the LORD continued, "I have marked well the plight of My people in Egypt and have heeded their outcry because of their taskmasters; yes, I am mindful of their sufferings. 8I have come down to rescue them from the Egyptians and to bring them out of that land to a good and spacious land, a land flowing with milk and honey, the region of the Canaanites, the Hittites, the Amorites, the Perizzites, the Hivites, and the Jebusites. 9Now the cry of the Israelites has reached Me; moreover, I have seen how the Egyptians oppress them. 10Come, therefore, I will send you to Pharaoh, and you shall free My people, the Israelites, from Egypt."

11But Moses said to God, "Who am I that I should go to Pharaoh and free the Israelites from Egypt?" 12And He said, "I will be with you; that shall be your sign that it was I who sent you. And when you have freed the people from Egypt, you shall worship God at this mountain."

13Moses said to God, "When I come to the Israelites and say to them, 'The God of your fathers has sent me to you,' and they ask me, 'What is His name?' what shall I say to them?"

רביעי **ג** וּמֹשֶׁה הָיָה רֹעֶה אֶת־צֹאן יִתְרוֹ חֹתְנוֹ כֹּהֵן מִדְיָן וַיִּנְהַג אֶת־הַצֹּאן אַחַר הַמִּדְבָּר וַיָּבֹא אֶל־הַר הָאֱלֹהִים חֹרֵבָה: 2וַיֵּרָא מַלְאַךְ יְהוָֹה אֵלָיו בְּלַבַּת־אֵשׁ מִתּוֹךְ הַסְּנֶה וַיַּרְא וְהִנֵּה הַסְּנֶה בֹּעֵר בָּאֵשׁ וְהַסְּנֶה אֵינֶנּוּ אֻכָּל: 3וַיֹּאמֶר מֹשֶׁה אָסֻרָה־נָּא וְאֶרְאֶה אֶת־הַמַּרְאֶה הַגָּדֹל הַזֶּה מַדּוּעַ לֹא־יִבְעַר הַסְּנֶה: 4וַיַּרְא יְהוָֹה כִּי סָר לִרְאוֹת וַיִּקְרָא אֵלָיו אֱלֹהִים מִתּוֹךְ הַסְּנֶה וַיֹּאמֶר מֹשֶׁה מֹשֶׁה וַיֹּאמֶר הִנֵּנִי: 5וַיֹּאמֶר אַל־תִּקְרַב הֲלֹם שַׁל־נְעָלֶיךָ מֵעַל רַגְלֶיךָ כִּי הַמָּקוֹם אֲשֶׁר אַתָּה עוֹמֵד עָלָיו אַדְמַת־קֹדֶשׁ הוּא: 6וַיֹּאמֶר אָנֹכִי אֱלֹהֵי אָבִיךָ אֱלֹהֵי אַבְרָהָם אֱלֹהֵי יִצְחָק וֵאלֹהֵי יַעֲקֹב וַיַּסְתֵּר מֹשֶׁה פָּנָיו כִּי יָרֵא מֵהַבִּיט אֶל־הָאֱלֹהִים: 7וַיֹּאמֶר יְהוָֹה רָאֹה רָאִיתִי אֶת־עֳנִי עַמִּי אֲשֶׁר בְּמִצְרָיִם וְאֶת־צַעֲקָתָם שָׁמַעְתִּי מִפְּנֵי נֹגְשָׂיו כִּי יָדַעְתִּי אֶת־מַכְאֹבָיו: 8וָאֵרֵד לְהַצִּילוֹ | מִיַּד מִצְרַיִם וּלְהַעֲלֹתוֹ מִן־הָאָרֶץ הַהִוא אֶל־אֶרֶץ טוֹבָה וּרְחָבָה אֶל־אֶרֶץ זָבַת חָלָב וּדְבָשׁ אֶל־מְקוֹם הַכְּנַעֲנִי וְהַחִתִּי וְהָאֱמֹרִי וְהַפְּרִזִּי וְהַחִוִּי וְהַיְבוּסִי: 9וְעַתָּה הִנֵּה צַעֲקַת בְּנֵי־יִשְׂרָאֵל בָּאָה אֵלָי וְגַם־רָאִיתִי אֶת־הַלַּחַץ אֲשֶׁר מִצְרַיִם לֹחֲצִים אֹתָם: 10וְעַתָּה לְכָה וְאֶשְׁלָחֲךָ אֶל־פַּרְעֹה וְהוֹצֵא אֶת־עַמִּי בְנֵי־יִשְׂרָאֵל מִמִּצְרָיִם: 11וַיֹּאמֶר מֹשֶׁה אֶל־הָאֱלֹהִים מִי אָנֹכִי כִּי אֵלֵךְ אֶל־פַּרְעֹה וְכִי אוֹצִיא אֶת־בְּנֵי יִשְׂרָאֵל מִמִּצְרָיִם: 12וַיֹּאמֶר כִּי־אֶהְיֶה עִמָּךְ וְזֶה־לְּךָ הָאוֹת כִּי אָנֹכִי שְׁלַחְתִּיךָ בְּהוֹצִיאֲךָ אֶת־הָעָם מִמִּצְרַיִם תַּעַבְדוּן אֶת־הָאֱלֹהִים עַל הָהָר הַזֶּה: 13וַיֹּאמֶר מֹשֶׁה אֶל־הָאֱלֹהִים הִנֵּה אָנֹכִי בָא אֶל־בְּנֵי יִשְׂרָאֵל וְאָמַרְתִּי לָהֶם אֱלֹהֵי אֲבוֹתֵיכֶם שְׁלָחַנִי אֲלֵיכֶם וְאָמְרוּ־לִי מַה־

2 Reprinted from the *JPS Hebrew-English Tanakh: The Holy Scriptures* by permission of the University of Nebraska Press (copyright 1985, 1999, 2000 by the Jewish Publication Society, Philadelphia).

[14] And God said to Moses, "Ehyeh-Asher-Ehyeh." He continued, "Thus shall you say to the Israelites, 'Ehyeh sent me to you.'" [15] And God said further to Moses, "Thus shall you speak to the Israelites: The LORD, the God of your fathers, the God of Abraham, the God of Isaac, and the God of Jacob, has sent me to you:

This shall be My name forever,
This My appellation for all eternity.

[16] "Go and assemble the elders of Israel and say to them: the LORD, the God of your fathers, the God of Abraham, Isaac, and Jacob, has appeared to me and said, 'I have taken note of you and of what is being done to you in Egypt, [17] and I have declared: I will take you out of the misery of Egypt to the land of the Canaanites, the Hittites, the Amorites, the Perizzites, the Hivites, and the Jebusites, to a land flowing with milk and honey.' [18] They will listen to you; then you shall go with the elders of Israel to the king of Egypt and you shall say to him, 'The LORD, the God of the Hebrews, manifested Himself to us. Now therefore, let us go a distance of three days into the wilderness to sacrifice to the LORD our God.' [19] Yet I know that the king of Egypt will let you go only because of a greater might. [20] So I will stretch out My hand and smite Egypt with various wonders which I will work upon them; after that he shall let you go. [21] And I will dispose the Egyptians favorably toward this people, so that when you go, you will not go away empty-handed. [22] Each woman shall borrow from her neighbor and the lodger in her house objects of silver and gold, and clothing, and you shall put these on your sons and daughters, thus stripping the Egyptians."

שְׁמוֹ מָה אֹמַר אֲלֵהֶם: 14 וַיֹּאמֶר אֱלֹהִים אֶל־מֹשֶׁה אֶהְיֶה אֲשֶׁר אֶהְיֶה וַיֹּאמֶר כֹּה תֹאמַר לִבְנֵי יִשְׂרָאֵל אֶהְיֶה שְׁלָחַנִי אֲלֵיכֶם: 15 וַיֹּאמֶר עוֹד אֱלֹהִים אֶל־מֹשֶׁה כֹּה־תֹאמַר אֶל־בְּנֵי יִשְׂרָאֵל יְהֹוָה אֱלֹהֵי אֲבֹתֵיכֶם אֱלֹהֵי אַבְרָהָם אֱלֹהֵי יִצְחָק וֵאלֹהֵי יַעֲקֹב שְׁלָחַנִי אֲלֵיכֶם זֶה־שְּׁמִי לְעֹלָם וְזֶה זִכְרִי לְדֹר דֹּר:

חמישי 16 לֵךְ וְאָסַפְתָּ אֶת־זִקְנֵי יִשְׂרָאֵל וְאָמַרְתָּ אֲלֵהֶם יְהֹוָה אֱלֹהֵי אֲבֹתֵיכֶם נִרְאָה אֵלַי אֱלֹהֵי אַבְרָהָם יִצְחָק וְיַעֲקֹב לֵאמֹר פָּקֹד פָּקַדְתִּי אֶתְכֶם וְאֶת־הֶעָשׂוּי לָכֶם בְּמִצְרָיִם: 17 וָאֹמַר אַעֲלֶה אֶתְכֶם מֵעֳנִי מִצְרַיִם אֶל־אֶרֶץ הַכְּנַעֲנִי וְהַחִתִּי וְהָאֱמֹרִי וְהַפְּרִזִּי וְהַחִוִּי וְהַיְבוּסִי אֶל־אֶרֶץ זָבַת חָלָב וּדְבָשׁ: 18 וְשָׁמְעוּ לְקֹלֶךָ וּבָאתָ אַתָּה וְזִקְנֵי יִשְׂרָאֵל אֶל־מֶלֶךְ מִצְרַיִם וַאֲמַרְתֶּם אֵלָיו יְהֹוָה אֱלֹהֵי הָעִבְרִיִּים נִקְרָה עָלֵינוּ וְעַתָּה נֵלֲכָה־נָּא דֶּרֶךְ שְׁלֹשֶׁת יָמִים בַּמִּדְבָּר וְנִזְבְּחָה לַיהֹוָה אֱלֹהֵינוּ: 19 וַאֲנִי יָדַעְתִּי כִּי לֹא־יִתֵּן אֶתְכֶם מֶלֶךְ מִצְרַיִם לַהֲלֹךְ וְלֹא בְּיָד חֲזָקָה: 20 וְשָׁלַחְתִּי אֶת־יָדִי וְהִכֵּיתִי אֶת־מִצְרַיִם בְּכֹל נִפְלְאֹתַי אֲשֶׁר אֶעֱשֶׂה בְּקִרְבּוֹ וְאַחֲרֵי־כֵן יְשַׁלַּח אֶתְכֶם: 21 וְנָתַתִּי אֶת־חֵן הָעָם־הַזֶּה בְּעֵינֵי מִצְרָיִם וְהָיָה כִּי תֵלֵכוּן לֹא תֵלְכוּ רֵיקָם: 22 וְשָׁאֲלָה אִשָּׁה מִשְּׁכֶנְתָּהּ וּמִגָּרַת בֵּיתָהּ כְּלֵי־כֶסֶף וּכְלֵי זָהָב וּשְׂמָלֹת וְשַׂמְתֶּם עַל־בְּנֵיכֶם וְעַל־בְּנֹתֵיכֶם וְנִצַּלְתֶּם אֶת־מִצְרָיִם:

READING 1.2: A Commentary by James L. Kugel

Biblical scholar James L. Kugel writes of Moses's first encounter with God:

At first, Moses is still in ordinary reality, but then, in a twinkling, he is in the midst of the extraordinary—and he is afraid. God then tells him … how He wants Moses to go back to Egypt and take the Israelites from their suffering; but Moses is reluctant, despite God's assurances.…

In his initial casting about for an excuse, Moses hits upon the fact that he himself does not know the specific name of this God. God had introduced Himself by saying, "I am the God of your father, the God of Abraham, the God of Isaac, and the God of Jacob," but He had not said what His name was. Of course, Moses is curious about the name, but he is also playing for time; he's frightened, but also intrigued. Who *is* this God, and what is happening to me? So he presents his question not as a real question but as an objection: "If I tell the Israelites that You appeared to me, the first thing they will ask is: 'What was His name?' Since I do not know the answer to that, I cannot possibly accept this mission."

To this question God responds with a polite "None of your business": *I am who I am,* He says, and this is reminiscent of the answer that the angel gave to Jacob after their fight, "Why should you be asking my name?" (Genesis 32:29).… In this case, however (as almost every biblical commentator since ancient times has pointed out), God's refusal to answer—"I am who I am"—nevertheless contains a clue to the true answer anyway, since *I am* in Hebrew (*'ehyeh*) sounds something like God's name (YHWH). So, God tells Moses, you won't be far wrong if you tell the Israelites, "*'Ehyeh* has sent me to you."…

Moses thus does get the answer he is looking for, and eventually he even accepts the mission.

To say this, however, is to miss something essential about this whole passage. After all, what it describes is nothing less than the moment when Moses' whole life changed. Up to this point, things had been going pretty well for him. True, he had to flee his native Egypt, but now he was comfortably settled in Midian, married to the daughter of one of its most prominent citizens, with nothing more to do all day than take care of his father-in-law's substantial flocks. All the turmoil he witnessed in Egypt was now far behind him; he was in new, far more tranquil surroundings. We do not know how old he was, but presumably he was still a fairly young man, since this incident occurs just after his marriage and the birth of his sons (Exodus 2:21–22). So it is surely no accident that, when God summons him to return to Egypt, he answers the way he does: "Who am I that I should go to Pharaoh and take the Israelites out of Egypt?" *Who am I?* is indeed the question of a still young man, not at all sure of the course his life may take. And so, God answers him in kind: "You wish to know who you are? I will tell you: *I am.* 'I-am' is sending you to Egypt." Staring into the crackling flames, Moses suddenly had his answer to both the questions he asked, "Who am I?" and "Who are You?"—and in that glimmering moment, the two answers seem to have come together.[3]

---

3   James L. Kugel, *How to Read the Bible: A Guide to Scripture Then and Now* (New York: Free Press, 2007), 210–12.

REFLECTIONS

- How does God answer when Moses asks, "Who am I?"
- How does that answer change Moses's life?
- Professor Kugel sums up the passage in the first four paragraphs and then writes that his summary misses something essential about the passage. What is missing? And what do the missing pieces add to our understanding of the passage?
- What lesson does Kugel seem to draw from this story? Do you agree? Why or why not?

READING 1.3: A Commentary by Jonathan Sacks

Jonathan Sacks, Britain's chief rabbi, writes of Moses's first encounter with God:

The first question Moses asked of God was *mi anokhi,* "Who am I?" On the surface, this was an expression of doubt as to his personal worthiness to lead the Israelites to freedom. But there is also an echo of an identity crisis, rare in those days though all too familiar now. Who, after all, was Moses? A child hidden in a basket of reeds, found and adopted by an Egyptian princess, given an Egyptian name and brought up in Pharaoh's palace. Many years later, when circumstances force him to leave Egypt and take flight to Midian, he comes to the rescue of Jethro's daughters, who tell their father, "An Egyptian man delivered us." Moses looked, spoke, and dressed like an Egyptian. Yet the text tells us that when he grew up he "went out to his brothers and saw their burdens." Somehow he knew that the enslaved Israelites were "his brothers." By upbringing he was an Egyptian; by birth he was a Jew.

The mind reels at such a choice. On the one hand lay a life of ease, position, and power as a prince in Pharaoh's court; on the other, the prospect of years of struggle and privation as a member of a nation of slaves. Yet when God tells him, "I am the Lord, the God of your father, the God of Abraham, the God of Isaac, and the God of Jacob," Moses' crisis is resolved and never reappears in that form. He now knows that he is part of an unfinished story that began with the patriarchs and continues through him. He may wear the clothes and speak the language of an Egyptian, but he is a Jew because that is who his ancestors were, and their hopes now rest on him. The modern Jewish question is unusual but not unprecedented: we are each faced with Moses' choice. By culture and upbringing we are part of the liberal democracies of the West, but by birth each of us is heir to the history of our ancestors and a destiny that joins our fate to theirs ...

To be a Jew, now as in the days of Moses, is to hear the call of those who came before us and know that we are guardians of their story.[4]

REFLECTIONS

- What identity crisis does Moses face? How does he deal with that crisis?
- How does that answer change Moses's life?
- What lesson does Sacks seem to draw from this story? Do you agree? Why or why not?

4   Jonathan Sacks, *A Letter in the Scroll: Understanding Our Jewish Identity and Exploring the Legacy of the Word's Oldest Religion* (New York: Simon & Schuster, 2000), 46–47.

What Does It Mean to Be a Jew in Today's World?

Most people view identity as a combination of many factors, including physical traits, values and beliefs, and social ties—connections to a family, an ethnic group, a community, or a nation. Although the ways we define ourselves and others seem familiar, those definitions can have long-lasting repercussions.

This lesson focuses on what it means to identify or be identified by others as a Jew in modern times. "In the past, and not all that long ago, all Jews belonged to a closely knit group of people who believed in the tenets of Judaism, obeyed its commandments, and lived in its religious fold," writes Adin Steinsaltz, a noted Jewish scholar.[5] He then points out that in our own time, most Jews do not regard themselves as religious and yet they continue to define themselves as Jews. So what is it that defines and unites all Jews, including those who do not keep any religious commandments? The readings in this lesson explore the question from a variety of points of view. Each emphasizes at least one aspect of Jewish identity.

Essential Question
- What does it mean to be Jewish?

Recommended Resources
- Reading 1.4: Kimchee on the Seder Plate
- Reading 1.5: "An Extraordinary Thing Began to Happen"
- Reading 1.6: "I Am Jewish"
- Reading 1.7: Growing Up Jewish
- Reading 1.8: "I Really Wanted a Hot Dog"
- Reading 1.9: "My Father's a Rabbi"
- *A Jew Is Not One Thing*, video (beginning at "and I ask myself…" at 22:20 to the end of the film). This video is available in Facing History's Resource Library.

Optional Resources
- *Facing History and Ourselves: Jews of Poland,* chapter 1
- *Yidl in the Middle: Growing Up Jewish in Iowa,* video (Filmmaker Marlene Booth probes her roots as a Jew in Iowa. Through home movies, period photos, her high-school reunion, and current interviews, she examines the complicated process of negotiating identity—as an American, a Jew, and a woman.)
- *Matzo and Mistletoe*, video, 49:00–55:45 (As the title implies, the video tells the story of filmmaker Kate Feiffer's personal struggle to uncover her Jewish identity.)

---

5   Adin Steinsaltz, *We Jews: Who Are We and What Should We Do?* trans. Yehuda Hanegbi and Rebecca Toueg (San Francisco: Jossey-Bass, 2005), 41.

Activity Ideas

For more information on specific teaching strategies highlighted in this lesson, see the Appendix.

GETTING STARTED

Our identity is the story we tell about ourselves. Ask students: What part does being Jewish play in the story you tell about yourself? What part does it play in the way others see you? How central is being a Jew to your identity? Do you think it will always be as central as it is today? What are the challenges and opportunities of living in a society where our religious and cultural identity differs from that of the majority? Have students complete the following sentence in their journals:

To me, being Jewish means…

Encourage students to reflect on their identity before discussing and then comparing responses with their *chavruta*. How does each pair account for both similarities and differences in their sentences?

INTERPRETING A QUOTATION

In 1928, Zora Neale Hurston, an African American writer, published an essay in which she wrote, "I feel most colored when thrown against a sharp white background."[6] What is she trying to say about what it means to be African American in the United States? To what does "the sharp white background" refer? What does that background suggest about her relationship with white Americans? Then have students consider how her experience is similar to their own experiences as Jews in the United States. When do they feel most Jewish? When do they feel least Jewish? Have students complete the sentence, "I feel most Jewish when…" What does that sentence add to their understanding of how being a Jew has shaped their identity?

For an artist's rendition of this quote, have students review Glenn Ligon's lithograph that can be found here: *http://www.wesleyan.edu/dac/coll/lign/wb2.html*. How does the image change as it moves downward? Why does Ligon use the line break the way he does? How does the background change? How does the artistic expression impact Hurston's words?

DEFINING JEWISHNESS

Historian Michael A. Meyer has written extensively about Jewish identity. In one essay he notes:

> Long before the word became fashionable among psychoanalysts and sociologists, Jews in the modern world were obsessed with the subject of *identity*. They were confronted by the problem that Jewishness seemed to fit none of the usual categories. Until the establishment of the state of Israel, the Jews were not a nation, at least not in the political sense; yet being Jewish was different from being German, French, or American. And even after 1948 most Jews remained nationally something other than Jewish. But neither could Jews define themselves by their religion alone. Few could ever seriously maintain that Judaism was, pure and simple, a religious faith on the model of Christianity. The easy answer was that Jewishness constituted some mixture of ethnicity and religion. But in what proportion? And was the whole more than simply a compound of these two elements?[7]

---

6   Zora Neale Hurston, "How It Feels to Be Colored Me," *The World Tomorrow* (magazine), May 1928, 215–16.
7   Michael A. Meyer, *Jewish Identity in the Modern World* (Seattle: University of Washington Press, 1999), 3.

Ask students to think about how they would answer the questions that Meyer raises. Have them record their initial responses in their journals. To encourage deeper reflection, you may wish to assign one or more of the various readings included in this lesson, as well as the last chapter of a video entitled *A Jew Is Not One Thing* and/or similar accounts (see "Optional Resources"). To include as wide a variety of resources as possible, divide the class into small groups, with each group responsible for sharing what members learned with the class as a whole.

Ask students to identify what each resource adds to their understanding of what it means to be a Jew. In what sense does it define being a Jew only in religious terms? In what sense does it view Jewishness as a mixture of ethnicity and religion? Are there other elements involved in Jewish identity? If so, what might they be?

EXPLORING CONSEQUENCES

In Reading 1.8, a young woman describes her efforts to maintain a strong Jewish identity in a community in which she is in the minority. She speaks eloquently of the tolerance she has found among students whose religious identity is equally strong even though their faith differs from her own. Ask students to reread the last paragraph. Why then does she say that we are "not able to get along"? What encourages people to "get along"? What makes it difficult? One answer to these questions lies in the last few sentences of her interview, which are not included in Reading 1.8. Read those sentences aloud to students or ask a volunteer to do so.

> One of my friends was raised Jewish but doesn't believe it so much anymore. That's who you get more grief from. She'll bring pork for lunch and say, "Umm, it's so-o-o good! Yum, yum, yum." She'll just shove it in my face.

Why do you think the young woman ended her remarks with this particular incident? What point is she trying to make? Have you or someone you know been mocked for being more or less observant than others in your class or a group? If so, how did you respond, and how would you have liked to respond? If not, how do you think you would have felt if you were mocked as she was, and how do you like to think you would have responded? What if someone else had seen the incident and intervened: What do you imagine they would have said? What encourages mutual respect? What makes it difficult to find common ground?

ASSESSMENT

To assess learning, have students reread their initial response to the prompt "To me, being Jewish means…" Ask them to revise the statement to reflect what they learned in this lesson. Or you may prefer to have students create a piece of art that completes the prompt "I feel most Jewish when…"

READING 1.4: Kimchee on the Seder Plate

Angela Warnick Buchdahl writes of her Jewish identity:

One year my mother put kimchee, a spicy, pickled cabbage condiment, on our seder plate. My Korean mother thought it was a reasonable substitution since both kimchee and horseradish elicit a similar sting in the mouth, the same clearing of the nostrils. She also liked kimchee on gefilte fish and matza. "Kimchee just like maror, but better," she said. I resigned myself to the fact that we were never going to be a "normal" Jewish family.

I grew up part of the "mixed multitude" of our people: an Ashkenazi, Reform Jewish father, a Korean Buddhist mother. I was born in Seoul and moved to Tacoma, Washington, at the age of five. Growing up, I knew my family was atypical, yet we were made to feel quite at home in our synagogue and community. My Jewish education began in my synagogue preschool, extended through cantorial and rabbinical school at Hebrew Union College (HUC), and continues today. I was the first Asian American to graduate from the rabbinical program at HUC, but definitely not the last—a Chinese American rabbi graduated the very next year, and I am sure others will follow.

As a child, I believed that my sister and I were the "only ones" in the Jewish community—the only ones with Asian faces, the only ones whose family trees didn't have roots in Eastern Europe, the only ones with kimchee on the seder plate. But as I grew older, I began to see myself reflected in the Jewish community. I was the only multiracial Jew at my Jewish summer camp in 1985; when I was a song-leader there a decade later, there were a dozen. I have met hundreds of people in multiracial Jewish families in the Northeast through the Multiracial Jewish Network. Social scientist Gary Tobin numbers interracial Jewish families in the hundreds of thousands in North America.

As I learned more about Jewish history and culture, I found it very powerful to learn that being of mixed race in the Jewish community was not just a modern phenomenon. We were a mixed multitude when we left Egypt and entered Israel, and the Hebrews continued to acquire different cultures and races throughout our Diaspora history. Walking through the streets of modern-day Israel, one sees the multicolored faces of Ethiopian, Russian, Yemenite, Iraqi, Moroccan, Polish, and countless other races of Jews—many facial particularities, but all Jewish. Yet, if you were to ask the typical secular Israeli on the street what it meant to be Jewish, she might respond, "It's not religious so much, it's my culture, my ethnicity." If Judaism is about culture, what then does it mean to be Jewish when Jews come from so many different cultures and ethnic backgrounds?

As the child of a non-Jewish mother, a mother who carried her own distinct ethnic and cultural traditions, I came to believe that I could never be "fully Jewish" since I could never be "purely" Jewish. I was reminded of this daily: when fielding the many comments like, "Funny, you don't look Jewish," or having to answer questions on my halakhic status as a Jew. My internal questions of authenticity loomed over my Jewish identity throughout my adolescence into early adulthood, as I sought to integrate my Jewish, Korean, and secular American identities.

It was only in a period of crisis, one college summer while living in Israel, that I fully understood what my Jewish identity meant to me. After a painful summer of feeling marginalized and invisible in Israel, I called my mother to declare that I no longer wanted to be a Jew. I did not look Jewish, I did not carry a Jewish name, and I no longer wanted the heavy burden of having to explain and prove myself every time I entered a new Jewish community. She simply responded by saying, "Is that possible?" It was only at that moment that I realized I could no sooner stop being a Jew than I could stop being Korean, or female, or me. I decided then to have a *giyur* (conversion ceremony), what I termed a reaffirmation ceremony in which I dipped in the *mikvah* [ritual bath] and reaffirmed my Jewish legacy. I have come to understand that anyone who has seriously considered her Jewish identity struggles with the many competing identities that the name "Jew" signifies.

What does it mean to be a "normal" Jewish family today? As we learn each other's stories we hear the challenges and joys of reconciling our sometimes competing identities of being Jewish while also feminist, Arab, gay, African-American, or Korean. We were a mixed multitude in ancient times, and we still are. May we continue to see the many faces of Israel as a gift that enriches our people.[8]

8   Angela Warnick Buchdahl, "My Personal Story: Kimchee on the Seder Plate," *Sh'ma: A Journal of Jewish Responsibility* (June 2003), *http://www.shma.com/2003/06/kimchee-on-the-seder-plate/*.

READING 1.5: "An Extraordinary Thing Began to Happen"

Jonathan Sacks recalls how he discovered that "being Jewish was not something private and personal but something collective and historical":

> I had just gone to university.... Until then I had been a Jew because—well, because that is what my parents were. I did what I did without asking why. I had my bar mitzvah, I went to Hebrew classes, and every Saturday I went to synagogue with my father. There was no reason not to, no reason to rebel.
>
> [University] was like a revelation.... Here was every kind of student, from every kind of background, studying every subject in every conceivable way. What mattered was critical intelligence, the ability to question everything.... Reality was confined to facts and inferences. Everything else was choice.... My parents' world seemed long ago and far away...
>
> Then, in May [of 1967], we began to hear disturbing news from the Middle East.... The State of Israel was exposed to attack on all fronts. Catastrophe seemed to be in the making. I, who had not lived through the Holocaust nor even thought much about it, became suddenly aware that a second tragedy might be about to overtake the Jewish people.
>
> It was then that an extraordinary thing began to happen. Throughout the university Jews suddenly became visible. Day after day they crowded into the little synagogue in the center of town.... Everyone wanted to help in some way, to express their solidarity, their identification with Israel's fate.... From the United States to the Soviet Union, Jews were riveted to their television screens or radios, anxious... as if it were their own lives at stake. The rest is history. The war was fought and won.... Life went back to normal.
>
> But not completely. For I had witnessed something in those days and weeks that didn't make sense in the rest of my world. It had nothing to do with politics or war or even prayer. It had to do with Jewish identity. Collectively the Jewish people had looked in the mirror and said, We are still Jews. And by that they meant more than a private declaration of faith.... It meant that they felt part of a people....
>
> Why? The Israelis were not people I knew.... Israel was a country two thousand miles away.... Yet I had no doubt that their danger was something I felt personally. It was then that I knew that being Jewish was not something private and personal but something collective and historical. It meant being part of an extended family, many of whose members I did not know, but to whom I nonetheless felt connected by bonds of kinship and responsibility.[9]

9   Jonathan Sacks, *A Letter in the Scroll: Understanding Our Jewish Identity and Exploring the Legacy of the World's Oldest Religion* (New York: Free Press, 2000), 26–29.

READING 1.6: "I Am Jewish"

Thomas Friedman was asked what the phrase "I am Jewish" means to him. His response:

> For me, the phrase "I am Jewish" means… a very important part of my identity, but not the only part of my identity. I see myself as an American, a journalist, a *New York Times* columnist, a husband, a father, a man of the world, a Jew. The last is by no means the least. My faith defines not only the pathway I choose to connect with God, but also, just as important, a big part of my cultural and communal root system. Being Jewish is a big part of my olive tree, the thing that anchors me in the world. But it is not the only root. Because being an American is also very much part of my olive tree. "American Jew," "Jewish American," "American Jewish writer for the *New York Times,*" it doesn't matter how you put it. They all capture me, and they are all important. They all locate where I've been and where I'm going.[10]

---

10   Thomas Friedman, "A Very Important Unit of My Identity," in *I Am Jewish: Personal Reflections Inspired by the Last Words of Daniel Pearl*, ed. Judea and Ruth Pearl (Woodstock, VT: Jewish Lights, 2004), 39.

READING 1.7: Growing Up Jewish

Sarah Greenberg describes what it means to "grow up Jewish" in a small Maryland town about 90 miles south of Washington, DC:

Our area is more rural than urban, and it has great natural beauty, but the Jewish population is very small. I was born here and I appreciate all that I know about the dominant religion, Christianity. But living here also inhibits my ability to express my Judaism. As I approached my bat mitzvah, I decided to interview other Jewish teens preparing for bar/bat mitzvah to see if they felt the same way. For comparison, I also interviewed my grandmother, who grew up in a small non-Jewish area of Pennsylvania.

In our community we have a one-room synagogue and a part-time rabbi. That one synagogue room serves as a sanctuary, program space, and school. Our synagogue membership is around 40 families and our religious school has about 35 kids. We meet for Shabbat services twice a month, but we do not always get 10 people….

I am the only Jewish kid in my grade at school—I'm in seventh grade. This situation is challenging. In sensing the differences between my peers and me, I feel alone and lonely. Thankfully, I do have Jewish friends from synagogue, but I do not see them as often as I would like.

In addition, through remarriages, many of my family members are not Jewish. My stepfather and his family are not Jewish and my stepmother's side of the family has mixed religions. I celebrate Jewish holidays with my parents and siblings and Christmas with my extended families.

When I interviewed my peers at Hebrew school about growing up Jewish in southern Maryland, I found that we each had similar experiences of feeling lonely in school. We all have felt frustrated at having to explain our religious practices to classmates and friends…. With more Jewish diversity, we would have an easier time practicing Judaism and nurturing our Jewish identities…

In listening to my grandmother's experience growing up in a predominantly Christian area, I heard a great deal about the anti-Semitism she faced in her teaching profession and social life…. While my peers and I do not experience anti-Semitic policies, we do face insulting comments and general disbelief that we are Jewish. It seems that somewhere beneath the surface lies an expectation that Jews are significantly different from everyone else.

… While I cherish many aspects of my growing-up experience, including the opportunities to understand the Christianity of my stepfamily and friends, living near more Jewish resources will be a factor in my decision about where to raise the family I hope to have someday.[11]

---

11   Sarah Greenberg, "Growing Up Jewish," *CJ: Voices of Conservative/Masorti Judaism* (Summer 2011), available at *http://www.wlcj.org/articlenav.php?id=424.*

READING 1.8: "I Really Wanted a Hot Dog"

A young woman told an interviewer what being a Jew meant to her:

> I keep kosher. But I don't do it as strictly as some people. Some people wait six hours from meat to milk—I wait two, sometimes less. Some people won't eat in a restaurant if it's not strictly CRC-approved kosher.*
>
> Today I was at our youth-group event, and I really wanted a hot dog, and it was a company that I knew was kosher. So then I had to ask about their bread—"Can I see the label on the bread to make sure there's no dairy in it?" And there wasn't. So I got a hot dog from a hot-dog stand, which is something I normally would not do.
>
> I only eat at certain restaurants. I hang out with a very religious group of kids so they understand. We're all different religions, but they all understand that I need to be doing this. You're brought up with the same traditions and the same values, regardless of whether or not it's the same religion. Like what things define a good person or a bad person? All these things are so parallel in all the religions, yet we seem not to be able to get along. It boggles my mind.

---

* The CRC refers to the Chicago Rabbinical Council. It certifies food as kosher in the Chicago area.

---

12   "I Really Wanted a Hot Dog," in Pearl Gaskins, *I Believe In…: Christian, Jewish, and Muslim Young People Speak About Their Faith* (Chicago: Cricket Books, 2004), 61.

READING 1.9: "My Father's a Rabbi"

A 15-year-old boy describes his struggle for religious identity:

My father's a rabbi. But I'm not the typical RK—rabbi's kid. Some RKs I know—they're just stuck up. They know that they own the place, basically. You can get kind of prissy and annoying. I try to be fair and accepting.

It's hard sometimes. You're always in the spotlight. When I went to Jewish school, everyone was like, "He's the rabbi's son. No wonder he's acing Jewish-studies class." But I learned just as much as everybody else from the class.

When my friends find out, they're like, "Oh, you're the rabbi's kid. You must be very religious and very holier-than-thou." But I'm normal. Dad's normal....

It's hard, too, because I don't want to look bad for my father. But I also have to remember that I'm not there just for him. Sometimes I wish I were just another member of the congregation, that I can just be at the synagogue and pray as opposed to politicking—being nice to everybody and being friendly and making the rounds.

But I feel it's not as bad as people may think it is. I try to hold myself well in the synagogue. I think I'm very lucky—I like my father, I like my mother. Being a rabbi's kid can be hard sometimes, but I don't regret it at all.

We're more traditional than most Reform families. When you think of Reform, you think of somebody not keeping the Sabbath, where I keep it all of the time....

I don't think it's right to have one definitive thing that makes somebody Jewish. I don't think it's fair to do that to anybody.... If you don't follow the laws but you try to be moral and just be a good person, then that's Jewish. Judaism teaches that you have to adapt to your time period—where you are and who you are.

I think my identity as a Jew is always changing. I don't think it will stop changing ever.... I'm definitely now in a process where I have no idea exactly where I am. I have no idea exactly where I stand or who I am or anything of that nature....

I think one good thing about Judaism is that it tries to get people to think for themselves. I find that Judaism is very individualistic, which is good. And I think if you study Torah and you study the law, you'll find the answers that can help you with your problems. But sometimes that's hard, which is why we have rabbis to help.

Another great thing about Judaism is that a big part of it is community—a great sense of community and a strong support system.... I believe that while individuals must have their own understanding of themselves as Jews, they must be part of the Jewish community. Throughout Jewish literature, we see the importance of a holy community, *Kehillat Kedushah*. This is vital and necessary to the survival of Judaism.[13]

---

13   "My Identity As a Jew Is Always Changing," in Pearl Gaskins, *I Believe In…: Christian, Jewish, and Muslim Young People Speak About Their Faith* (Chicago: Cricket Books, 2004), 36–38.

"Us" and "Them"

"When we identify one thing as unlike the others," observes Martha Minow, a legal scholar, "we are dividing the world; we use our language to exclude, to distinguish—to discriminate." She goes on to say:

> Of course, there are "real differences" in the world; each person differs in countless ways from each other person. But when we simplify and sort, we focus on some traits rather than others, and we assign consequences to the presence and absence of the traits we make significant. We ask, "What's the new baby?"—and we expect as an answer, boy or girl. That answer, for most of history, has spelled consequences for the roles and opportunities available to that individual.[14]

Our identity includes not only the stories we tell about ourselves but also the stories others tell about us and the labels that they attach to us. Both shape our identity in small ways and large, thus raising two questions: In what proportions? And is the whole more than the sum of these elements? The readings in this lesson explore those questions. They also introduce several important terms: *stereotyping, prejudice*, and *discrimination*.

We tend to see ourselves as unique individuals even as we tend to see others as representatives of various groups. Although it is natural to do so, stereotyping is offensive. Stereotypes are more than labels or judgments about an individual based on the real or imagined characteristics of a group. Stereotyping reduces individuals to categories. Therefore stereotyping can lead to prejudice and discrimination. The word *prejudice* comes from the word *pre-judge*. We pre-judge when we have an opinion about an individual based on his or her membership in a particular group. A prejudice attaches value to differences to the benefit of one's own group and at the expense of other groups. Discrimination occurs when prejudices are translated into actions. Not every stereotype results in discrimination. But all stereotypes tend to divide a society into "us" and "them."

Essential Questions
- How does the way that others see us affect the way we see ourselves?
- How do "their" perceptions of "us" affect the choices we make?

Recommended Resources
- *The Bear That Wasn't* by Frank Tashlin (abridged version), both video and text online at *http://www.facinghistory.org/hhb/bear-wasnt*
- Reading 1.10: "We Don't Control America" and Other Myths
- Reading 1.11: "It's a Courageous Thing to Do"

---

14   Martha Minow, *Making All the Difference: Inclusion, Exclusion and American Law* (Ithaca, NY: Cornell University Press, 1990), 3.

Activity Ideas

For more information on specific teaching strategies highlighted in this lesson, see the Appendix.

GETTING STARTED

In *The Bear That Wasn't*, Frank Tashlin tells of a bear who finds himself among people and other bears who deny an important part of his identity. The story highlights the ways the society in which we live can shape how we see ourselves and others. If students have read the book as part of a Facing History and Ourselves unit, you may wish to review the story as a way of introducing this lesson. If students are not yet familiar with the book, you may want to have students take turns reading it aloud. Alternatively, the class might watch an animated film version of the story on YouTube.

To initiate a discussion, point out that the bears in the zoo as well as the factory officials insisted that the Bear was not a bear. What reasons do they give? What do their answers suggest about what makes a bear a bear? Is being a bear a matter of appearance? What other factors may be involved? Then have students give examples of the way society influences how they see themselves and others. For example: What messages does our society send about the way a girl or a boy is supposed to think, act, and dress? How do these messages influence the behavior of both girls and boys? What messages does our society send about what it means to be a Jew? How do those messages influence our behavior?

DEFINING TERMS

We tend to see ourselves as unique even as "we" stereotype "them." A *stereotype* is the mental image "we" use to categorize or label "them." Reading 1.10 contains brief interviews with three young Jewish women who describe some of the stereotypes people have of Jews. Ask students to underline those stereotypes. What do those images suggest about the way some people view all Jews? How might those images affect the way they treat Jews? How might they affect the way Jews see themselves?

Based on the reading and their own experiences, have students create a working definition of the word *stereotype*. A working definition is a definition that we expand and revise as we encounter new information and deepen our understanding. The following is an example of a working definition based on Reading 1.11:

Stereotype:

- an overly simplistic generalization about a group that allows others to categorize them and treat them accordingly
- can be positive or negative
- ignores the uniqueness of individuals
- a picture in our heads
- a mental image that reduces an individual to a label

Have students also create working definitions of such key terms as *prejudice* and *discrimination*. As they complete the lesson, ask them to add to and/or edit those definitions. They may also want to include pictures. Sometimes a drawing captures an idea better than a long, complicated definition can.

MAKING INFERENCES

Stereotypes affect not only the way "they" see "us" but also the way *we* see ourselves. Ask students to read an interview with a young Jew (Reading 1.11). Why does the speaker regard the decision to wear a *kippah* as "courageous"? Why is he reluctant to make that decision? What do your answers suggest about the way that "they" shape *our* identity in small ways and large? What stereotypes do "we" hold about "them"? How might we break down those stereotypes so that they can see who we really are and we can see who they are? Why is it important to do so?

ASSESSMENT

Ask students to write a letter in response to one of the individuals featured in this lesson. What advice would you give that individual? What would you like him or her to know about your own experiences with stereotypes? The letters should show an understanding of key terms and the essential questions posed in this lesson.

READING 1.10: "We Don't Control America" and Other Myths

Miriam observes:

> Last year I tutored at this nursing school. This woman was from Guatemala. I'm sure she's educated, but she didn't speak English. My job was to teach her enough English so she could pass the test to get in. One day she said, "Miriam, are you Jewish?" I said, "Yeah." She said, "You know how I knew? Because you're very smart and you dress modestly." Then she said, "The Jews are the people of God— it says so in the Bible. That's why they're very smart and wealthy."

> I didn't know what to say. If you're Jewish, there is definitely an emphasis on being smart and succeeding in school. If people think that, then OK. But it's a problem to think that all Jews are wealthy when they're not. I was in Argentina last quarter. They have this huge economic crisis and a lot of extreme poverty. Synagogues are feeding lots and lots of hungry people who are Jews. No one can pay tuition anymore at the Jewish schools. Anti-Semitism is more of an issue there. A woman from Uruguay told a friend of mine that Jews run everything in Argentina.

> People's willingness to believe things like that is weird. That's where I think stereotypes become a problem. It's not OK to say, "All Jews are wealthier," or "The Jews run things," or "There's something about the Jews."[15]

Darcy notes:

> Sometimes it's just innocent questions: people don't know better. A Jewish girlfriend of mine was asked if it's true that Jews freeze the placentas of their babies and then eat them. No. But there are definitely versions of the blood libel still around—[the lie] that Jews use the blood of Christian children to make their matzo for Passover....

> In America, they complain that we control all the money of the world—just ridiculous stuff. People are convinced that I can do whatever I want because I have unlimited resources. I'm Jewish, so I must be incredibly wealthy. No, actually I'm not. I'm at school on a scholarship.

> I have a classmate who is Egyptian. She came with me to synagogue once and was looking through the prayer book, which is in Hebrew and English. She was looking for the part where it says we should kill all the Arabs, because that's what she was always taught.

> But there isn't anything in the prayer book or anything else about that because Jews don't believe that. We don't teach our children to hate Arabs or that they or any other non-Jews must die.

---

15   "There's Something About the Jews," in Pearl Gaskins, *I Believe In…: Christian, Jewish, and Muslim Young People Speak About Their Faith* (Chicago: Cricket Books, 2004), 92.

She also thinks that Jews rule the U.S., which a lot of people think. We don't control America. In fact, until very recently, in many ways we were similar to blacks. It was fashionable to dislike Jews. We got blackballed from country clubs. If you look at charters for covenant-controlled communities, the old charters will actually list in their rules: "No blacks, no Jews. Mow your lawn once a week." They just put it in like it was a normal thing.[16]

Kerri Strug writes:

I have heard the same question over and over since I received my gold medal in gymnastics on the Olympic podium. "You're Jewish?" people ask in a surprised tone. Perhaps it is my appearance or the stereotype that Jews and sports don't mix that makes my Jewish heritage so unexpected. I think about the attributes that helped me reach that podium: perseverance when faced with pain, years of patience and hope in an uncertain future, and a belief and devotion to something greater than myself. It makes it hard for me to believe that I did not look Jewish up on the podium. In my mind, those are attributes that have defined Jews throughout history.[17]

---

16   "There's Something About the Jews," in Gaskins, *I Believe In...*
17   Kerri Strug, "You're Jewish?" in *I Am Jewish: Personal Reflections Inspired by the Last Words of Daniel Pearl,* ed. Judea and Ruth Pearl (Woodstock, VT: Jewish Lights, 2004), 98.

READING 1.11: "It's a Courageous Thing to Do"

A student reflects on why it takes courage to wear a *yarmulke* or *kippah*:

When I was in high school one of my friends was wearing a yarmulke, and he was in the gym locker room and someone just grabbed it off his head and ran. In high school, teenagers are immature, ignorant, whatever.

I admire people who wear yarmulkes publicly. It's a courageous thing to do. Wearing it is a way for someone to say, "I'm a Jew." It's the biggest symbol. People who wear yarmulkes are generally more observant. For some kids who grow up in observant households, since day one they wear a kippah. But for a small minority out there, it's something they do as a way of showing Jewish pride.

I have friends who used to not wear them, and in their teenage years they said, "This is something I want to do." It's tough for someone to make that jump. I have a friend who used to go around wearing a baseball cap. You can wear a baseball cap—that counts as a yarmulke. Then he said, "You know what? I'm Jewish. I'm proud to be Jewish." So now he wears a kippah.

Especially if you're in a public forum, wearing a kippah requires a lot of courage, and you have to have a lot of pride in your religion. Some people in the business or professional worlds won't wear a kippah, because, unfortunately, a bit of anti-Semitism and prejudice exist there.... For some people in the professional world, it changes the way that people think of them, and perceptions are important.

Every once in a while, I think, "Maybe I should do it." I think I've ultimately never had the courage. The reason it's difficult, at least for myself in a tolerant community like this one, is that there's the fear—you don't want to stick out. But also, I'm satisfied with the level of my observance right now. Wearing a kippah is not the only way of making a statement of Jewish pride.[18]

---

18 "It Takes a Lot of Courage to Wear a Kippah," in Pearl Gaskins, *I Believe In…: Christian, Jewish and Muslim Young People Speak About Their Faith* (Chicago: Cricket Books, 2004), 12–13.

Membership: What Do We Do With the Stranger?

Teaching Focus

Unit 2 explores questions of membership and belonging by focusing on the ways societies define their *universe of obligation*. Sociologist Helen Fein coined the term to describe the circle of individuals and groups toward whom a society has obligations, for whom its rules apply, and in whose name justice is sought.[1] It is a concept that can be traced to biblical times, even though Fein uses the term to describe the way modern nations view their responsibilities. The idea of a universe of obligation also has meaning for us as individuals. Some scholars link the concept to the idea of *areyvut,* a word that literally means "a guarantor"—someone who accepts legal responsibility for the actions of another. That idea is also related to acts of kindness, charity, and *tikkun olam.*

Lesson 1: What Do We Do With a Difference?
Lesson 2: A Biblical Perspective on *Areyvut*
Lesson 3: A Historical Perspective on Universe of Obligation

Essential Questions

- Who decides who belongs and who does not? And why does belonging matter?
- Why do we distinguish between "us" and "them"? How do those distinctions affect the way "we" treat "them"?
- What is the relationship between the concept of a universe of obligation and the concept of *areyvut*?

---

1   Helen Fein, *Accounting for Genocide: National Responses and Jewish Victimization during the Holocaust* (New York: Free Press, 1979), 4.

Student Outcomes

Students will . . .

- examine the impact of the distinctions societies and individuals create between "us" and "them."
- create working definitions of *universe of obligation* and *areyvut.*
- apply the two concepts to the choices made by various societies and the individuals who live in those societies.

These lessons may be used to extend, reinforce, and enhance concepts developed in:

- Chapters 2, 3, and 5 in *Facing History and Ourselves: Holocaust and Human Behavior*
- Chapters 2 and 3 in *Facing History and Ourselves: Jews of Poland*

What Do We Do With a Difference?

According to an old Yiddish saying, life is with people. Everywhere on Earth, to be human means to live with others. In groups, we meet our most basic needs. We gather with others to work, learn, play, and pray. In groups, we satisfy our yearning to belong, receive comfort in times of trouble, and find companions that share our dreams and value our beliefs. Membership is rarely universal. Almost every group has customs, rules, or laws that spell out who belongs and who does not. Those definitions reveal who holds power in a society. And they determine who is a part of its universe of obligation—the individuals and groups who benefit from rules of the larger society and on whose behalf justice is sought. For Jews and other minorities, the way the larger society defines membership has always been of vital importance. It signals not only how they will be seen by others but also how they are likely to be treated. Will they be welcomed or expelled? Will they be tolerated or attacked? This lesson examines those questions by exploring two concepts: *universe of obligation* and *areyvut* (the idea of individual responsibility for others in a society).

Essential Questions
- What does it mean to be included in a society's universe of obligation?
- What does it mean to be seen as beyond that universe of obligation?
- What is the relationship between *areyvut* and a universe of obligation?

Recommended Resources
- Reading 2.1: "What Do We Do With a Variation?"
- Reading 2.2: The Etiquette of Democracy
- Reading 2.3: Quotations on the Problem of the Stranger

Activity Ideas
For more information on specific teaching strategies highlighted in this lesson, see the Appendix.

GETTING STARTED
Invite one or more volunteers to read aloud the poem "What Do We Do With a Variation?" (Reading 2.1). Ask students how they would answer the question James Berry raises. You may wish to point out that he uses the word *we* in every stanza. Whom does he seem to include in that word? Who is not included? Who decides what "we" do? Encourage students to record their initial responses to the questions raised by the poem in their journals. Explain that they will reexamine, revise, and/or expand those responses as the lesson continues.

BUILDING WORKING DEFINITIONS

Share Helen Fein's definition of the term *universe of obligation* with the class. To help students visualize the concept, you may wish to draw a large circle on the board and explain that it represents our nation's universe of obligation. What individuals and groups would you place at the center or heart of the circle? What individuals and groups would you place along the outer edge of the circle? What individuals or groups do you think are beyond the nation's universe of obligation?

Individuals also have circles of obligation and responsibility. The Hebrew word for that concept is *areyvut*, which literally means "guarantor"—someone who takes legal responsibility for the actions of another person. That idea has been expanded to include those who provide emotional and physical support for others, as well as legal and/or financial backing. The concept of *areyvut* is closely related to other important Jewish principles, including *chesed* (acts of kindness), *tzedakah* (charity), and *tikkun olam* (the repair or perfecting of the world). Have students share examples of *areyvut* or create a drawing that illustrates the concept. Who is a part of your sense of *areyvut*? Then ask the class to compare and contrast their working definition of the term with their working definition of *universe of obligation*. What are the main differences between the two concepts? In what respects do the two overlap?

EXAMINING A TURNING POINT

Ask students to read a portion of an essay written by political scientist Stephen Carter (Reading 2.2). He describes a time when a simple act made "all the difference" in his life. Have students read the first page of his essay and answer the question at the bottom of the page. After they have recorded their ideas in their journals, distribute copies of the second page of Reading 2.2 so that students can find out what actually happened next. Ask them: Were you surprised at the way the incident ends? If so, why were you surprised? If not, what clues tipped you off as to what was likely to happen next?

What does the story reveal about the way Carter thought the United States defined its universe of obligation in 1966? What stereotypes may have shaped his views? How did Sara Kestenbaum's welcome complicate those views? Carter describes her behavior as "an act of civility." He defines *civility* as "the sum of the many sacrifices we are called to make for the sake of living together."[2] How does the concept of civility relate to *areyvut*? What does the story add to our understanding of both concepts? Ask students to reread their working definitions of *universe of obligation* and *areyvut* and encourage them to expand or revise those definitions based on their discussions of Carter's essay.

ANALYZING QUOTATIONS

Explain to students that many rabbis have noted that there is only one verse in the Torah that commands: "You shall love your neighbor as yourself," but there are 36 that command us to "love the stranger"— the outsider, the alien, the one who is least like "us." It is a concept that both Jews and non-Jews have struggled to understand and apply to their lives. Have students work with their *chavruta*. Distribute one of the quotations in Reading 2.3 to half of the pairs and the second to the other half. Ask each pair to tape its quotation to a large sheet of paper and then use markers to carry on a silent conversation about the quotation (see **BIG PAPER** teaching strategy in the Appendix).

After students have silently engaged in a conversation about their quotation with their *chavruta*, encourage them to walk around the room and read and comment in writing on what others have had to say about both quotations. The next step is to break the silence and discuss the two quotations as a class. You may begin the discussion with the following guiding questions:

- What does each quotation suggest about who should be part of our universe of obligation?
- What does each add to our understanding of *areyvut* and the role it should play in our lives?
- How do the two quotations complement one another? How do they differ?
- What do the two add to our working definitions of *universe of obligation* and *areyvut*?

ASSESSMENT

The written comments students make in response to the quotations can be used to evaluate their understanding of the two concepts. Another way to measure learning is by having students edit or revise their working definitions of the two concepts after completing the Big Paper activity.

---

2   Stephen L. Carter, *Civility: Manners, Morals, and the Etiquette of Democracy* (New York: HarperPerennial, 1998).

READING 2.1: "What Do We Do With a Variation?"

What do we do with a difference?
Do we stand and discuss its oddity
or do we ignore it?

Do we shut our eyes to it
or poke it with a stick?
Do we clobber it to death?

Do we move around it in rage
and enlist the rage of others?
Do we will it to go away?

Do we look at it in awe
or purely in wonderment?
Do we work for it to disappear?

Do we pass it stealthily
Or change route away from it?
Do we will it to become like ourselves?

What do we do with a difference?
Do we communicate to it,
let application acknowledge it
for barriers to fall down? [3]

—James Berry

---

3   James Berry, "What Do We Do With a Variation?" in *When I Dance* (San Diego: Harcourt Brace Jovanovich, 1991), 86.

READING 2.2: The Etiquette of Democracy (part 1 of 2)

Stephen L. Carter, a political scientist, writes about a memorable day in his life:

> In the summer of 1966, my parents moved with their five children to a large house near the corner of 35th and Macomb Streets in Cleveland Park, a neighborhood in the middle of Northwest Washington, D.C., and, in those days, a lily-white enclave. My father, trained as a lawyer, was working for the federal government, and this was an area of the city where many lawyers and government officials lived. There were senators, there were lobbyists, there were undersecretaries of this and that. My first impression was of block upon block of grim, forbidding old homes, each of which seemed to feature a massive dog and spoiled children in the uniforms of various private schools. My two brothers and two sisters and I sat on the front steps, missing our playmates, as the movers carried in our furniture. Cars passed what was now our house, slowing for a look, as did people on foot. We waited for somebody to say hello, to welcome us. Nobody did.
>
> We children had no previous experience of white neighborhoods. But we had heard unpleasant rumors. The gang of boys I used to hang out with in Southwest Washington traded tall tales of places where white people did evil things to us, mostly in the South, where none of us had ever lived, nor wanted to.
>
> I watched the strange new people passing us and wordlessly watching back, and I knew we were not welcome here. I knew we would not be liked here. I knew we would have no friends here. I knew we should not have moved here. I knew...[4]

Carter describes what happened next as a "simple act that changed my life." What do you think happened next?

---

4   From an article published in *The Christian Century,* April 8, 1998, 366–371. Originally published in Stephen L. Carter, *Civility: Manners, Morals, and the Etiquette of Democracy* (New York: HarperPerennial, 1998), 61–62.

READING 2.2: The Etiquette of Democracy (part 2 of 2)

Carter continues his story:

> And all at once, a white woman arriving home from work at the house across the street from ours turned and smiled with obvious delight and waved and called out, "Welcome!" in a booming, confident voice I would come to love. She bustled into her house, only to emerge, minutes later, with a huge tray of cream cheese and jelly sandwiches, which she carried to our porch and offered around with her ready smile, simultaneously feeding and greeting the children of a family she had never met—and a black family at that—with nothing to gain for herself except perhaps the knowledge that she had done the right thing. We were strangers, black strangers, and she went out of her way to make us feel welcome. This woman's name was Sara Kestenbaum. Sara died much too soon, but she remains, in my experience, one of the great exemplars of all that is best about civility.
> Sara Kestenbaum's special contribution to civility back in 1966 was to create for us a sense of belonging where none had existed before. And she did so even though she had never seen any of us in her life. She managed, in the course of a single day, to turn us from strangers into friends, a remarkable gift that few share. (My wife is one of the few.) But we must never require friendship as the price of civility, and the great majority of us who lack that gift nevertheless hold the same obligation of civility.
>
> This story illustrates what I mean when I say that civility is the set of sacrifices we make for the sake of our fellow passengers. Sara Kestenbaum was generous to us, giving of herself with no benefit to herself, and she demonstrated not merely a welcome that nobody else offered, but a faith in us, a trust that we were people to whom one could and should be generous....
> Saying hello to a stranger on the street or driving with a bit more care are acts of generosity. Conceding the basic goodwill of my fellow citizens, even when I disagree with them, is an act of trust. By greeting us as she did, in the midst of a white neighborhood and a racially charged era, Sara was generous when nobody forced her to be, and trusting when there was no reason to be. Of such risks is true civility constructed.[5]

---

5   Carter, 62–63.

READING 2.3: Quotations on the Problem of the Stranger

"When a stranger resides with you in your land, you should not wrong him. The stranger who resides with you shall be to you as one of your citizens; you shall love him as yourself, for you were strangers in the land of Egypt: I the LORD am your God."

—Leviticus 19:33–34

"No man* is an island entire of itself; every man is a piece of the continent, a part of the main; if a clod be washed away by the sea, Europe is the less, as well as if a promontory were, as well as a manor of thy friend or of thine own were; any man's death diminishes me, because I am involved in mankind. And therefore never send to know for whom the bell tolls; it tolls for thee."

—John Donne, "Devotion XVII," *Devotions upon Emergent Occasions* (1624)

---

* The word *man* was commonly used in earlier centuries to refer to a human being. Its use reflects a particular time period.

A Biblical Perspective on *Areyvut*

This lesson focuses on the biblical account of Joseph and his brothers. It can be read as an illustration of the ties that bind us to a family, a tribe, or a nation. It is also a powerful reminder that the stranger—the person not like "us"—can be anyone, even a member of our own family. The focus in this reading of Joseph's story is not Joseph but Judah, one of his ten older brothers. Students will examine three passages that trace Judah's growing sense of *areyvut*.

Essential Questions
- How are members of a family tied to one another?
- What strengthens those ties?
- What strains those ties?

Recommended Resources
- Reading 2.4: Genesis 37, 43–45
- Reading 2.5: "They Saw Him from Afar"
- Reading 2.6: Interpreting the Story of Joseph and His Brothers

Activity Ideas
For more information on specific teaching strategies highlighted in this lesson, see the Appendix.

GETTING STARTED
Explain to students that they will be reading the story of Joseph and his brothers. Ask what students already know about the story. You may wish to have them list the things they know in their journals, along with any questions they have about the story. Remind students that the story centers on relations within a family, particularly relations among siblings. It is a topic that most students know intimately. What unites brothers and sisters? What issues tend to divide them and even strain their relationship? Explain that even though the Torah focuses on Joseph, we will pay special attention to the behavior of his brothers—particularly Judah.

ANALYZING THE TEXT
You may wish to have students read the entire story of Joseph and his brothers (Genesis 37–45), or you may prefer to tell the story to the class so that you can focus solely on the relevant passages—Genesis 37, 43, 44, and 45 (Reading 2.4). Here is a summary you can use:

Joseph was the eleventh of Jacob's twelve sons. Because Joseph was his father's favorite, his brothers were jealous of him. They particularly hated his accounts of dreams in which he described his brothers as bowing to him. To get back at him, they plotted to murder him. At the last minute, Judah intervened. He suggested selling Joseph into slavery instead; the brothers agreed.

Joseph was eventually purchased by a high-ranking Egyptian named Potiphar and in time assumed an important position in the man's household. He served faithfully until his master's wife slandered him. As a result of her lie, he was sent to prison. While in prison, he interpreted the dreams of the Pharaoh's baker and wine-taster. A few years later, after Pharaoh had a series of troubling dreams, the wine-taster brought Joseph to his attention as someone who could explain those dreams. Joseph was brought before Pharaoh and promptly interpreted the ruler's dreams as a warning that seven years of plenty would be followed by seven years of famine and hunger. Pharaoh was pleased with Joseph's interpretation and put him in charge of storing food during the first seven years so that there would be enough food for all of Egypt through the years of famine. As a result, Joseph became the highest-ranking person in Egypt after Pharaoh.

During the seven years of famine, Judah and his brothers came to Egypt to purchase grain for their starving family. Joseph recognized them but did not reveal his identity. Instead he invited them to dinner. While they were at his home, he secretly placed a valuable cup in one of the bags of grain they purchased. Soon after they left, he ordered his guards to chase after them and accuse them of theft. Their bags were searched and the stolen object was found. When the brothers insisted they were innocent, Joseph said he would believe them only if they brought their youngest brother Benjamin to him. He kept one brother as a hostage until the others returned with Benjamin.

Not long after Benjamin arrived in Egypt, Joseph once again hid an object in a bag belonging to the brothers. This time Joseph demanded that Benjamin pay for the theft by becoming his slave. When Judah offered to become a slave in Benjamin's place, Joseph revealed his true identity. His brothers then asked for forgiveness for what they had done to Joseph. He accepted their apology. The brothers returned home and brought their families, including their elderly father, back to Egypt.

After students have read or heard the story, ask what questions they have about it and discuss possible answers. Then direct their attention to Judah's role in the story by having students carefully read Genesis 37, 43, and 44. The three chapters trace the development of Judah's sense of *areyvut*. Have students record the facts of Judah's story in their journals before asking them to interpret the reading with their *chavruta*. Ask the partners to identify the specific verses that reveal Judah's sense of *areyvut*. What may have motivated his actions in each instance? Which verse(s) show a limited sense of *areyvut*? Which show an expanded sense? Which show the fulfillment of *areyvut*?

- "How will it profit us to kill him? Let us sell him instead...." Genesis 37:26–27
- "I will be his guarantor [*a'arvenu*]... If I do not return Benjamin to you I will have sinned to you all my days...." Genesis 43:8–10
- "For your servant made himself responsible [*arav*, related to *areyvut*] for the boy.... Now, let me be a slave to you instead of the boy...." Genesis 44:30–34

EXAMINING AN INTERPRETATION

In reading the story of Joseph and his brothers, a nineteenth-century Hasidic teacher reflected on a single verse in Genesis 37: "They saw him from afar, and before he came close to them they conspired to kill him." In Reading 2.5, Isaac of Worka reminds readers of the difference between seeing a person from afar and seeing that same individual up close. His reading of the text may prompt a discussion of the differences between a stereotype (an overgeneralized image formed at a distance) and a face-to-face encounter with a person. It can also be used to draw attention to the value of a close reading of a passage over "skimming" the text.

MAKING COMPARISONS AND CONTRASTS

The story of Joseph and his brothers is one of four stories in Genesis that deal with quarrels between brothers. Rabbi Joseph Telushkin has commented on the similarities and differences among the four (Reading 2.6). Have students read Telushkin's comments with a partner and then discuss what the four stories teach about the factors that encourage the growth and expansion of *areyvut*. According to Telushkin, what may be the obstacles to *areyvut*? Do you agree? If so, why? If not, what do you think the obstacles are? What does James L. Kugel, a biblical scholar, add to our understanding of why the story of Joseph and his brothers ends differently from the other three stories?

ASSESSMENT

Ask students to use the three passages featured in this lesson to write Judah's story in their own words. What do those passages teach us about the development of a sense of *areyvut*? What do they teach us about the importance of *areyvut*? Have students write a title for their story that reflects the main idea. As another way of assessing students' understanding, have them use what they learned to revise, expand, and/or update their working definition of *areyvut*. Those definitions should reflect the growth of Judah's sense of *areyvut*.

READING 2.4: Genesis 37, 43–45 (part 1 of 11)[6]

VA-YEISHEV

37 Now Jacob was settled in the land where his father had sojourned, the land of Canaan. [2]This, then, is the line of Jacob:

At seventeen years of age, Joseph tended the flocks with his brothers, as a helper to the sons of his father's wives Bilhah and Zilpah. And Joseph brought bad reports of them to their father. [3]Now Israel loved Joseph best of all his sons, for he was the child of his old age; and he had made him an ornamented tunic. [4]And when his brothers saw that their father loved him more than any of his brothers, they hated him so that they could not speak a friendly word to him.

[5]Once Joseph had a dream which he told to his brothers; and they hated him even more. [6]He said to them, "Hear this dream which I have dreamed: [7]There we were binding sheaves in the field, when suddenly my sheaf stood up and remained upright; then your sheaves gathered around and bowed low to my sheaf." [8]His brothers answered, "Do you mean to reign over us? Do you mean to rule over us?" And they hated him even more for his talk about his dreams.

[9]He dreamed another dream and told it to his brothers, saying, "Look, I have had another dream: And this time, the sun, the moon, and eleven stars were bowing down to me." [10]And when he told it to his father and brothers, his father berated him. "What," he said to him, "is this dream you have dreamed? Are we to come, I and your mother and your brothers, and bow low to you to the ground?" [11]So his brothers were wrought up at him, and his father kept the matter in mind.

[12]One time, when his brothers had gone to pasture their father's flock at Shechem, [13]Israel said to Joseph, "Your brothers are pasturing at Shechem. Come, I will send you to them." He

וישב

לז וַיֵּשֶׁב יַעֲקֹב בְּאֶרֶץ מְגוּרֵי אָבִיו בְּאֶרֶץ כְּנָעַן: 2אֵלֶּה | תֹּלְדוֹת יַעֲקֹב יוֹסֵף בֶּן־שְׁבַע־עֶשְׂרֵה שָׁנָה הָיָה רֹעֶה אֶת־אֶחָיו בַּצֹּאן וְהוּא נַעַר אֶת־בְּנֵי בִלְהָה וְאֶת־בְּנֵי זִלְפָּה נְשֵׁי אָבִיו וַיָּבֵא יוֹסֵף אֶת־דִּבָּתָם רָעָה אֶל־אֲבִיהֶם: 3וְיִשְׂרָאֵל אָהַב אֶת־יוֹסֵף מִכָּל־בָּנָיו כִּי־בֶן־זְקֻנִים הוּא לוֹ וְעָשָׂה לוֹ כְּתֹנֶת פַּסִּים: 4וַיִּרְאוּ אֶחָיו כִּי־אֹתוֹ אָהַב אֲבִיהֶם מִכָּל־אֶחָיו וַיִּשְׂנְאוּ אֹתוֹ וְלֹא יָכְלוּ דַּבְּרוֹ לְשָׁלֹם: 5וַיַּחֲלֹם יוֹסֵף חֲלוֹם וַיַּגֵּד לְאֶחָיו וַיּוֹסִפוּ עוֹד שְׂנֹא אֹתוֹ: 6וַיֹּאמֶר אֲלֵיהֶם שִׁמְעוּ־נָא הַחֲלוֹם הַזֶּה אֲשֶׁר חָלָמְתִּי: 7וְהִנֵּה אֲנַחְנוּ מְאַלְּמִים אֲלֻמִּים בְּתוֹךְ הַשָּׂדֶה וְהִנֵּה קָמָה אֲלֻמָּתִי וְגַם־נִצָּבָה וְהִנֵּה תְסֻבֶּינָה אֲלֻמֹּתֵיכֶם וַתִּשְׁתַּחֲוֶיןָ לַאֲלֻמָּתִי: 8וַיֹּאמְרוּ לוֹ אֶחָיו הֲמָלֹךְ תִּמְלֹךְ עָלֵינוּ אִם־מָשׁוֹל תִּמְשֹׁל בָּנוּ וַיּוֹסִפוּ עוֹד שְׂנֹא אֹתוֹ עַל־חֲלֹמֹתָיו וְעַל־דְּבָרָיו: 9וַיַּחֲלֹם עוֹד חֲלוֹם אַחֵר וַיְסַפֵּר אֹתוֹ לְאֶחָיו וַיֹּאמֶר הִנֵּה חָלַמְתִּי חֲלוֹם עוֹד וְהִנֵּה הַשֶּׁמֶשׁ וְהַיָּרֵחַ וְאַחַד עָשָׂר כּוֹכָבִים מִשְׁתַּחֲוִים לִי: 10וַיְסַפֵּר אֶל־אָבִיו וְאֶל־אֶחָיו וַיִּגְעַר־בּוֹ אָבִיו וַיֹּאמֶר לוֹ מָה הַחֲלוֹם הַזֶּה אֲשֶׁר חָלָמְתָּ הֲבוֹא נָבוֹא אֲנִי וְאִמְּךָ וְאַחֶיךָ לְהִשְׁתַּחֲוֹת לְךָ אָרְצָה: 11וַיְקַנְאוּ־בוֹ אֶחָיו וְאָבִיו שָׁמַר אֶת־הַדָּבָר: שני 12וַיֵּלְכוּ אֶחָיו לִרְעוֹת אֶת*־צֹאן אֲבִיהֶם בִּשְׁכֶם: 13וַיֹּאמֶר יִשְׂרָאֵל אֶל־יוֹסֵף הֲלוֹא אַחֶיךָ רֹעִים בִּשְׁכֶם לְכָה וְאֶשְׁלָחֲךָ

v. 12. נקוד על א׳ ת׳

6 Reprinted from the *JPS Hebrew-English Tanakh: The Holy Scriptures* by permission of the University of Nebraska Press (copyright 1985, 1999, 2000 by the Jewish Publication Society, Philadelphia).

answered, "I am ready." ¹⁴And he said to him, "Go and see how your brothers are and how the flocks are faring, and bring me back word." So he sent him from the valley of Hebron.

When he reached Shechem, ¹⁵a man came upon him wandering in the fields. The man asked him, "What are you looking for?" ¹⁶He answered, "I am looking for my brothers. Could you tell me where they are pasturing?" ¹⁷The man said, "They have gone from here, for I heard them say: Let us go to Dothan." So Joseph followed his brothers and found them at Dothan.

¹⁸They saw him from afar, and before he came close to them they conspired to kill him. ¹⁹They said to one another, "Here comes that dreamer! ²⁰Come now, let us kill him and

throw him into one of the pits; and we can say, 'A savage beast devoured him.' We shall see what comes of his dreams!" ²¹But when Reuben heard it, he tried to save him from them. He said, "Let us not take his life." ²²And Reuben went on, "Shed no blood! Cast him into that pit out in the wilderness, but do not touch him yourselves"—intending to save him from them and restore him to his father. ²³When Joseph came up to his brothers, they stripped Joseph of his tunic, the ornamented tunic that he was wearing, ²⁴and took him and cast him into the pit. The pit was empty; there was no water in it.

²⁵Then they sat down to a meal. Looking up, they saw a caravan of Ishmaelites coming from

אֲלֵיהֶ֖ם וַיֹּ֣אמֶר ל֑וֹ הִנֵּֽנִי׃ ¹⁴וַיֹּ֣אמֶר ל֗וֹ לֶךְ־
נָ֨א רְאֵ֜ה אֶת־שְׁל֤וֹם אַחֶ֙יךָ֙ וְאֶת־שְׁל֣וֹם
הַצֹּ֔אן וַהֲשִׁבֵ֖נִי דָּבָ֑ר וַיִּשְׁלָחֵ֙הוּ֙ מֵעֵ֣מֶק
חֶבְר֔וֹן
וַיָּבֹ֖א שְׁכֶֽמָה׃ ¹⁵וַיִּמְצָאֵ֣הוּ אִ֔ישׁ וְהִנֵּ֥ה
תֹעֶ֖ה בַּשָּׂדֶ֑ה וַיִּשְׁאָלֵ֧הוּ הָאִ֛ישׁ לֵאמֹ֖ר
מַה־תְּבַקֵּֽשׁ׃ ¹⁶וַיֹּ֕אמֶר אֶת־אַחַ֖י אָנֹכִ֣י
מְבַקֵּ֑שׁ הַגִּֽידָה־נָּ֣א לִ֔י אֵיפֹ֖ה הֵ֥ם רֹעִֽים׃
¹⁷וַיֹּ֤אמֶר הָאִישׁ֙ נָסְע֣וּ מִזֶּ֔ה כִּ֤י שָׁמַ֙עְתִּי֙
אֹֽמְרִ֔ים נֵלְכָ֖ה דֹּתָ֑יְנָה וַיֵּ֤לֶךְ יוֹסֵף֙ אַחַ֣ר
אֶחָ֔יו וַיִּמְצָאֵ֖ם בְּדֹתָֽן׃
¹⁸וַיִּרְא֥וּ אֹת֖וֹ מֵרָחֹ֑ק וּבְטֶ֙רֶם֙ יִקְרַ֣ב אֲלֵיהֶ֔ם
וַיִּֽתְנַכְּל֥וּ אֹת֖וֹ לַהֲמִיתֽוֹ׃ ¹⁹וַיֹּֽאמְר֖וּ אִ֣ישׁ
אֶל־אָחִ֑יו הִנֵּ֗ה בַּ֛עַל הַחֲלֹמ֥וֹת הַלָּזֶ֖ה בָּֽא׃
²⁰וְעַתָּ֣ה ׀ לְכ֣וּ וְנַֽהַרְגֵ֗הוּ וְנַשְׁלִכֵ֙הוּ֙ בְּאַחַ֣ד
הַבֹּר֔וֹת וְאָמַ֕רְנוּ חַיָּ֥ה רָעָ֖ה אֲכָלָ֑תְהוּ
וְנִרְאֶ֕ה מַה־יִּהְי֖וּ חֲלֹמֹתָֽיו׃ ²¹וַיִּשְׁמַ֣ע
רְאוּבֵ֔ן וַיַּצִּלֵ֖הוּ מִיָּדָ֑ם וַיֹּ֕אמֶר לֹ֥א נַכֶּ֖נּוּ
נָֽפֶשׁ׃ ²²וַיֹּ֨אמֶר אֲלֵהֶ֣ם ׀ רְאוּבֵ֗ן אַל־
תִּשְׁפְּכוּ־דָם֒ הַשְׁלִ֣יכוּ אֹת֗וֹ אֶל־הַבּ֤וֹר הַזֶּה֙
אֲשֶׁ֣ר בַּמִּדְבָּ֔ר וְיָ֖ד אַל־תִּשְׁלְחוּ־ב֑וֹ לְמַ֗עַן
הַצִּ֤יל אֹתוֹ֙ מִיָּדָ֔ם לַהֲשִׁיב֖וֹ אֶל־אָבִֽיו׃
שלישי ²³וַֽיְהִ֕י כַּֽאֲשֶׁר־בָּ֥א יוֹסֵ֖ף אֶל־אֶחָ֑יו
וַיַּפְשִׁ֤יטוּ אֶת־יוֹסֵף֙ אֶת־כֻּתָּנְתּ֔וֹ אֶת־
כְּתֹ֥נֶת הַפַּסִּ֖ים אֲשֶׁ֥ר עָלָֽיו׃ ²⁴וַיִּ֨קָּחֻ֔הוּ
וַיַּשְׁלִ֥כוּ אֹת֖וֹ הַבֹּ֑רָה וְהַבּ֣וֹר רֵ֔ק אֵ֥ין בּ֖וֹ
מָֽיִם׃
²⁵וַיֵּשְׁבוּ֮ לֶֽאֱכָל־לֶחֶם֒ וַיִּשְׂא֤וּ עֵֽינֵיהֶם֙

Gilead, their camels bearing gum, balm, and ladanum to be taken to Egypt. [26]Then Judah said to his brothers, "What do we gain by killing our brother and covering up his blood? [27]Come, let us sell him to the Ishmaelites, but let us not do away with him ourselves. After all, he is our brother, our own flesh." His brothers agreed. [28]When Midianite traders passed by, they pulled Joseph up out of the pit. They sold Joseph for twenty pieces of silver to the Ishmaelites, who brought Joseph to Egypt.

[29]When Reuben returned to the pit and saw that Joseph was not in the pit, he rent his clothes. [30]Returning to his brothers, he said, "The boy is gone! Now, what am I to do?" [31]Then they took Joseph's tunic, slaughtered

a kid, and dipped the tunic in the blood. [32]They had the ornamented tunic taken to their father, and they said, "We found this. Please examine it; is it your son's tunic or not?" [33]He recognized it, and said, "My son's tunic! A savage beast devoured him! Joseph was torn by a beast!" [34]Jacob rent his clothes, put sackcloth on his loins, and observed mourning for his son many days. [35]All his sons and daughters sought to comfort him; but he refused to be comforted, saying, "No, I will go down mourning to my son in Sheol." Thus his father bewailed him.

[36]The Midianites, meanwhile, sold him in Egypt to Potiphar, a courtier of Pharaoh and his chief steward.

וַיִּרְאוּ וְהִנֵּה אֹרְחַת יִשְׁמְעֵאלִים בָּאָה מִגִּלְעָד וּגְמַלֵּיהֶם נֹשְׂאִים נְכֹאת וּצְרִי וָלֹט הוֹלְכִים לְהוֹרִיד מִצְרָיְמָה: 26 וַיֹּאמֶר יְהוּדָה אֶל־אֶחָיו מַה־בֶּצַע כִּי נַהֲרֹג אֶת־ אָחִינוּ וְכִסִּינוּ אֶת־דָּמוֹ: 27 לְכוּ וְנִמְכְּרֶנּוּ לַיִּשְׁמְעֵאלִים וְיָדֵנוּ אַל־תְּהִי־בוֹ כִּי־אָחִינוּ בְשָׂרֵנוּ הוּא וַיִּשְׁמְעוּ אֶחָיו: 28 וַיַּעַבְרוּ אֲנָשִׁים מִדְיָנִים סֹחֲרִים וַיִּמְשְׁכוּ וַיַּעֲלוּ אֶת־יוֹסֵף מִן־הַבּוֹר וַיִּמְכְּרוּ אֶת־יוֹסֵף לַיִּשְׁמְעֵאלִים בְּעֶשְׂרִים כָּסֶף וַיָּבִיאוּ אֶת־ יוֹסֵף מִצְרָיְמָה:

29 וַיָּשָׁב רְאוּבֵן אֶל־הַבּוֹר וְהִנֵּה אֵין־יוֹסֵף בַּבּוֹר וַיִּקְרַע אֶת־בְּגָדָיו: 30 וַיָּשָׁב אֶל־אֶחָיו וַיֹּאמַר הַיֶּלֶד אֵינֶנּוּ וַאֲנִי אָנָה אֲנִי־בָא:

31 וַיִּקְחוּ אֶת־כְּתֹנֶת יוֹסֵף וַיִּשְׁחֲטוּ שְׂעִיר עִזִּים וַיִּטְבְּלוּ אֶת־הַכֻּתֹּנֶת בַּדָּם: 32 וַיְשַׁלְּחוּ אֶת־כְּתֹנֶת הַפַּסִּים וַיָּבִיאוּ אֶל־אֲבִיהֶם וַיֹּאמְרוּ זֹאת מָצָאנוּ הַכֶּר־ נָא הַכְּתֹנֶת בִּנְךָ הִוא אִם־לֹא: 33 וַיַּכִּירָהּ וַיֹּאמֶר כְּתֹנֶת בְּנִי חַיָּה רָעָה אֲכָלָתְהוּ טָרֹף טֹרַף יוֹסֵף: 34 וַיִּקְרַע יַעֲקֹב שִׂמְלֹתָיו וַיָּשֶׂם שַׂק בְּמָתְנָיו וַיִּתְאַבֵּל עַל־בְּנוֹ יָמִים רַבִּים: 35 וַיָּקֻמוּ כָל־בָּנָיו וְכָל־בְּנֹתָיו לְנַחֲמוֹ וַיְמָאֵן לְהִתְנַחֵם וַיֹּאמֶר כִּי־אֵרֵד אֶל־בְּנִי אָבֵל שְׁאֹלָה וַיֵּבְךְ אֹתוֹ אָבִיו: 36 וְהַמְּדָנִים מָכְרוּ אֹתוֹ אֶל־מִצְרָיִם לְפוֹטִיפַר סְרִיס פַּרְעֹה שַׂר הַטַּבָּחִים: פ

43 But the famine in the land was severe. ²And when they had eaten up the rations which they had brought from Egypt, their father said to them, "Go again and procure some food for us." ³But Judah said to him, "The man warned us, 'Do not let me see your faces unless your brother is with you.' ⁴If you will let our brother go with us, we will go down and procure food for you; ⁵but if you will not let him go, we will not go down, for the man said to us, 'Do not let me see your faces unless your brother is with you.'" ⁶And Israel said, "Why did you serve me so ill as to tell the man that you had another brother?" ⁷They replied, "But the man kept asking about us and our family, saying, 'Is your father still living? Have you another brother?' And we answered him accordingly. How were we to know that he would say, 'Bring your brother here'?"

⁸Then Judah said to his father Israel, "Send the boy in my care, and let us be on our way, that we may live and not die—you and we and our children. ⁹I myself will be surety for him; you may hold me responsible: if I do not bring him back to you and set him before you, I shall stand guilty before you forever. ¹⁰For we could have been there and back twice if we had not dawdled."

¹¹Then their father Israel said to them, "If it must be so, do this: take some of the choice products of the land in your baggage, and carry them down as a gift for the man—some balm

מג וְהָרָעָב כָּבֵד בָּאָרֶץ: ²וַיְהִי
כַּאֲשֶׁר כִּלּוּ לֶאֱכֹל אֶת־הַשֶּׁבֶר אֲשֶׁר
הֵבִיאוּ מִמִּצְרָיִם וַיֹּאמֶר אֲלֵיהֶם אֲבִיהֶם
שֻׁבוּ שִׁבְרוּ־לָנוּ מְעַט־אֹכֶל: ³וַיֹּאמֶר אֵלָיו
יְהוּדָה לֵאמֹר הָעֵד הֵעִד בָּנוּ הָאִישׁ
לֵאמֹר לֹא־תִרְאוּ פָנַי בִּלְתִּי אֲחִיכֶם
אִתְּכֶם: ⁴אִם־יֶשְׁךָ מְשַׁלֵּחַ אֶת־אָחִינוּ
אִתָּנוּ נֵרְדָה וְנִשְׁבְּרָה לְךָ אֹכֶל: ⁵וְאִם־
אֵינְךָ מְשַׁלֵּחַ לֹא נֵרֵד כִּי־הָאִישׁ אָמַר
אֵלֵינוּ לֹא־תִרְאוּ פָנַי בִּלְתִּי אֲחִיכֶם
אִתְּכֶם: ⁶וַיֹּאמֶר יִשְׂרָאֵל לָמָה הֲרֵעֹתֶם
לִי לְהַגִּיד לָאִישׁ הַעוֹד לָכֶם אָח:

⁷וַיֹּאמְרוּ שָׁאוֹל שָׁאַל־הָאִישׁ לָנוּ
וּלְמוֹלַדְתֵּנוּ לֵאמֹר הַעוֹד אֲבִיכֶם חַי הֲיֵשׁ
לָכֶם אָח וַנַּגֶּד־לוֹ עַל־פִּי הַדְּבָרִים הָאֵלֶּה
הֲיָדוֹעַ נֵדַע כִּי יֹאמַר הוֹרִידוּ אֶת־
אֲחִיכֶם:

⁸וַיֹּאמֶר יְהוּדָה אֶל־יִשְׂרָאֵל אָבִיו שִׁלְחָה
הַנַּעַר אִתִּי וְנָקוּמָה וְנֵלֵכָה וְנִחְיֶה וְלֹא
נָמוּת גַּם־אֲנַחְנוּ גַם־אַתָּה גַּם־טַפֵּנוּ:
⁹אָנֹכִי אֶעֶרְבֶנּוּ מִיָּדִי תְּבַקְשֶׁנּוּ אִם־לֹא
הֲבִיאֹתִיו אֵלֶיךָ וְהִצַּגְתִּיו לְפָנֶיךָ וְחָטָאתִי
לְךָ כָּל־הַיָּמִים: ¹⁰כִּי לוּלֵא הִתְמַהְמָהְנוּ
כִּי־עַתָּה שַׁבְנוּ זֶה פַעֲמָיִם:

¹¹וַיֹּאמֶר אֲלֵהֶם יִשְׂרָאֵל אֲבִיהֶם אִם־כֵּן
אֵפוֹא זֹאת עֲשׂוּ קְחוּ מִזִּמְרַת הָאָרֶץ
בִּכְלֵיכֶם וְהוֹרִידוּ לָאִישׁ מִנְחָה מְעַט צֳרִי

and some honey, gum, ladanum, pistachio nuts, and almonds. ¹²And take with you double the money, carrying back with you the money that was replaced in the mouths of your bags; perhaps it was a mistake. ¹³Take your brother too; and go back at once to the man. ¹⁴And may El Shaddai dispose the man to mercy toward you, that he may release to you your other brother, as well as Benjamin. As for me, if I am to be bereaved, I shall be bereaved."

¹⁵So the men took that gift, and they took with them double the money, as well as Benjamin. They made their way down to Egypt, where they presented themselves to Joseph. ¹⁶When Joseph saw Benjamin with them, he said to his house steward, "Take the men into the house; slaughter and prepare an animal, for the men will dine with me at noon." ¹⁷The man did as Joseph said, and he brought the men into Joseph's house. ¹⁸But the men were frightened at being brought into Joseph's house. "It must be," they thought, "because of the money replaced in our bags the first time that we have been brought inside, as a pretext to attack us and seize us as slaves, with our pack animals." ¹⁹So they went up to Joseph's house steward and spoke to him at the entrance of the house. ²⁰"If you please, my lord," they said, "we came down once before to procure food. ²¹But when

וּמְעַט צְרִי דְּבַשׁ נְכֹאת וָלֹט בָּטְנִים וּשְׁקֵדִים:
¹² וְכֶסֶף מִשְׁנֶה קְחוּ בְיֶדְכֶם וְאֶת־הַכֶּסֶף הַמּוּשָׁב בְּפִי אַמְתְּחֹתֵיכֶם תָּשִׁיבוּ בְיֶדְכֶם אוּלַי מִשְׁגֶּה הוּא: ¹³ וְאֶת־אֲחִיכֶם קָחוּ וְקוּמוּ שׁוּבוּ אֶל־הָאִישׁ: ¹⁴ וְאֵל שַׁדַּי יִתֵּן לָכֶם רַחֲמִים לִפְנֵי הָאִישׁ וְשִׁלַּח לָכֶם אֶת־אֲחִיכֶם אַחֵר וְאֶת־בִּנְיָמִין וַאֲנִי כַּאֲשֶׁר שָׁכֹלְתִּי שָׁכָלְתִּי:
¹⁵ וַיִּקְחוּ הָאֲנָשִׁים אֶת־הַמִּנְחָה הַזֹּאת וּמִשְׁנֶה־כֶּסֶף לָקְחוּ בְיָדָם וְאֶת־בִּנְיָמִן וַיָּקֻמוּ וַיֵּרְדוּ מִצְרַיִם וַיַּעַמְדוּ לִפְנֵי יוֹסֵף:
ש ¹⁶ וַיַּרְא יוֹסֵף אִתָּם אֶת־בִּנְיָמִין וַיֹּאמֶר לַאֲשֶׁר עַל־בֵּיתוֹ הָבֵא אֶת־הָאֲנָשִׁים הַבָּיְתָה וּטְבֹחַ טֶבַח וְהָכֵן כִּי אִתִּי יֹאכְלוּ הָאֲנָשִׁים בַּצָּהֳרָיִם: ¹⁷ וַיַּעַשׂ הָאִישׁ כַּאֲשֶׁר אָמַר יוֹסֵף וַיָּבֵא הָאִישׁ אֶת־הָאֲנָשִׁים בֵּיתָה יוֹסֵף: ¹⁸ וַיִּירְאוּ הָאֲנָשִׁים כִּי הוּבְאוּ בֵּית יוֹסֵף וַיֹּאמְרוּ עַל־דְּבַר הַכֶּסֶף הַשָּׁב בְּאַמְתְּחֹתֵינוּ בַּתְּחִלָּה אֲנַחְנוּ מוּבָאִים לְהִתְגֹּלֵל עָלֵינוּ וּלְהִתְנַפֵּל עָלֵינוּ וְלָקַחַת אֹתָנוּ לַעֲבָדִים וְאֶת־חֲמֹרֵינוּ:
¹⁹ וַיִּגְּשׁוּ אֶל־הָאִישׁ אֲשֶׁר עַל־בֵּית יוֹסֵף וַיְדַבְּרוּ אֵלָיו פֶּתַח הַבָּיִת: ²⁰ וַיֹּאמְרוּ בִּי אֲדֹנִי יָרֹד יָרַדְנוּ בַּתְּחִלָּה לִשְׁבָּר־אֹכֶל:

we arrived at the night encampment and opened our bags, there was each one's money in the mouth of his bag, our money in full. So we have brought it back with us. ²²And we have brought down with us other money to procure food. We do not know who put the money in our bags." ²³He replied, "All is well with you; do not be afraid. Your God, the God of your father, must have put treasure in your bags for you. I got your payment." And he brought out Simeon to them.

²⁴Then the man brought the men into Joseph's house; he gave them water to bathe their feet, and he provided feed for their asses. ²⁵They laid out their gifts to await Joseph's arrival at noon, for they had heard that they were to dine there.

²⁶When Joseph came home, they presented to him the gifts that they had brought with them into the house, bowing low before him to the ground. ²⁷He greeted them, and he said, "How is your aged father of whom you spoke? Is he still in good health?" ²⁸They replied, "It is well with your servant our father; he is still in

²¹וַיְהִי כִּי־בָאנוּ אֶל־הַמָּלוֹן וַנִּפְתְּחָה אֶת־אַמְתְּחֹתֵינוּ וְהִנֵּה כֶסֶף־אִישׁ בְּפִי אַמְתַּחְתּוֹ כַּסְפֵּנוּ בְּמִשְׁקָלוֹ וַנָּשֶׁב אֹתוֹ בְּיָדֵנוּ: ²²וְכֶסֶף אַחֵר הוֹרַדְנוּ בְיָדֵנוּ לִשְׁבָּר־אֹכֶל לֹא יָדַעְנוּ מִי־שָׂם כַּסְפֵּנוּ בְּאַמְתְּחֹתֵינוּ: ²³וַיֹּאמֶר שָׁלוֹם לָכֶם אַל־תִּירָאוּ אֱלֹהֵיכֶם וֵאלֹהֵי אֲבִיכֶם נָתַן לָכֶם מַטְמוֹן בְּאַמְתְּחֹתֵיכֶם כַּסְפְּכֶם בָּא אֵלָי וַיּוֹצֵא אֲלֵהֶם אֶת־שִׁמְעוֹן:

²⁴וַיָּבֵא הָאִישׁ אֶת־הָאֲנָשִׁים בֵּיתָה יוֹסֵף וַיִּתֶּן־מַיִם וַיִּרְחֲצוּ רַגְלֵיהֶם וַיִּתֵּן מִסְפּוֹא לַחֲמֹרֵיהֶם: ²⁵וַיָּכִינוּ אֶת־הַמִּנְחָה עַד־בּוֹא יוֹסֵף בַּצָּהֳרָיִם כִּי שָׁמְעוּ כִּי־שָׁם יֹאכְלוּ לָחֶם:

²⁶וַיָּבֹא יוֹסֵף הַבַּיְתָה וַיָּבִיאוּ* לוֹ אֶת־הַמִּנְחָה אֲשֶׁר־בְּיָדָם הַבָּיְתָה וַיִּשְׁתַּחֲווּ־לוֹ אָרְצָה: ²⁷וַיִּשְׁאַל לָהֶם לְשָׁלוֹם וַיֹּאמֶר הֲשָׁלוֹם אֲבִיכֶם הַזָּקֵן אֲשֶׁר אֲמַרְתֶּם הַעוֹדֶנּוּ חָי: ²⁸וַיֹּאמְרוּ שָׁלוֹם לְעַבְדְּךָ

v. 26. א׳ דגושה

good health." And they bowed and made obeisance.

²⁹Looking about, he saw his brother Benjamin, his mother's son, and asked, "Is this your youngest brother of whom you spoke to me?" And he went on, "May God be gracious to you, my boy." ³⁰With that, Joseph hurried out, for he was overcome with feeling toward his brother and was on the verge of tears; he went into a room and wept there. ³¹Then he washed his face, reappeared, and—now in control of himself—gave the order, "Serve the meal." ³²They served him by himself, and them by themselves, and the Egyptians who ate with him by themselves; for the Egyptians could not dine with the Hebrews, since that would be abhorrent to the Egyptians. ³³As they were seated by his direction, from the oldest in the order of his seniority to the youngest in the order of his youth, the men looked at one another in astonishment. ³⁴Portions were served them from his table; but Benjamin's portion was several times that of anyone else. And they drank their fill with him.

לְאָבִינוּ עוֹדֶנּוּ חָי וַיִּקְּדוּ וישתחו וַיִּשְׁתַּחֲוּוּ:
²⁹וַיִּשָּׂא עֵינָיו וַיַּרְא אֶת־בִּנְיָמִין אָחִיו בֶּן־אִמּוֹ וַיֹּאמֶר הֲזֶה אֲחִיכֶם הַקָּטֹן אֲשֶׁר אֲמַרְתֶּם אֵלָי וַיֹּאמַר אֱלֹהִים יָחְנְךָ בְּנִי:
שביעי ³⁰וַיְמַהֵר יוֹסֵף כִּי־נִכְמְרוּ רַחֲמָיו אֶל־אָחִיו וַיְבַקֵּשׁ לִבְכּוֹת וַיָּבֹא הַחַדְרָה וַיֵּבְךְּ שָׁמָּה: ³¹וַיִּרְחַץ פָּנָיו וַיֵּצֵא וַיִּתְאַפַּק וַיֹּאמֶר שִׂימוּ לָחֶם: ³²וַיָּשִׂימוּ לוֹ לְבַדּוֹ וְלָהֶם לְבַדָּם וְלַמִּצְרִים הָאֹכְלִים אִתּוֹ לְבַדָּם כִּי לֹא יוּכְלוּן הַמִּצְרִים לֶאֱכֹל אֶת־הָעִבְרִים לֶחֶם כִּי־תוֹעֵבָה הִוא לְמִצְרָיִם: ³³וַיֵּשְׁבוּ לְפָנָיו הַבְּכֹר כִּבְכֹרָתוֹ וְהַצָּעִיר כִּצְעִרָתוֹ
וַיִּתְמְהוּ הָאֲנָשִׁים אִישׁ אֶל־רֵעֵהוּ:
³⁴וַיִּשָּׂא מַשְׂאֹת מֵאֵת פָּנָיו אֲלֵהֶם וַתֵּרֶב מַשְׂאַת בִּנְיָמִן מִמַּשְׂאֹת כֻּלָּם חָמֵשׁ יָדוֹת וַיִּשְׁתּוּ וַיִּשְׁכְּרוּ עִמּוֹ:

44 Then he instructed his house steward as follows, "Fill the men's bags with food, as much as they can carry, and put each one's money in the mouth of his bag. [2]Put my silver goblet in the mouth of the bag of the youngest one, together with his money for the rations." And he did as Joseph told him.

[3]With the first light of morning, the men were sent off with their pack animals. [4]They had just left the city and had not gone far, when Joseph said to his steward, "Up, go after the men! And when you overtake them, say to them, 'Why did you repay good with evil? [5]It is the very one from which my master drinks and which he uses for divination. It was a wicked thing for you to do!'"

[6]He overtook them and spoke those words to them. [7]And they said to him, "Why does my lord say such things? Far be it from your servants to do anything of the kind! [8]Here we brought back to you from the land of Canaan the money that we found in the mouths of our bags. How then could we have stolen any silver or gold from your master's house! [9]Whichever of your servants it is found with shall die; the rest of us, moreover, shall become slaves to my lord." [10]He replied, "Although what you are proposing is right, only the one with whom it is found shall be my slave; but the rest of you shall go free."

[11]So each one hastened to lower his bag to the ground, and each one opened his bag. [12]He searched, beginning with the oldest and ending with the youngest; and the goblet turned up in Benjamin's bag. [13]At this they rent their clothes. Each reloaded his pack animal, and they returned to the city.

[14]When Judah and his brothers reentered the house of Joseph, who was still there, they threw themselves on the ground before him. [15]Joseph said to them, "What is this deed that you have done? Do you not know that a man like me practices divination?" [16]Judah replied,

מד וַיְצַו אֶת־אֲשֶׁר עַל־בֵּיתוֹ לֵאמֹר מַלֵּא אֶת־אַמְתְּחֹת הָאֲנָשִׁים אֹכֶל כַּאֲשֶׁר יוּכְלוּן שְׂאֵת וְשִׂים כֶּסֶף־אִישׁ בְּפִי אַמְתַּחְתּוֹ: 2וְאֶת־גְּבִיעִי גְּבִיעַ הַכֶּסֶף תָּשִׂים בְּפִי אַמְתַּחַת הַקָּטֹן וְאֵת כֶּסֶף שִׁבְרוֹ וַיַּעַשׂ כִּדְבַר יוֹסֵף אֲשֶׁר דִּבֵּר: 3הַבֹּקֶר אוֹר וְהָאֲנָשִׁים שֻׁלְּחוּ הֵמָּה וַחֲמֹרֵיהֶם: 4הֵם יָצְאוּ אֶת־הָעִיר לֹא הִרְחִיקוּ וְיוֹסֵף אָמַר לַאֲשֶׁר עַל־בֵּיתוֹ קוּם רְדֹף אַחֲרֵי הָאֲנָשִׁים וְהִשַּׂגְתָּם וְאָמַרְתָּ אֲלֵהֶם לָמָּה שִׁלַּמְתֶּם רָעָה תַּחַת טוֹבָה: 5הֲלוֹא זֶה אֲשֶׁר יִשְׁתֶּה אֲדֹנִי בּוֹ וְהוּא נַחֵשׁ יְנַחֵשׁ בּוֹ הֲרֵעֹתֶם אֲשֶׁר עֲשִׂיתֶם: 6וַיַּשִּׂגֵם וַיְדַבֵּר אֲלֵהֶם אֶת־הַדְּבָרִים הָאֵלֶּה: 7וַיֹּאמְרוּ אֵלָיו לָמָּה יְדַבֵּר אֲדֹנִי כַּדְּבָרִים הָאֵלֶּה חָלִילָה לַעֲבָדֶיךָ מֵעֲשׂוֹת כַּדָּבָר הַזֶּה: 8הֵן כֶּסֶף אֲשֶׁר מָצָאנוּ בְּפִי אַמְתְּחֹתֵינוּ הֱשִׁיבֹנוּ אֵלֶיךָ מֵאֶרֶץ כְּנָעַן וְאֵיךְ נִגְנֹב מִבֵּית אֲדֹנֶיךָ כֶּסֶף אוֹ זָהָב: 9אֲשֶׁר יִמָּצֵא אִתּוֹ מֵעֲבָדֶיךָ וָמֵת וְגַם־אֲנַחְנוּ נִהְיֶה לַאדֹנִי לַעֲבָדִים: 10וַיֹּאמֶר גַּם־עַתָּה כְדִבְרֵיכֶם כֶּן־הוּא אֲשֶׁר יִמָּצֵא אִתּוֹ יִהְיֶה־לִּי עָבֶד וְאַתֶּם תִּהְיוּ נְקִיִּם: 11וַיְמַהֲרוּ וַיּוֹרִדוּ אִישׁ אֶת־אַמְתַּחְתּוֹ אָרְצָה וַיִּפְתְּחוּ אִישׁ אַמְתַּחְתּוֹ: 12וַיְחַפֵּשׂ בַּגָּדוֹל הֵחֵל וּבַקָּטֹן כִּלָּה וַיִּמָּצֵא הַגָּבִיעַ בְּאַמְתַּחַת בִּנְיָמִן: 13וַיִּקְרְעוּ שִׂמְלֹתָם וַיַּעֲמֹס אִישׁ עַל־חֲמֹרוֹ וַיָּשֻׁבוּ הָעִירָה: 14וַיָּבֹא יְהוּדָה וְאֶחָיו בֵּיתָה יוֹסֵף וְהוּא עוֹדֶנּוּ שָׁם וַיִּפְּלוּ לְפָנָיו אָרְצָה: 15וַיֹּאמֶר לָהֶם יוֹסֵף מָה־הַמַּעֲשֶׂה הַזֶּה אֲשֶׁר עֲשִׂיתֶם הֲלוֹא יְדַעְתֶּם כִּי־נַחֵשׁ יְנַחֵשׁ אִישׁ אֲשֶׁר כָּמֹנִי: 16וַיֹּאמֶר יְהוּדָה מַה־

"What can we say to my lord? How can we plead, how can we prove our innocence? God has uncovered the crime of your servants. Here we are, then, slaves of my lord, the rest of us as much as he in whose possession the goblet was found." [17]But he replied, "Far be it from me to act thus! Only he in whose possession the goblet was found shall be my slave; the rest of you go back in peace to your father."

נֹאמַר לַאדֹנִי מַה־נְּדַבֵּר וּמַה־נִּצְטַדָּק הָאֱלֹהִים מָצָא אֶת־עֲוֹן עֲבָדֶיךָ הִנֶּנּוּ עֲבָדִים לַאדֹנִי גַּם־אֲנַחְנוּ גַּם אֲשֶׁר־נִמְצָא הַגָּבִיעַ בְּיָדוֹ: [17]וַיֹּאמֶר חָלִילָה לִּי מֵעֲשׂוֹת זֹאת הָאִישׁ אֲשֶׁר נִמְצָא הַגָּבִיעַ בְּיָדוֹ הוּא יִהְיֶה־לִּי עָבֶד וְאַתֶּם עֲלוּ לְשָׁלוֹם אֶל־אֲבִיכֶם: פ

45 Joseph could no longer control himself before all his attendants, and he cried out,

מה וְלֹא־יָכֹל יוֹסֵף לְהִתְאַפֵּק לְכֹל הַנִּצָּבִים עָלָיו וַיִּקְרָא הוֹצִיאוּ כָל־אִישׁ

v. 29. חסר א'

"Have everyone withdraw from me!" So there was no one else about when Joseph made himself known to his brothers. [2]His sobs were so loud that the Egyptians could hear, and so the news reached Pharaoh's palace.

[3]Joseph said to his brothers, "I am Joseph. Is my father still well?" But his brothers could not answer him, so dumfounded were they on account of him.

[4]Then Joseph said to his brothers, "Come forward to me." And when they came forward, he said, "I am your brother Joseph, he whom you sold into Egypt. [5]Now, do not be distressed or reproach yourselves because you sold me hither; it was to save life that God sent me ahead of you. [6]It is now two years that there has been famine in the land, and there are still five years to come in which there shall be no

מֵעָלָי וְלֹא־עָמַד אִישׁ אִתּוֹ בְּהִתְוַדַּע יוֹסֵף אֶל־אֶחָיו: [2]וַיִּתֵּן אֶת־קֹלוֹ בִּבְכִי וַיִּשְׁמְעוּ מִצְרַיִם וַיִּשְׁמַע בֵּית פַּרְעֹה:
[3]וַיֹּאמֶר יוֹסֵף אֶל־אֶחָיו אֲנִי יוֹסֵף הַעוֹד אָבִי חָי וְלֹא־יָכְלוּ אֶחָיו לַעֲנוֹת אֹתוֹ כִּי נִבְהֲלוּ מִפָּנָיו:
[4]וַיֹּאמֶר יוֹסֵף אֶל־אֶחָיו גְּשׁוּ־נָא אֵלַי וַיִּגָּשׁוּ וַיֹּאמֶר אֲנִי יוֹסֵף אֲחִיכֶם אֲשֶׁר־מְכַרְתֶּם אֹתִי מִצְרָיְמָה: [5]וְעַתָּה | אַל־תֵּעָצְבוּ וְאַל־יִחַר בְּעֵינֵיכֶם כִּי־מְכַרְתֶּם אֹתִי הֵנָּה כִּי לְמִחְיָה שְׁלָחַנִי אֱלֹהִים לִפְנֵיכֶם: [6]כִּי־זֶה שְׁנָתַיִם הָרָעָב בְּקֶרֶב הָאָרֶץ וְעוֹד חָמֵשׁ שָׁנִים אֲשֶׁר אֵין־חָרִישׁ

yield from tilling. 7God has sent me ahead of you to ensure your survival on earth, and to save your lives in an extraordinary deliverance. 8So, it was not you who sent me here, but God; and He has made me a father to Pharaoh, lord of all his household, and ruler over the whole land of Egypt.

9"Now, hurry back to my father and say to him: Thus says your son Joseph, 'God has made me lord of all Egypt; come down to me without delay. 10You will dwell in the region of Goshen, where you will be near me—you and your children and your grandchildren, your flocks and herds, and all that is yours. 11There I will provide for you—for there are yet five years of famine to come—that you and your household and all that is yours may not suffer want.' 12You can see for yourselves, and my brother Benjamin for himself, that it is indeed I who am speaking to you. 13And you must tell my father everything about my high station in Egypt and all that you have seen; and bring my father here with all speed."

14With that he embraced his brother Benjamin around the neck and wept, and Benjamin wept on his neck. 15He kissed all his brothers

וְקָצִיר: 7וַיִּשְׁלָחֵנִי אֱלֹהִים לִפְנֵיכֶם לָשׂוּם לָכֶם שְׁאֵרִית בָּאָרֶץ וּלְהַחֲיוֹת לָכֶם לִפְלֵיטָה גְּדֹלָה: 8וְעַתָּה לֹא-אַתֶּם שְׁלַחְתֶּם אֹתִי הֵנָּה כִּי הָאֱלֹהִים וַיְשִׂימֵנִי לְאָב לְפַרְעֹה וּלְאָדוֹן לְכָל-בֵּיתוֹ וּמֹשֵׁל בְּכָל-אֶרֶץ מִצְרָיִם: 9מַהֲרוּ וַעֲלוּ אֶל-אָבִי וַאֲמַרְתֶּם אֵלָיו כֹּה אָמַר בִּנְךָ יוֹסֵף שָׂמַנִי אֱלֹהִים לְאָדוֹן לְכָל-מִצְרָיִם רְדָה אֵלַי אַל-תַּעֲמֹד: 10וְיָשַׁבְתָּ בְאֶרֶץ-גֹּשֶׁן וְהָיִיתָ קָרוֹב אֵלַי אַתָּה וּבָנֶיךָ וּבְנֵי בָנֶיךָ וְצֹאנְךָ וּבְקָרְךָ וְכָל-אֲשֶׁר-לָךְ: 11וְכִלְכַּלְתִּי אֹתְךָ שָׁם כִּי-עוֹד חָמֵשׁ שָׁנִים רָעָב פֶּן-תִּוָּרֵשׁ אַתָּה וּבֵיתְךָ וְכָל-אֲשֶׁר-לָךְ: 12וְהִנֵּה עֵינֵיכֶם רֹאוֹת וְעֵינֵי אָחִי בִנְיָמִין כִּי-פִי הַמְדַבֵּר אֲלֵיכֶם: 13וְהִגַּדְתֶּם לְאָבִי אֶת-כָּל-כְּבוֹדִי בְּמִצְרַיִם וְאֵת כָּל-אֲשֶׁר רְאִיתֶם וּמִהַרְתֶּם וְהוֹרַדְתֶּם אֶת-אָבִי הֵנָּה: 14וַיִּפֹּל עַל-צַוְּארֵי בִנְיָמִן-אָחִיו וַיֵּבְךְּ וּבִנְיָמִן בָּכָה עַל-צַוָּארָיו: 15וַיְנַשֵּׁק לְכָל-

and wept upon them; only then were his brothers able to talk to him.

16The news reached Pharaoh's palace: "Joseph's brothers have come." Pharaoh and his courtiers were pleased. 17And Pharaoh said to Joseph, "Say to your brothers, 'Do as follows: load up your beasts and go at once to the land of Canaan. 18Take your father and your households and come to me; I will give you the best of the land of Egypt and you shall live off the fat of the land.' 19And you are bidden [to add], 'Do as follows: take from the land of Egypt wagons for your children and your wives, and bring your father here. 20And never mind your belongings, for the best of all the land of Egypt shall be yours.'"

21The sons of Israel did so; Joseph gave them wagons as Pharaoh had commanded, and he supplied them with provisions for the journey. 22To each of them, moreover, he gave a change of clothing; but to Benjamin he gave three hundred pieces of silver and several changes of clothing. 23And to his father he sent the following: ten he-asses laden with the best things of Egypt, and ten she-asses laden with grain, bread, and provisions for his father on the journey. 24As he sent his brothers off on their way, he told them, "Do not be quarrelsome on the way."

25They went up from Egypt and came to their father Jacob in the land of Canaan. 26And they told him, "Joseph is still alive; yes, he is ruler over the whole land of Egypt." His heart went numb, for he did not believe them. 27But when they recounted all that Joseph had said to them, and when he saw the wagons that Joseph had sent to transport him, the spirit of their father Jacob revived. 28"Enough!" said Israel. "My son Joseph is still alive! I must go and see him before I die."

אֶחָיו וַיֵּבְךְּ עֲלֵהֶם וְאַחֲרֵי כֵן דִּבְּרוּ אֶחָיו
אִתּוֹ:

16 וְהַקֹּל נִשְׁמַע בֵּית פַּרְעֹה לֵאמֹר בָּאוּ
אֲחֵי יוֹסֵף וַיִּיטַב בְּעֵינֵי פַרְעֹה וּבְעֵינֵי
עֲבָדָיו: 17 וַיֹּאמֶר פַּרְעֹה אֶל־יוֹסֵף אֱמֹר
אֶל־אַחֶיךָ זֹאת עֲשׂוּ טַעֲנוּ אֶת־בְּעִירְכֶם
וּלְכוּ־בֹאוּ אַרְצָה כְּנָעַן: 18 וּקְחוּ אֶת־
אֲבִיכֶם וְאֶת־בָּתֵּיכֶם וּבֹאוּ אֵלָי וְאֶתְּנָה
לָכֶם אֶת־טוּב אֶרֶץ מִצְרַיִם וְאִכְלוּ אֶת־
חֵלֶב הָאָרֶץ: 19 וְאַתָּה צֻוֵּיתָה זֹאת עֲשׂוּ
קְחוּ־לָכֶם מֵאֶרֶץ מִצְרַיִם עֲגָלוֹת לְטַפְּכֶם
וְלִנְשֵׁיכֶם וּנְשָׂאתֶם אֶת־אֲבִיכֶם וּבָאתֶם:
20 וְעֵינְכֶם אַל־תָּחֹס עַל־כְּלֵיכֶם כִּי־טוּב
כָּל־אֶרֶץ מִצְרַיִם לָכֶם הוּא:

21 וַיַּעֲשׂוּ־כֵן בְּנֵי יִשְׂרָאֵל וַיִּתֵּן לָהֶם יוֹסֵף
עֲגָלוֹת עַל־פִּי פַרְעֹה וַיִּתֵּן לָהֶם צֵדָה
לַדָּרֶךְ: 22 לְכֻלָּם נָתַן לָאִישׁ חֲלִפוֹת
שְׂמָלֹת וּלְבִנְיָמִן נָתַן שְׁלֹשׁ מֵאוֹת כֶּסֶף

23 וּלְאָבִיו שָׁלַח וְחָמֵשׁ חֲלִפֹת שְׂמָלֹת:
כְּזֹאת עֲשָׂרָה חֲמֹרִים נֹשְׂאִים מִטּוּב
מִצְרָיִם וְעֶשֶׂר אֲתֹנֹת נֹשְׂאֹת בָּר וָלֶחֶם
וּמָזוֹן לְאָבִיו לַדָּרֶךְ: 24 וַיְשַׁלַּח אֶת־אֶחָיו
וַיֵּלֵכוּ וַיֹּאמֶר אֲלֵהֶם אַל־תִּרְגְּזוּ בַּדָּרֶךְ:
25 וַיַּעֲלוּ מִמִּצְרָיִם וַיָּבֹאוּ אֶרֶץ* כְּנַעַן אֶל־
יַעֲקֹב אֲבִיהֶם: 26 וַיַּגִּדוּ לוֹ לֵאמֹר עוֹד
יוֹסֵף חַי וְכִי־הוּא מֹשֵׁל בְּכָל־אֶרֶץ
מִצְרָיִם וַיָּפָג לִבּוֹ כִּי לֹא־הֶאֱמִין לָהֶם:
27 וַיְדַבְּרוּ אֵלָיו אֵת כָּל־דִּבְרֵי יוֹסֵף אֲשֶׁר
דִּבֶּר אֲלֵהֶם וַיַּרְא אֶת־הָעֲגָלוֹת אֲשֶׁר־
שָׁלַח יוֹסֵף לָשֵׂאת אֹתוֹ וַתְּחִי רוּחַ יַעֲקֹב
אֲבִיהֶם: 28 וַיֹּאמֶר יִשְׂרָאֵל רַב עוֹד־יוֹסֵף
בְּנִי חָי אֵלְכָה וְאֶרְאֶנּוּ בְּטֶרֶם אָמוּת:

READING 2.5: "They Saw Him from Afar"

"They [Joseph's brothers] saw him from afar, and before he came close to them they conspired to kill him."

—Genesis 37:18

Isaac of Worka, a Hasidic teacher, writes:

> The reason why the brothers wanted to kill Joseph is that they saw him only from afar. Had they seen him in true nearness, they would have understood his essence, and they would have loved him.
>
> In every man there is a spark of the Divine Soul. The power of evil in man darkens this flame and almost puts it out. Brotherly love among men rekindles the soul and brings it closer to its source.[7]

REFLECTIONS

- What are we most likely to notice about an individual when we see that person "from afar"?
- What are we unable to see "from afar"?
- What do your answers suggest about what encourages an expanded sense of *areyvut*?
- What do your answers suggest about the obstacles to developing an expanded sense of *areyvut*?

---

7   Isaac of Worka, quoted in Arthur Hertzberg, ed., *Judaism: The Classic Introduction to One of the Great Religions of the Modern World* (New York: Free Press, 1991), 168–169.

READING 2.6: Interpreting the Story of Joseph and His Brothers

A number of interpreters have pointed out that the story of Joseph and his brothers is one of several in Genesis that involve a quarrel between brothers. Rabbi Joseph Telushkin writes:

> Four sets of brothers fight in Genesis—Cain and Abel, Isaac and Ishmael, Jacob and Esau, and Joseph and his brothers—but only in this last case is there a complete reconciliation.
>
> Concerning the first pair, Cain murders Abel.
>
> Abraham expels his son Ishmael from his house, so that he will exert no negative influence on his younger brother, Isaac: The brothers meet only once more, to bury their father.
>
> Esau wants to murder Jacob, but when the two brothers finally meet twenty years later, they fall on each other's neck, kiss, make peace, and bury the hatchet. Apparently, though, each remembers where the hatchet is buried, because they never see each other again.
>
> And finally, there are Joseph and his brothers. "I am Joseph," he reveals to them and soon thereafter, they move from Canaan to Egypt to live with him.[8]

Why did Joseph wait so long to reveal himself to his brothers? Why did he weep after doing so? James Kugel, a biblical scholar, offers one explanation:

> Interpreters noted that, although Joseph had ample opportunity to take revenge on his brothers for their cruelty—all those years of slavery and imprisonment were their doing, after all—he did not. If he did throw a scare into them for a while, even that had a purpose. Joseph manipulated events, interpreters said, so that Judah—the same brother that looked on unfeelingly as Joseph was sold into slavery—found himself potentially in the same position once again. This was the moment when Benjamin, Joseph's younger brother, was accused of theft and about to be jailed. But this time Judah did not stand idly by: he volunteered himself in Benjamin's place. For Joseph, this was proof positive that at least one brother had learned his lesson, and Joseph burst into tears.[9]

REFLECTIONS

- How is the story of Joseph and his brothers similar to other biblical stories that involve a conflict between brothers?
- In what ways does Joseph's story differ from the others?
- What does that difference teach us about the links between *areyvut* and reconciliation?
- What does it teach about forgiveness?

---

8   Joseph Telushkin, *Jewish Literacy: The Most Important Things to Know About the Jewish Religion, Its People, and Its History* (New York: William Morrow, 1991), 42.
9   James L. Kugel, *How to Read the Bible: A Guide to Scripture Then and Now* (New York: Free Press, 2007), 178–179.

A Historical Perspective on Universe of Obligation

Lesson 3 focuses on the concept of a "universe of obligation" in Europe, with a focus on Germany. It examines the treatment of Jews in Germany at the end of the eleventh century, in the age of the Enlightenment, and in early 1930s, soon after Adolf Hitler became chancellor. In each example, Jews are seen as outsiders—as a people beyond "our" universe of obligation. Students are encouraged to examine a variety of documents that spell out not only who belonged and who did not but also what it meant to be seen as a stranger, an outsider, at a particular time in history.

Note: The focus is on Germany in this lesson because the units that follow examine the events that led to the Holocaust. It should be noted, however, that antisemitism was not limited to Germany at any period in history.

Essential Questions
- How did Germans define their universe of obligation at various times in history?
- How did those definitions affect relationships between Germans and Jews?
- What did it mean to Jews in Germany to be seen as outsiders in places where their families had lived for generations?

Recommended Resources
- Reading 2.7a: Germany at the Time of the Crusades: Historical Background
- Reading 2.7b: Germany at the Time of the Crusades: Examining the Speyer Charter
- Reading 2.7c: Germany at the Time of the Crusades: The Crusaders and the Jews
- Reading 2.8a: Germany in the Age of the Enlightenment: Historical Background
- Reading 2.8b: Germany in the Age of the Enlightenment: Who Belongs, According to Royal Decrees and German Law
- Reading 2.8c: Germany in the Age of the Enlightenment: The Debate in Germany About Citizenship
- Reading 2.9a: Germany in the 1920s and 1930s: Historical Background
- Reading 2.9b: Germany in the 1920s and 1930s: Dismantling Democracy
- Reading 2.9c: Germany in the 1920s and 1930s: The Impact of Anti-Jewish Laws
- *Childhood Memories,* chapter 5 (video testimony of Walter, a Jewish student in Nazi Germany)

Optional Resources

- "The Hangman," in *Facing History and Ourselves: Holocaust and Human Behavior*, 204–205
- Chapter 4, *Facing History and Ourselves: Holocaust and Human Behavior* (primary source documents related to Germany immediately after Hitler took power)
- Chapters 4 and 9, *A Convenient Hatred: The History of Antisemitism* (additional information about Jewish life during the Crusades and the Enlightenment). This book is available through our Resource Library.

Activity Ideas

For more information on specific teaching strategies highlighted in this lesson, see the Appendix.

GETTING STARTED

Have students review their working definition of the concept of a universe of obligation. What does it mean to be included in that universe in our country? What does it mean to be excluded? Read aloud the preamble to the US Constitution:

> We the people of the United States, in order to form a more perfect union, establish justice, insure domestic tranquility, provide for the common defense, promote the general welfare, and secure the blessings of liberty to ourselves and our posterity, do ordain and establish this Constitution for the United States of America.

Ask students what individuals and groups were included in the words "we the people" 200 years ago. Who was included 100 years ago? Who is included today? One way to prompt such a discussion is by reading students a few lines from a 1974 speech by Barbara Jordan, the first African American woman to serve in the US House of Representatives. She stated:

> "We, the people." It's a very eloquent beginning. But when that document was completed on the seventeenth of September in 1787, I was not included in that "We, the people." I felt somehow for many years that George Washington and Alexander Hamilton just left me out by mistake. But through the process of amendment, interpretation, and court decision, I have finally been included in "We, the people."[10]

What is Jordan suggesting about the link between the nation's universe of obligation and her own life story? Explain that in this lesson, we will be examining how Germans defined their universe of obligation at three different times in history and how those definitions affected Jewish life.

---

10   Barbara Jordan, opening statement to the House Judiciary Committee, proceedings on the impeachment of Richard Nixon, July 25, 1974, available at *http://gos.sbc.edu/j/jordan3.html.*

ANALYZING INFORMATION

Each reading in this lesson focuses on a particular time in German history. You may wish to have students examine all three time periods, or you may prefer to focus on one or two periods. Regardless of the strategy you choose, you will want your students to address the following questions:

- Who belonged? Who did not belong? Who determined membership?
- How did the way Germans defined their universe of obligation shape the attitudes and actions of individuals and groups?
- What did it mean to be an outsider at this time in history?
- How did the way Germany seemed to define its universe of obligation challenge, compromise, or reinforce many Germans' sense of *areyvut*?

You may wish to divide the class into small groups. Have each group examine documents from a single time period, and then teach the class as a whole what members learned from those documents about Germany and the concept of a universe of obligation. Encourage them to use drawings as well as words to relay information and ideas.

REVISING A WORKING DEFINITION

Ask students to reread their working definition of *universe of obligation*. Have them revise or expand their definitions to reflect what they have learned in this lesson.

ASSESSMENT

In 1933, Martin Niemöller, a Protestant minister, voted for the Nazi Party. By 1938, he was in a concentration camp. After the war, he is believed to have said the following:

> In Germany, the Nazis came for the Communists, and I didn't speak up because I wasn't a Communist. Then they came for the Jews, and I didn't speak up because I wasn't a Jew. Then the came for the trade unionists, and I didn't speak up because I wasn't a trade unionist. Then they came for the Catholics, and I didn't speak up because I was a Protestant. Then they came for me, and by that time there was no one left to speak for me.[11]

Maurice Ogden's poem entitled "The Hangman" could be substituted for the quotation, as it expresses many of the same ideas. Ask students to edit or revise their working definition of *universe of obligation* to reflect the observations of Niemöller and/or Ogden and the readings included in this lesson. What are the consequences of a decision to exclude some people from "our" universe of obligation?

---

11   Attributed to lectures delivered by Martin Niemöller. Different versions of the quotation exist.

READING 2.7a: Germany at the Time of the Crusades: Historical Background

In the seventh century, only a few Jews lived in what is now Germany. Many more arrived in the eighth and ninth centuries. It was a time when the region's economy was beginning to recover from centuries of wars and invasions. Because people there had had to concentrate for so long on protecting themselves from invaders, few had the skills, experience, or contacts to revive trade with countries along the Mediterranean Sea. Therefore, a number of rulers turned to Jewish merchants who had lived along the Mediterranean for generations for help in stimulating the economy. They were experienced in doing business with people of many faiths.

The newcomers found themselves in a society where powerful men, each with an army of warriors or knights loyal only to him, ruled much of the region. Those leaders kept the peace and protected the less powerful in their territory in exchange for goods and/or services. This system is known today as "feudalism"; it was roughly arranged like a pyramid, with a king or an emperor at the top. Below him were his vassals: the most powerful nobles in the kingdom. Those nobles, in turn, had their own vassals, and so on down the line to the lowest vassals of all: warriors who had no land or soldiers of their own. One's rank in society depended on the value of the services provided. At the lowest level, serfs held the right to farm a few strips of land for themselves in return for their work on the lord's estate. At a much higher level, a duke held the right to the income of his large estate in return for providing the king with a certain number of warriors for 40 days each year.

The only unifying force in Europe in the days of feudalism was the Roman Catholic Church, headed by the pope. The Church struggled to unite Christians by keeping alive Roman laws and learning. Although the Church had members of all ranks, it was organized in much the way kingdoms were—with the pope at the top of the pyramid and bishops and abbots roughly equal to nobles and knights. In fact, they often came from the same families.

Many bishops owned large estates, had many vassals, and relied on serfs to work their land. These Church leaders took part in the struggles for power that occurred often throughout Europe. A few even went to war themselves. Church leaders also helped kings and other rulers manage their affairs; they were able to read and write at a time when most people in Europe, including many kings, were illiterate.

How did Jews fit into this world? After all, they could not take an oath of loyalty to a great lord and become his vassals; to do so, they would have had to swear their loyalty on the relics of Christian saints, which meant at least partially accepting Christianity. And they certainly had not moved north to become serfs. They had settled in Germany and other parts of northern Europe because they saw opportunities there for a better life. The answer to their dilemma was a charter, a written document issued by a ruler that spelled out the rights, obligations, and privileges of both the ruler and a group of people who wanted to live under his/her rule. At this time in history, most people did not move as individuals but as members of an extended family or a group of extended families.

READING 2.7b: Germany at the Time of the Crusades: Examining the Speyer Charter

How did Jews make the most of their opportunities in Europe? How did they deal with the challenges they faced? Clues can be found in a charter issued in 1087 by Bishop Rudiger of Speyer to the Jews he had invited to settle in the city he ruled. Bishop Rudiger wrote, in part:

1. Those Jews whom I have gathered I placed outside the neighborhood and residential area of the other burghers.* In order that [the Jews] not be easily disrupted by the insolence of the mob, I have encircled them with a wall.

2. The site of their residential area I have acquired properly—first the hill partially by purchase and partially by exchange; then the valley I received by gift of the heirs. I have given [the Jews] that area on the condition that they annually pay three and one-half pounds in Speyer currency for the shared use of the monks.

3. I have accorded the free right of exchanging gold and silver and of buying and selling everything they use—both within their residential area and outside, beyond the gate down to the wharf and on the wharf itself. I have given them the same right throughout the entire city.

4. I have, moreover, given [the Jews] out of the land of the Church burial ground to be held in perpetuity.

5. I have also added that, if a Jew from elsewhere has quartered with them, he shall pay no toll.

6. Just as the mayor of the city serves among the burghers, so too shall the Jewish leader adjudicate** any quarrel which might arise among [the Jews] or against them. If he is unable to determine the issue, then the case shall come before the bishop of the town or his chamberlain.***

7. [The Jews] must discharge the responsibility of watch, guard, and fortification only in their own area. The responsibility of guarding they may discharge along with their servants.

8. [The Jews] may legally have nurses and servants from among our people.

9. [The Jews] may legally sell to Christians meat, which they consider unfit for themselves according to the sanctity of their law. Christians may legally buy such meats.

In short, in order to achieve the height of kindness, I have granted them a legal status more generous than any the Jewish people have in any city of the German kingdom.

---

* Burghers were Christian artisans and merchants who were citizens of the town.
** pass judgment on
*** an official in charge of the bishop's household

Lest one of my successors dare to deny this grant and concession and force them to a greater tax, claiming that the Jews themselves usurped this status and did not receive it from the bishop, I have given them this charter of aforesaid grant as proper testimony. In order that the meaning of this matter remains throughout the generations, I have strengthened it by signing it and by the imposition of my seal.[12]

Three years after Bishop Rudiger issued the Speyer charter, Jews there sought additional protection. They asked Henry IV, the Holy Roman emperor, to approve the terms of their charter. In 1090, Henry issued a document that affirmed the rights listed in the Speyer charter for all of his Jewish subjects.

---

12 "The Latin Document," in *Urkunden zur Geschichte der Stadt,* ed. Alfred Hilgard (Strassburg, 1885), 11–12, quoted in *Church, State, and Jew in the Middle Ages,* ed. Robert Chazan (New York: Behrman House, 1980), 58–59.

READING 2.7c: Germany at the Time of the Crusades: The Crusaders and the Jews

The importance of charters can be seen in the experiences of the Jews in Speyer and other German communities soon after the pope issued a call for a crusade, or holy war, in 1096 to restore the Holy Land to Christian rule by defeating the Muslims.

Thousands of Christians answered the pope's call. Many Christians were eager to fight for their faith because of a reform movement in the Catholic Church in the eleventh century. It changed the way many Christians felt about their religion. Earlier, they had seen Jesus primarily as a distant figure whom they viewed as an all-powerful deity who had risen from death. Now many priests focused their teaching on Jesus's suffering and his dual role as a figure both human and divine. As a result, people in Germany and elsewhere came to view Jesus as a man who identified with the poor and the powerless, a man who died painfully on the cross at the hands of his enemy—and that enemy was, in their minds, "the Jews." It was at this time that the "deicide charge" took root in Christianity. A growing number of Christians now believed that Jews as a people were collectively guilty for the crucifixion of Jesus.

The Church leaders reinforced that belief. It was the theme of many statues and other art found in most Christian churches. It was also expressed in sermons and other teachings. Not surprisingly, a number of crusaders decided that it was "preposterous to set out on a long journey to kill God's enemies far away, while God's worst enemies, the Jews, are dwelling in ease close at hand." Among those crusaders was a landowner known as Count Emicho. In May and June of 1096, he and his followers systematically attacked Jewish communities in the valley of the Rhine River, including Speyer. A Jewish chronicler noted that on the morning of Saturday, May 3, Emicho led a surprise attack on the synagogue in Speyer. When he and his men burst into the building, they found it empty. Someone had warned the Jews. Outraged, the crusaders searched the town with the help of a number of burghers. In the end, they found and killed eleven Jews. Where were the others?

The current bishop, Johann, was determined to live up to the charter written by his predecessor, Bishop Rudiger. He used his soldiers to escort the Jews of Speyer to a safe place in the countryside. Then, after the crusaders left town, Bishop Johann tried and punished all of the burghers who had taken part in killing the eleven Jews. Jews in other cities were not as fortunate. Although many tried to fight back, they were hopelessly outnumbered. Dozens of Jewish communities were completely wiped out. No one was ever punished for those crimes.

READING 2.8a: Germany in the Age of the Enlightenment: Historical Background

"There is no such thing as a Christian commonwealth. Neither Pagan nor [Muslim], nor Jew, ought to be excluded from the civil rights of the commonwealth because of his religion."

—John Locke (England, 1689)

"All religions are equal and good, if only the people that practice them are honest people; and if Turks and heathens came and wanted to live here in this country, we would build them mosques and churches."

—King Frederick (Prussia, 1740)

"Men are born, and always continue, free and equal in respect of their rights."

—Declaration of the Rights of Man and Citizen (France, 1789)

These three quotations reflect a dramatic change in the way some educated Europeans thought about ethnic and religious differences. John Locke was an English philosopher whose ideas influenced both the American and French revolutions. Frederick II was the king of Prussia, the most powerful German state in the 1700s, and the Declaration of the Rights of Man and Citizen expressed the ideals of the French Revolution.

By the early 1700s, these new ideas were seen as making a new age. It was believed that in this new age scientific knowledge would replace old superstitions and progress would be more valued than tradition. Not everyone welcomed such changes. In an essay written in 1784, Immanuel Kant, a German philosopher, expressed his belief that these people, too, would eventually come to accept the changes:

> As matters now stand, a great deal is still lacking in order for men as a whole to … apply [reason] confidently to religious issues. But we do have clear indications that the way is now being opened for men to proceed freely in this direction and that the obstacles to general enlightenment … are gradually diminishing. In this regard, this age is the age of enlightenment.[13]

According to Kant, the motto of this new era, which came to be known as the Enlightenment, was "Dare to know!"—*Sapere aude!* in Latin. He described the movement's leaders as those who dared to "reject the authority of tradition, and to think and inquire." Modern science grew out of that daring. So did the efforts of many Jews to win liberty and equality.

---

13   Immanuel Kant, "An Answer to the Question: What Is the Enlightenment?" (1784), in *Internet Modern History Sourcebook*, ed. Paul Halsall (1997), available at *http://www.fordham.edu/halsall/mod/Kant-whatis.html.*

The treatment of Jews during these years reveals that "enlightenment" is not easily achieved. In a world that valued equality and liberty, one group could exclude another only by demonstrating a "natural difference." In other words, discrimination had to be justified by "scientific" evidence showing that human nature differs according to age, gender, and "race." Until the 1700s, the word *race* had been widely used to refer to a people, a tribe, or a nation. By the end of that century, however, it was being used to describe a distinct group of human beings with inherited physical traits and moral qualities that set them apart from other "races." Increasingly, Jews were no longer seen as members of a religious group but rather as members of a separate "race."

READING 2.8b: Germany in the Age of the Enlightenment: Who Belongs, According to Royal Decrees and German Law

The Enlightenment in what is now Germany was a time when trade expanded and money became increasingly central to everyday life. Even a few generations earlier, ordinary people had bartered for goods and services they could not produce themselves. Now they had more opportunities to earn money, and with enough gold, even a serf could buy freedom and land. Money was also the key to power for rulers eager to finance lavish palaces and large armies, so they were always on the lookout for newcomers willing and able to expand trade and build industry.

In 1669, a group of Jews who had recently been expelled from Vienna asked Frederick I of Prussia for permission to settle in Berlin because "the earth and the entire world, which, after all, God created for all humans, appears to be shutting us out."[14] Their plea was written in the language of reason and a common humanity; Frederick responded with a business deal. He offered the 50 richest Jews permission to live in Berlin in exchange for a payment of 2,000 thalers apiece, a huge sum in those days (roughly $90,000 per person in today's dollars). They were also required to develop industry in Prussia. Other Jewish refugees were not welcome; Frederick had no interest in poor Jews.

The Jews who settled in Berlin in 1669, like most Jews in Prussia and other German states, lived under a bewildering number of laws that applied only to them. Those laws, written centuries earlier, determined where Jews could live, what clothing they could wear, and on which streets they could walk. Until 1710, they also had to wear a yellow patch on their clothes to distinguish them from Germans. By then Frederick William was king, and he, like his father, saw Jews mainly in terms of their economic value. That year he announced that any Jew who paid him 8,000 thalers could remove the yellow patch.

In 1740 Frederick II became king. Unlike his father and grandfather, he considered himself "enlightened." Although he, like them, ruled with a heavy hand, he established the first code of laws in Germany, eliminated torture, and reduced corruption in the courts. He also enacted laws designed to protect most religious minorities, but the only Jews he tolerated were the wealthiest.

What happened to the vast majority of Jews who were not rich? They had few rights and at best just barely made a living. Historians estimate that about 10 percent were homeless. They could not live in Berlin or other German cities unless a privileged Jew was willing to support them. If he died, they could be expelled. The same was true of their wives and children.

What happened to those who were expelled? Some had enough money to purchase a residence permit in another town. Others had relatives willing to shelter them. Those who lacked money or connections had no choice, as a Christian observer wrote in 1783, but to "roam through life as beggars or be rogues."[15] For the most part, the homeless traveled through the countryside in large ragtag groups—townspeople described them as "hordes of wretched creatures with their children, carrying their entire possessions on their backs."[16] They were truly outcasts.

---

14   Quoted in Amos Elon, *The Pity of It All: A History of the Jews in Germany, 1743–1933* (New York: Metropolitan Books, 2002), 14.
15   Ibid., 29.
16   Ibid.

READING 2.8c: Germany in the Age of the Enlightenment: The Debate in Germany About Citizenship

Between 1799 and 1815, the various German states fought a series of wars against France. During those wars, many people in those states began to think of themselves as Germans rather than as Prussians, Bavarians, or members of some other state. Before long, they were debating what it meant to be a German—and who belonged in Germany and who did not. In 1819, the debate turned violent.

That year, a professor at the University of Wurzburg in Bavaria urged an end to discrimination against Jews. His outraged students responded by attacking him and then taking to the streets. For several days they, along with others in the town, ran through the city, destroying Jewish homes and businesses and shouting, "*Hep! Hep!* Death to all Jews!" The letters *h, e,* and *p* form an acronym for the Latin phrase *Hieroslyma est perdita*— "Jerusalem is lost." It was believed to have been the battle cry of the crusaders who had attacked Jews as they made their way to the Holy Land more than 500 years earlier.

When the riots ended in Wurzburg, two people were dead and more than 20 were wounded. By then the violence had spread to other parts of Bavaria and, from there, to other German states. Most Germans did not join the rioters. Instead they locked their doors and shut the windows to keep out the noise. In only a few cities did ordinary citizens try to help the victims. In Heidelberg, a city in southwestern Germany, two professors and their students contained the mob until the police arrived.

Soon after soldiers came to restore order in Karlsruhe, a city in Baden, anonymous fliers blanketed the city. They were written in response to an earlier flier that had called for the massacre of Jews. The new message read, "Emperors, kings, dukes, beggars, Catholics, and Jews are all human and as such our equals."[17] To emphasize that idea, the grand-duke of Baden showed his solidarity with the city's Jews by spending the night at the home of a prominent Jew. The gesture helped restore calm to the city.

The riots stopped as suddenly as they had begun. No one ever took responsibility for the violence. But many Jews noted that for at least ten years before the riots, a number of professors had been preaching the myth that the Germans were a "pure" people or "race" struggling for freedom from "the Jews," whom they regarded as a "race" of dangerous outsiders. One professor insisted that "the Jews" posed so great a threat that they ought to be exterminated "root and branch." After the riots, some people accused him of sparking the violence. He denied the charge, claiming that he had "only" called for the extermination "root and branch" of Judaism, not of Jews.

Those who shared the professor's views did not believe that Jews could ever be "true Germans." Others insisted that Jews could become Germans if they were "properly educated" and converted to Christianity. Many Jews questioned the sincerity of such views. During the wars against France, Jews had joined their German neighbors in the fight. In Prussia alone, 71 Jewish soldiers had earned the Iron Cross, a medal given for bravery in battle. Despite their patriotism, once the war was over, one German state after another revoked the rights Jews had received under French rule. Prussia's minister of justice justified the move by noting that the Jews' "temporary bravery" "did not rule out a lower degree of morality."[18] Jews in Germany were not granted citizenship until 1871, the year Germany united. But discriminatory laws a based on religion and "race" remained until the 1920s.

---

17   Quoted in Amos Elon, *The Pity of It All: A History of the Jews in Germany*, 1743–1933 (New York: Metropolitan Books, 2002), 106.
18   Ibid., 108.

READING 2.9a: Germany in the 1920s and 1930s: Historical Background

In 1914, a world war began. Germany, Austria-Hungary, and their allies fought against Britain, France, and their allies. In a single week in November 1918, many Germans learned not only that the war was coming to an end but also that they were on the losing side. On November 9, Kaiser Wilhelm II gave up his throne and fled to the Netherlands. Within hours, the Social Democrats, then the largest political party in Germany's parliament, replaced the monarchy with a republic. The new government faced incredible challenges, including the possibility of a revolution. The capital, Berlin, was so unsettled that lawmakers met in Weimar (about 180 miles to the southwest), and the newly established government was therefore known as the Weimar Republic.

Then, on November 11, just two days after Germany became a republic, World War I ended with a cease-fire. Only then did many Germans realize that they had lost the war. Some were even more stunned when they learned the terms of the peace treaty signed at Versailles, just outside Paris, in 1919. Germany had to give up its colonies abroad and some territory at home, and the size of its army was restricted. The treaty also held Kaiser Wilhelm responsible for the war and required that Germany pay reparations to the victors.

As anger over the terms of the treaty grew, Germans increasingly insisted that someone had "stabbed the nation in the back." General Erich Ludendorff, a war hero, told lawmakers that Germany had been betrayed not by the men who had led the nation into war but by some Social Democrats, the Catholic Center Party, the socialists, and the Jews. At the time, Germany's 500,000 Jews accounted for less than one percent of a total population of about 61 million.

Despite such talk, most Germans in 1919 knew that Germany had lost the war not because it was "stabbed in the back," but because the entry of the United States into the war in 1917 gave France and Britain the advantage. The United States declared war because of German attacks on its ships—attacks ordered by Ludendorff and other German generals. In the end, Germany's new constitution guaranteed equal rights to all citizens, including Jews. And some Jews took advantage of the opportunity that those rights afforded them. As a result, Ludendorff and other extreme nationalists now referred to the Weimar Republic as the "Jew republic." Yet of the 250 Germans who served as ministers between 1919 and 1933, only four were Jews. For many nationalists, even one Jew in government was one too many.

Among the extreme nationalists who saw Jews as a threat to Germany was a drifter who had moved to Munich from Austria just before the war. His name was Adolf Hitler. In the early 1920s, he, like many other veterans, was angry and bitter about the way the war had ended. Like some of them, he joined an extremist political group later known as the National Socialist German Workers' Party (the Nazi Party, for short). He quickly became its leader.

Hitler believed that world history was a struggle between absolute good (represented by Germans and other members of the so-called Aryan race) and absolute evil (represented by "the Jewish race"), with the world's future dependent on the outcome of that struggle. When he took power in 1933, he set out to turn Germany into a racial state by ending so-called Jewish racial domination of the nation.

READING 2.9b: Germany in the 1920s and 1930s: Dismantling Democracy

To build a racial state, Adolf Hitler and his Nazi Party set out to isolate Jews from their non-Jewish neighbors little by little, step by step.

1933:
- Hitler appointed chancellor of Germany (January 30).
- Creation of the Ministry of Public Enlightenment and Propaganda to make sure that every film, radio program, book, magazine, picture, and musical composition showed Hitler and the Nazis as heroic guardians of the German *Volk*.
- Hitler granted emergency power as a result of a fire in the building where the German parliament met (February 28).
- Opening of Dachau, the first concentration camp, with others soon to follow (March 22).
- Parliament passed the Enabling Act, which gave Hitler dictatorial powers.
- A one-day boycott of Jewish businesses (April 1).
- Orders ending protection of Jews by the police and courts.
- Passage of the Law for the Restoration of the Professional Civil Service, which removed "non-Aryans" from government jobs. The only exceptions were Jewish veterans, their fathers, and their sons.
- Public burning of books written by Jews and anti-Nazis (May 10).
- Removal of all Jewish doctors from the national health system.
- Strict limits on the number of Jews who could attend a public high school or teach in one.
- Establishment of a Department of Racial Hygiene.

1934:
- Jews banned from the German Labour Front.
- Jews denied national health insurance.
- Exclusion of all Jewish students from exams to become physicians, dentists, pharmacists, or lawyers.
- Jews removed from the arts.
- Adolf Hitler became the sole leader of Germany with the support of 90 percent of German voters (August).

1935:
- Exclusion of Jews from the military.
- Passage of a law that defined a German citizen as a person "of German or kindred blood who proves by his conduct that he is willing and suited loyally to serve the German people and the Reich."[19]
- Passage of a law that outlawed marriages between Jews and Germans.[20] People of "German blood" who were already married to Jews were encouraged to dissolve those marriages.

---

19   Quoted in Lucy S. Dawidowicz, ed., *A Holocaust Reader* (Behrman House Publishing, 1976), 47–48.
20   Ibid.

- Announcement of a decree that defined a Jew as a person with three Jewish grandparents. A person with one Jewish parent was not considered a Jew unless he or she belonged to a Jewish community, the non-Jewish parent was dead, or the state did not approve of his or her behavior. According to some estimates, Germany was home to as many as 300,000 *Mischlinge*—persons of "mixed race"—and another 100,000 who were affected to some extent by racial laws.[21]
- Jews no longer allowed to vote or to participate in government.
- Restrictions placed on Jews who wished to travel abroad.
- Jewish students removed from German schools and universities.
- Jews banned from parks, restaurants, and swimming pools.

In the years that followed, the government dissolved Jewish businesses. Jews who owned large companies had to turn over their holdings "in trust" to "Aryans." Between 1933 and 1937, more than 129,000 Jews left the country. Of those who remained, one in every three was reduced to extreme poverty.

---

21 Quoted in Marion A. Kaplan, *Between Dignity and Despair: Jewish Life in Nazi Germany* (New York: Oxford University Press, 1998), 75.

READING 2.9c: Germany in the 1920s and 1930s: The Impact of Anti-Jewish Laws

Edwin Landau recalled the events of January 30, 1933, the day Adolf Hitler became chancellor of Germany:

> On the radio we heard the big torchlight procession of the Nazis marching past the Chancellery of the Reich, heard the tumultuous jubilation of the multitudes and became very depressed. We did not dare go into the street of our town that evening, for there, too, there was unparalleled jubilation, and outside one heard of the shouts of the marching Nazis, "Death to the Jews!"

> And on the next day the swastika flags were fluttering from the houses and next to them also the black, white, and red flags of the monarchy. But now one could tell who of one's acquaintants was a Nazi follower. On the faces of some citizens one saw a look that earlier one had not noticed. Many Catholics were already also joining in. And the youth went marching at the head. Then one heard the great declaration of the new government and the speeches of the new ministers…

> The war against the Jews was the first item of the agenda that was implemented. Fate took its course. In our town, too, the Nazi gangs made the streets unsafe.[22]

Carl Schwabe, a veteran of World War I and the manager of a department store owned by his family in the town of Hanau, recalled the boycott on April 1, 1933:

> The boycott lasted one day. I will never forget it. The street was filled with people. Young fellows howling, older people curious, many incensed. In front of each Jewish store the SA men in brown were lined up. The leaders, in snappy new uniforms, checked the guards. I closed up and went home. After all, we were not yet so humbled, so trampled down as not to have been seized by a raging anger and the shame that something like that was possible in Germany. My wife and I went to a nearby forest, and in the evening we visited a district court judge, with whom we were on friendly terms. There we met friends, and a Protestant pastor who came somewhat later said: "Some nice company I'm finding here, a Catholic district court judge, a Social Democratic director and two Jewish couples! High time the police put an end to this scandal!" It did so soon enough.

> Soon after the boycott the first laws appeared throwing Jews out of the professions that until then they had practiced with the greatest success and to everyone's satisfaction. Lawyers, doctors, and officials who had not worked before 1914 or had not been frontline soldiers in the war had to leave professional life.… My brother-in-law in Stutgart had worked during the war as a surgeon and orthopedist in Canstatt. His superiors had not let him leave the hospital for the front because they considered him indispensable. Now he lost his main practice. His wife had gone to an epidemic disease hospital at the front as a medical student and taken her exams before the war. Since she had not worked as a doctor she was granted the privilege of a frontline soldier. The two emigrated to Palestine.[23]

---

22   Edwin Landau, "My Life Before and After Hitler," manuscript (Ramat Gan, 1940), quoted in *Jewish Life in Germany: Memoirs from Three Centuries*, ed. Monika Richarz, trans. Stella P. Rosenfeld and Sydney Rosenfeld (Bloomington, IN: Indiana University Press, 1991), 310.
23   Carl Schwabe, "My Life in Germany Before and After January 30, 1933," manuscript (London, 1939), quoted in *Jewish Life in Germany*, 328.

Hanna Bergas, a public-school teacher, described her last day of teaching in April 1933:

> When I arrived at the school building … the principal [said] "Good morning" in his customary, friendly way, stopped me, and asked me to come to his room…. When we were seated, he said, in a serious, embarrassed tone of voice, he had orders to ask me not to go into my classroom. I probably knew, he said, that I was not permitted to teach any more at a German school. I did know, but was it to happen so abruptly? … Mr. B. was extremely sorry…. I collected myself [and] my belongings…. There was nobody … to say goodbye to, because everybody else had gone to the classroom…. In the afternoon … colleagues, pupils, their mothers came, some in a sad mood, others angry with their country, lovely bouquets of flowers, large and small, in their arms. In the evening, the little house was full of fragrance and colors, like for a funeral, I thought; and indeed, this was the funeral of my teaching at a German public school.[24]

A diary entry by Hertha Nathorff:

> June 1933: Meeting of the League of German Women Doctors. As usual, I went today, after all this is where the most respected and best known women colleagues in Berlin gather. "Strange atmosphere today," I thought, "and so many strange faces." A colleague whom I did not know said to me, "You must also be one of us?" and showed me the swastika on the lapel of her coat. Before I could answer, she stood up and fetched a gentleman into our meeting, who said that he had to demand the [Nazification] of the League in the name of the government…. Another colleague … my predecessor in the Red Cross … who had been dismissed … because of unfitness and other not very nice human qualities … stood up and said, "Now I ask the German colleagues to go into the next room for a discussion." Colleague S., a good Catholic, … asked: "What does that mean—German colleagues?" "All who are not Jews, of course," was the answer. Now it had been said. Silently, we "Jewish and half-Jewish" doctors stood up and with us some "German" doctors—silently we left the room—pale, outraged to our innermost selves. We then went … to discuss what we should do now. "We should quit the League as a united group," some said. I was opposed. I will gladly allow them the honor of throwing us out, but I will at least not voluntarily abandon my claim to membership…. I am so agitated, so sad and confused, and I am ashamed for my "German" colleagues.[25]

Erna Albersheim, "a half Jew" according the Nazis, wrote in the mid-1930s:

> This Aryan business was getting on my nerves. Jews were afraid to associate with me and Aryans also. I sometimes felt like a leper…. My intimate friends all came. I was very careful for their sakes and never invited Jews and Aryans at the same time.[26]

24   Hanna Bergas (first-person account, Leo Baeck Institute), quoted in *Between Dignity and Despair: Jewish Life in Nazi Germany* by Marion A. Kaplan (Oxford University Press, 1998), 25.

25   Hertha Nathorff, *Das Tagebuch der Hertha Nathorff (Diary of Hertha Nathorff)*, ed. Wolfgang Benz (Munich, 1987), 40, quoted in *Between Dignity and Despair*, 26–27.

26   Erna Albersheim (first-person account), E MS Ger 90, Houghton Library, Harvard University, quoted in *Between Dignity and Despair*, 42.

Conscience and Courage in the Face of Authority

Teaching Focus

In Unit 2, students consider the ways societies define their universe of obligation and individuals in those societies define their sense of *areyvut*. In this unit, students will examine the consequences of those definitions, both in biblical times and in Adolf Hitler's Europe. Both periods raise important questions about the duties and obligations of membership. In Unit 2, political scientist Stephen Carter defines the price of belonging as "the sum of the many sacrifices we are called to make for the sake of living together." In his view, those sacrifices call for "generosity, even when it is costly, and trust, even when there is risk."

Lesson 1: Moral Courage in Pharaoh's Egypt
Lesson 2: The Push to Conform and the Pull of Conscience in Hitler's Europe

Essential Questions
- Who creates a society's customs, rules, and laws?
- Under what circumstances do we all have a duty to conform to those customs, rules, and laws?
- Under what circumstances do we all have a duty to question and even challenge those customs, rules, and laws?
- How do we decide when to obey and when to resist?

Student Outcomes
Students will . . .
- identify the factors that characterize a moral dilemma.
- explore the consequences of moral choices at various times in history.
- make inferences and draw conclusions based on the reading of Jewish texts.
- explore *midrash* as a product and a process.

These lessons may be used to extend, reinforce, and enhance concepts developed in:
- Chapters 5 and 8 in *Facing History and Ourselves: Holocaust and Human Behavior*
- Chapter 5 in *Facing History and Ourselves: Jews of Poland*

Moral Courage in Pharaoh's Egypt

In this lesson, students explore the idea of moral courage in Exodus 1 and 2—the story of Pharaoh's enslavement of the Israelites and his decree calling for the murder of all of their male babies. Rabbi Jonathan Sacks explains:

> Moral courage can sometimes be found in the heart of darkness. That the Torah itself tells the story [of Exodus] the way it does has enormous implications. It means that when it comes to people, we must never generalize, never stereotype. The Egyptians were not all evil; even from Pharaoh himself a heroine was born. Nothing could signal more powerfully that the Torah is not an ethnocentric text; that we must recognize virtue wherever we find it, even among our enemies; and the basic core of human values—humanity, compassion, courage—is truly universal.[1]

This lesson focuses on the choices made by a number of courageous individuals. Among them were Shiphrah and Puah, two midwives who refused to comply with Pharaoh's decree because they "feared God." Their response made it possible for Moses's mother to place her son in a basket in the reeds along the Nile in the hope that he would be rescued. As his sister stood watch, Pharaoh's daughter found the basket and made the fateful decision to save the child, even though she recognized that he was an Israelite. Once Moses became an adult, he too defied authority by intervening to protect defenseless individuals threatened by a stronger force. Students are encouraged to examine the factors that encourage obedience to the rules and laws that bind a community or a nation. They will also consider the factors that have led some individuals to challenge, resist, or rebel against some of those rules or laws. These stories raise important questions that still resonate in the world today.

Essential Questions
- What does it mean to "fear God"?
- What encourages obedience to authority?
- What prompts people to question or defy authority?
- What are the consequences of obedience and resistance?

Recommended Resources
- Reading 3.1: Exodus 1–2
- Reading 3.2: *Pardes*: A Fourfold Method (an essay on methods the rabbis have used to interpret Torah)
- Reading 3.3: Because They Feared God (three interpretations of the choices made by Shiphrah and Puah by Rabbis Jonathan Sacks, Joseph Telushkin, and Harold M. Schulweis)
- Reading 3.4: A Modern Perspective on Pharaoh's Daughter (an interpretation by Rabbi Jonathan Sacks)

---

1   Jonathan Sacks, *Covenant & Conversation: A Weekly Reading of the Jewish Bible* (New Milford, CT: Maggid Books and the Orthodox Union, 2009–2010), 28.

Activity Ideas

For more information on specific teaching strategies useful in carrying out the various activities outlined in this lesson, see the Appendix.

GETTING STARTED

Explain to students that every group—large and small alike—has its own rules or laws. What purpose do these rules serve? In every society, there are times when individuals disagree with some of those rules. What options do they have? How do they decide whether to challenge those rules or simply break them? What does it take to defy the rules? US Senator Robert F. Kennedy once said of those who wish to change their society:

> Few… are willing to brave the disapproval of their fellows, the censure of their colleagues, the wrath of their society. Moral courage is a rarer commodity than bravery in battle or great intelligence. Yet it is the one essential, vital quality of those who seek to change a world which yields most painfully to change.[2]

What is the connection between moral courage and "following one's conscience"? The modern Hebrew word for "conscience" is *matzpun.* There is no word in biblical Hebrew that translates as "conscience," and yet the idea is central to biblical teachings. Some rabbis believe that the phrase *yirat elohim,* or "fear of God," comes very close to the idea of conscience. Rabbi Harold Schulweis defines this quality as "the hidden inner compass that guides our lives and must be searched for and recovered repeatedly."[3] What are the links between one's conscience and one's sense of *areyvut?* Encourage students to write their initial responses in their journals. Explain that they will revisit those responses later in this unit.

SUMMARIZING THE TEXT

Assign students Exodus 1 and 2 in Hebrew and/or English (Reading 3.1). As they read, ask them to list words or phrases that seem significant or raise questions of meaning. If students began a timeline of Moses's life in Unit 1, this would be a good time to add to it. If students have not yet created such a timeline, you may want to have them do so now. Explain that it is a way of organizing and highlighting the key events in the two chapters, which roughly span the years from just before Moses's own birth through the birth of his first child. After students have created or updated the timeline, ask them to use it to write a paragraph that summarizes the key events in each chapter. Have students write a title for the paragraph that highlights the theme of both chapters—that is, what lesson they teach and/or what they have in common.

INTERPRETING THE TEXT

Divide the class into three groups and assign one passage from Reading 3.1 to each group:

- Shiphrah and Puah (1:8–22)
- Pharaoh's daughter (2:1–10)
- Moses (2:11–22)

---

2   Robert F. Kennedy, "Day of Affirmation," speech given to the National Union of South African Students, South Africa, June 6, 1966.

3   Harold M. Schulweis, *Conscience: The Duty to Obey and the Duty to Disobey* (Woodstock, VT: Jewish Lights, 2008), 5.

After each group has its assigned portion of the text, ask group members to answer the following questions:

- What problem or dilemma did the individual or individuals face in this part of the story?
- How did each try to resolve that problem?
- What were the consequences of the choice each made?
- If you could interview the individual or individuals, what questions would you ask about their choice?
- What did you learn from their choice?

Have each group share its answers with the class. After each group has presented its ideas, discuss the similarities and differences in both the motivations for and the outcomes of the choices all four individuals made.

EXPLORING *MIDRASH*

It has been said that Jews read the Torah or the Bible with a question mark. The result is *midrash*—a search for answers to religious questions. Based on a Hebrew root that means "to study, seek out, or investigate," *midrash* is a method of interpretation that assumes that every word—indeed, every letter—has meaning. But the word *midrash* describes not only a method of understanding text; but also the name given to a collection of rabbinic commentaries on the five volumes of the Torah. *Midrash aggadah* focuses on biblical narratives, and *midrash halakhah* interprets legal passages. An essay by Sandy Sasso (Reading 3.2) describes the fourfold process the rabbis used to interpret text. It is called *pardes*, based on the first letter of each step in the process. To help students learn more about the process, assign the reading. After completing it, encourage students to reread Exodus 1 and 2 (Reading 3.1) with their *chavruta*. What does the author's discussion of *midrashim* related to Exodus 1 and 2 add to our understanding of the text? What new questions does it raise?

EXAMINING WORDS AND PHRASES

According to Jewish tradition, every word in the Torah is intentional and purposeful. Nothing is accidental or unimportant—not the choice of words, the spelling of the words, or the order of events. Everything has a meaning and an explanation. How then do we understand the phrase *hameyaldot ha'ivriyot,* used to describe Shiphrah and Puah? The phrase can be translated as either "the Hebrew midwives" or "the midwives to the Hebrews." What is the difference between the two translations? How does that difference alter the meaning of the story? If students need help in coming up with an explanation, you may want to have them read the first set of comments by Rabbi Jonathan Sacks in Reading 3.3.

The two midwives are also described as having defied Pharaoh's decree because they "fear God." What does it mean to "fear God" (*yirat elohim*)? Have students brainstorm ideas. Encourage them to consult a dictionary or thesaurus to find synonyms for the word *fear (fright, terror, concern, awe,* etc.) Then ask students to discover how others have understood the phrase by assigning Reading 3.3. Have students use their own ideas, as well as the comments they have heard and read, to explain the phrase, either by writing their own definition of the phrase, drawing a picture that explains it, or identifying a piece of music or art that reflects its meaning.

MAKING INFERENCES

Remind students that an *inference* is sometimes described as the feeling we get that something is true based on our reading or observations. For example, if you were in line to buy tickets for a movie and noticed that everyone coming out of the theater was looking sad or even crying, what conclusion would you be likely to reach about the film? That conclusion is an *inference*. Inferences are not facts we can point to in our reading or in our observations, but something that seems to be true based on the facts at hand or our own experience. An inference is a conclusion that makes sense in terms of what we have learned so far.

After assigning Reading 3.4, have students work with their *chavruta* to circle the inferences the author makes. Have students locate the evidence and/or reasoning the author uses to support those inferences. Which level of interpretation is the author using—*peshat, remez, drash, sod*, or some combination of the four? What does the interpretation add to our understanding of the role that Pharaoh's daughter plays in Jewish history? What does it add to our understanding of her as a person? The author makes a number of inferences about Moses's mother and sister. What do those inferences add to our understanding of moral courage? How are the choices of Moses's mother and sister similar to those made by Pharaoh's daughter? What is the main difference?

COMPARING AND CONTRASTING CHOICES

Exodus 2 describes three incidents that took place in Moses's life not long before his encounter with God at the burning bush. Ask students who else was involved in each incident, what action Moses took, and what happened as a result of his action. Then have students use their lists to describe what we can infer about Moses and his sense of *areyvut* from the first incident. What does the second add to our understanding of the man? What does the third add? What do your answers suggest as to why all three incidents are included in Exodus 2?

Have students use their lists to write a paragraph in which they give the moral or lesson of each story. Ask the class to decide what the combination of all three stories reveals about Moses as a person and his sense of *areyvut*. How do you think the three relate to his first encounter with God (Unit 1)? What inferences can we draw from these accounts? How do those lessons apply to our own lives today?

ASSESSMENT

Have students review the summary they wrote after their initial read of Exodus 1 and 2. Then ask them to revise and expand it so that it serves as their commentary on the two chapters. It should be based at least in part on the various commentaries included in this lesson and class discussions about those commentaries.

1 These are the names of the sons of Israel who came to Egypt with Jacob, each coming with his household: ²Reuben, Simeon, Levi, and Judah; ³Issachar, Zebulun, and Benjamin; ⁴Dan and Naphtali, Gad and Asher. ⁵The total number of persons that were of Jacob's issue came to seventy, Joseph being already in Egypt. ⁶Joseph died, and all his brothers, and all that generation. ⁷But the Israelites were fertile and prolific; they multiplied and increased very greatly, so that the land was filled with them.

⁸A new king arose over Egypt who did not know Joseph. ⁹And he said to his people, "Look, the Israelite people are much too numerous for us. ¹⁰Let us deal shrewdly with them, so that they may not increase; otherwise in the event of war they may join our enemies in fighting against us and rise from the ground." ¹¹So they set taskmasters over them to oppress them with forced labor; and they built garrison cities for Pharaoh: Pithom and Rameses. ¹²But the more they were oppressed, the more they increased and spread out, so that the [Egyptians] came to dread the Israelites.

¹³The Egyptians ruthlessly imposed upon the Israelites ¹⁴the various labors that they made them perform. Ruthlessly they made life bitter for them with harsh labor at mortar and bricks and with all sorts of tasks in the field.

אַ וְאֵ֗לֶּה שְׁמוֹת֙ בְּנֵ֣י יִשְׂרָאֵ֔ל הַבָּאִ֖ים מִצְרָ֑יְמָה אֵ֣ת יַעֲקֹ֔ב אִ֥ישׁ וּבֵית֖וֹ בָּֽאוּ׃ ² רְאוּבֵ֣ן שִׁמְע֔וֹן לֵוִ֖י וִֽיהוּדָֽה׃ ³ יִשָּׂשכָ֥ר זְבוּלֻ֖ן וּבִנְיָמִֽן׃ ⁴ דָּ֥ן וְנַפְתָּלִ֖י גָּ֥ד וְאָשֵֽׁר׃ ⁵ וַֽיְהִ֗י כָּל־נֶ֛פֶשׁ יֹצְאֵ֥י יֶֽרֶךְ־יַעֲקֹ֖ב שִׁבְעִ֣ים נָ֑פֶשׁ וְיוֹסֵ֖ף הָיָ֥ה בְמִצְרָֽיִם׃ ⁶ וַיָּ֤מָת יוֹסֵף֙ וְכָל־אֶחָ֔יו וְכֹ֖ל הַדּ֥וֹר הַהֽוּא׃ ⁷ וּבְנֵ֣י יִשְׂרָאֵ֗ל פָּר֧וּ וַֽיִּשְׁרְצ֛וּ וַיִּרְבּ֥וּ וַיַּֽעַצְמ֖וּ בִּמְאֹ֣ד מְאֹ֑ד וַתִּמָּלֵ֥א הָאָ֖רֶץ אֹתָֽם׃ פ ⁸ וַיָּ֥קָם מֶֽלֶךְ־חָדָ֖שׁ עַל־מִצְרָ֑יִם אֲשֶׁ֥ר לֹֽא־יָדַ֖ע אֶת־יוֹסֵֽף׃ ⁹ וַיֹּ֖אמֶר אֶל־עַמּ֑וֹ הִנֵּ֗ה עַ֚ם בְּנֵ֣י יִשְׂרָאֵ֔ל רַ֥ב וְעָצ֖וּם מִמֶּֽנּוּ׃ ¹⁰ הָ֥בָה נִֽתְחַכְּמָ֖ה ל֑וֹ פֶּן־יִרְבֶּ֗ה וְהָיָ֞ה כִּֽי־תִקְרֶ֤אנָה מִלְחָמָה֙ וְנוֹסַ֤ף גַּם־הוּא֙ עַל־שֹׂ֣נְאֵ֔ינוּ וְנִלְחַם־בָּ֖נוּ וְעָלָ֥ה מִן־הָאָֽרֶץ׃ ¹¹ וַיָּשִׂ֤ימוּ עָלָיו֙ שָׂרֵ֣י מִסִּ֔ים לְמַ֥עַן עַנֹּת֖וֹ בְּסִבְלֹתָ֑ם וַיִּ֜בֶן עָרֵ֤י מִסְכְּנוֹת֙ לְפַרְעֹ֔ה אֶת־פִּתֹ֖ם וְאֶת־רַעַמְסֵֽס׃ ¹² וְכַאֲשֶׁר֙ יְעַנּ֣וּ אֹת֔וֹ כֵּ֥ן יִרְבֶּ֖ה וְכֵ֣ן יִפְרֹ֑ץ וַיָּקֻ֕צוּ מִפְּנֵ֖י בְּנֵ֥י יִשְׂרָאֵֽל׃ ¹³ וַיַּעֲבִ֧דוּ מִצְרַ֛יִם אֶת־בְּנֵ֥י יִשְׂרָאֵ֖ל בְּפָֽרֶךְ׃ ¹⁴ וַיְמָרְר֨וּ אֶת־חַיֵּיהֶ֜ם בַּעֲבֹדָ֣ה קָשָׁ֗ה בְּחֹ֙מֶר֙ וּבִלְבֵנִ֔ים וּבְכָל־עֲבֹדָ֖ה בַּשָּׂדֶ֑ה אֵ֚ת כָּל־עֲבֹ֣דָתָ֔ם אֲשֶׁר־עָבְד֥וּ בָהֶ֖ם בְּפָֽרֶךְ׃

4   Reprinted from the *JPS Hebrew-English Tanakh: The Holy Scriptures* by permission of the University of Nebraska Press (copyright 1985, 1999, 2000 by the Jewish Publication Society, Philadelphia).

READING 3.1: Exodus 1–2 (part 2 of 4)

15The king of Egypt spoke to the Hebrew mid-wives, one of whom was named Shiphrah and the other Puah, 16saying, "When you deliver the Hebrew women, look at the birthstool: if it is a boy, kill him; if it is a girl, let her live." 17The midwives, fearing God, did not do as the king of Egypt had told them; they let the boys live. 18So the king of Egypt summoned the midwives and said to them, "Why have you done this thing, letting the boys live?" 19The midwives said to Pharaoh, "Because the Hebrew women are not like the Egyptian women: they are vigorous. Before the midwife can come to them, they have given birth." 20And God dealt well with the midwives; and the people multiplied and increased greatly. 21And because the midwives feared God, He established households for them. 22Then Pharaoh charged all his people, saying, "Every boy that is born you shall throw into the Nile, but let every girl live."

15 וַיֹּ֙אמֶר֙ מֶ֣לֶךְ מִצְרַ֔יִם לַֽמְיַלְּדֹ֖ת הָֽעִבְרִיֹּ֑ת אֲשֶׁ֨ר שֵׁ֤ם הָֽאַחַת֙ שִׁפְרָ֔ה וְשֵׁ֥ם הַשֵּׁנִ֖ית פּוּעָֽה׃ 16 וַיֹּ֗אמֶר בְּיַלֶּדְכֶן֙ אֶת־הָֽעִבְרִיּ֔וֹת וּרְאִיתֶ֖ן עַל־הָאָבְנָ֑יִם אִם־בֵּ֥ן הוּא֙ וַהֲמִתֶּ֣ן אֹת֔וֹ וְאִם־בַּ֥ת הִ֖יא וָחָֽיָה׃ 17 וַתִּירֶ֤אןָ הַֽמְיַלְּדֹת֙ אֶת־הָ֣אֱלֹהִ֔ים וְלֹ֣א עָשׂ֔וּ כַּֽאֲשֶׁ֛ר דִּבֶּ֥ר אֲלֵיהֶ֖ן מֶ֣לֶךְ מִצְרָ֑יִם וַתְּחַיֶּ֖יןָ אֶת־הַיְלָדִֽים׃ שני 18 וַיִּקְרָ֤א מֶֽלֶךְ־מִצְרַ֙יִם֙ לַֽמְיַלְּדֹ֔ת וַיֹּ֣אמֶר לָהֶ֔ן מַדּ֥וּעַ עֲשִׂיתֶ֖ן הַדָּבָ֣ר הַזֶּ֑ה וַתְּחַיֶּ֖יןָ אֶת־הַיְלָדִֽים׃ 19 וַתֹּאמַ֤רְןָ הַֽמְיַלְּדֹת֙ אֶל־פַּרְעֹ֔ה כִּ֣י לֹ֧א כַנָּשִׁ֛ים הַמִּצְרִיֹּ֖ת הָֽעִבְרִיֹּ֑ת כִּֽי־חָי֣וֹת הֵ֔נָּה בְּטֶ֨רֶם תָּב֧וֹא אֲלֵהֶ֛ן הַֽמְיַלֶּ֖דֶת וְיָלָֽדוּ׃ 20 וַיֵּ֥יטֶב אֱלֹהִ֖ים לַֽמְיַלְּדֹ֑ת וַיִּ֧רֶב הָעָ֛ם וַיַּֽעַצְמ֖וּ מְאֹֽד׃ 21 וַיְהִ֕י כִּֽי־יָֽרְא֥וּ הַֽמְיַלְּדֹ֖ת אֶת־הָֽאֱלֹהִ֑ים וַיַּ֥עַשׂ לָהֶ֖ם בָּתִּֽים׃ 22 וַיְצַ֣ו פַּרְעֹ֔ה לְכָל־עַמּ֖וֹ לֵאמֹ֑ר כָּל־הַבֵּ֣ן הַיִּלּ֗וֹד הַיְאֹ֙רָה֙ תַּשְׁלִיכֻ֔הוּ וְכָל־הַבַּ֖ת תְּחַיּֽוּן׃ ס

2 A certain man of the house of Levi went and married a Levite woman. [2]The woman conceived and bore a son; and when she saw how beautiful he was, she hid him for three months. [3]When she could hide him no longer, she got a wicker basket for him and caulked it with bitumen and pitch. She put the child into it and placed it among the reeds by the bank of the Nile. [4]And his sister stationed herself at a distance, to learn what would befall him.

[5]The daughter of Pharaoh came down to bathe in the Nile, while her maidens walked along the Nile. She spied the basket among the reeds and sent her slave girl to fetch it. [6]When she opened it, she saw that it was a child, a boy crying. She took pity on it and said, "This must be a Hebrew child." [7]Then his sister said to Pharaoh's daughter, "Shall I go and get you a Hebrew nurse to suckle the child for you?" [8]And Pharaoh's daughter answered, "Yes." So the girl went and called the child's mother. [9]And Pharaoh's daughter said to her, "Take this child and nurse it for me, and I will pay your wages." So the woman took the child and nursed it. [10]When the child grew up, she brought him to Pharaoh's daughter, who made him her son. She named him Moses, explaining, "I drew him out of the water."

[11]Some time after that, when Moses had

ב וַיֵּ֥לֶךְ אִ֖ישׁ מִבֵּ֣ית לֵוִ֑י וַיִּקַּ֖ח אֶת־בַּת־לֵוִֽי׃ 2 וַתַּ֥הַר הָאִשָּׁ֖ה וַתֵּ֣לֶד בֵּ֑ן וַתֵּ֤רֶא אֹתוֹ֙ כִּי־ט֣וֹב ה֔וּא וַֽתִּצְפְּנֵ֖הוּ שְׁלֹשָׁ֥ה יְרָחִֽים׃ 3 וְלֹא־יָכְלָ֣ה עוֹד֮ הַצְּפִינוֹ֒ וַתִּֽקַּֽח־לוֹ֙ תֵּ֣בַת גֹּ֔מֶא וַתַּחְמְרָ֥ה בַחֵמָ֖ר וּבַזָּ֑פֶת וַתָּ֤שֶׂם בָּהּ֙ אֶת־הַיֶּ֔לֶד וַתָּ֥שֶׂם בַּסּ֖וּף עַל־שְׂפַ֥ת הַיְאֹֽר׃ 4 וַתֵּתַצַּ֥ב אֲחֹת֖וֹ מֵרָחֹ֑ק לְדֵעָ֕ה מַה־יֵּעָשֶׂ֖ה לֽוֹ׃

5 וַתֵּ֤רֶד בַּת־פַּרְעֹה֙ לִרְחֹ֣ץ עַל־הַיְאֹ֔ר וְנַעֲרֹתֶ֥יהָ הֹלְכֹ֖ת עַל־יַ֣ד הַיְאֹ֑ר וַתֵּ֤רֶא אֶת־הַתֵּבָה֙ בְּת֣וֹךְ הַסּ֔וּף וַתִּשְׁלַ֥ח אֶת־אֲמָתָ֖הּ וַתִּקָּחֶֽהָ׃ 6 וַתִּפְתַּח֙ וַתִּרְאֵ֣הוּ אֶת־הַיֶּ֔לֶד וְהִנֵּה־נַ֖עַר בֹּכֶ֑ה וַתַּחְמֹ֣ל עָלָ֔יו וַתֹּ֕אמֶר מִיַּלְדֵ֥י הָֽעִבְרִ֖ים זֶֽה׃ 7 וַתֹּ֣אמֶר אֲחֹתוֹ֮ אֶל־בַּת־פַּרְעֹה֒ הַאֵלֵ֗ךְ וְקָרָ֤אתִי לָךְ֙ אִשָּׁ֣ה מֵינֶ֔קֶת מִ֖ן הָעִבְרִיֹּ֑ת וְתֵינִ֥ק לָ֖ךְ אֶת־הַיָּֽלֶד׃ 8 וַתֹּֽאמֶר־לָ֥הּ בַּת־פַּרְעֹ֖ה לֵ֑כִי וַתֵּ֙לֶךְ֙ הָֽעַלְמָ֔ה וַתִּקְרָ֖א אֶת־אֵ֥ם הַיָּֽלֶד׃ 9 וַתֹּ֧אמֶר לָ֣הּ בַּת־פַּרְעֹ֗ה הֵילִ֜יכִי אֶת־הַיֶּ֤לֶד הַזֶּה֙ וְהֵינִקִ֣הוּ לִ֔י וַאֲנִ֖י אֶתֵּ֣ן אֶת־שְׂכָרֵ֑ךְ וַתִּקַּ֧ח הָאִשָּׁ֛ה הַיֶּ֖לֶד וַתְּנִיקֵֽהוּ׃ 10 וַיִּגְדַּ֣ל הַיֶּ֗לֶד וַתְּבִאֵ֙הוּ֙ לְבַת־פַּרְעֹ֔ה וַֽיְהִי־לָ֖הּ לְבֵ֑ן וַתִּקְרָ֤א שְׁמוֹ֙ מֹשֶׁ֔ה וַתֹּ֕אמֶר כִּ֥י מִן־הַמַּ֖יִם מְשִׁיתִֽהוּ׃

שלישי 11 וַיְהִ֣י ׀ בַּיָּמִ֣ים הָהֵ֗ם וַיִּגְדַּ֤ל מֹשֶׁה֙ וַיֵּצֵ֣א

grown up, he went out to his kinsfolk and witnessed their labors. He saw an Egyptian beating a Hebrew, one of his kinsmen. [12]He turned this way and that and, seeing no one about, he struck down the Egyptian and hid him in the sand. [13]When he went out the next day, he found two Hebrews fighting; so he said to the offender, "Why do you strike your fellow?" [14]He retorted, "Who made you chief and ruler over us? Do you mean to kill me as you killed the Egyptian?" Moses was frightened, and thought: Then the matter is known! [15]When Pharaoh learned of the matter, he sought to kill Moses; but Moses fled from Pharaoh. He arrived in the land of Midian, and sat down beside a well.

[16]Now the priest of Midian had seven daughters. They came to draw water, and filled the troughs to water their father's flock; [17]but shepherds came and drove them off. Moses rose to their defense, and he watered their flock. [18]When they returned to their father Reuel, he said, "How is it that you have come back so soon today?" [19]They answered, "An Egyptian rescued us from the shepherds; he even drew water for us and watered the flock." [20]He said to his daughters, "Where is he then? Why did you leave the man? Ask him in to break bread." [21]Moses consented to stay with the man, and he gave Moses his daughter Zipporah as wife. [22]She bore a son whom he named Gershom, for he said, "I have been a stranger in a foreign land."

[23]A long time after that, the king of Egypt died. The Israelites were groaning under the bondage and cried out; and their cry for help from the bondage rose up to God. [24]God heard their moaning, and God remembered His covenant with Abraham and Isaac and Jacob. [25]God looked upon the Israelites, and God took notice of them.

אֶל־אֶחָ֗יו וַיַּ֖רְא בְּסִבְלֹתָ֑ם וַיַּ֗רְא אִ֣ישׁ מִצְרִ֔י מַכֶּ֥ה אִישׁ־עִבְרִ֖י מֵאֶחָֽיו׃ 12 וַיִּ֤פֶן כֹּה֙ וָכֹ֔ה וַיַּ֖רְא כִּ֣י אֵ֣ין אִ֑ישׁ וַיַּךְ֙ אֶת־הַמִּצְרִ֔י וַֽיִּטְמְנֵ֖הוּ בַּחֽוֹל׃ 13 וַיֵּצֵא֙ בַּיּ֣וֹם הַשֵּׁנִ֔י וְהִנֵּ֛ה שְׁנֵֽי־אֲנָשִׁ֥ים עִבְרִ֖ים נִצִּ֑ים וַיֹּ֙אמֶר֙ לָֽרָשָׁ֔ע לָ֥מָּה תַכֶּ֖ה רֵעֶֽךָ׃ 14 וַ֠יֹּאמֶר מִ֣י שָֽׂמְךָ֞ לְאִ֨ישׁ שַׂ֤ר וְשֹׁפֵט֙ עָלֵ֔ינוּ הַלְהָרְגֵ֙נִי֙ אַתָּ֣ה אֹמֵ֔ר כַּאֲשֶׁ֥ר הָרַ֖גְתָּ אֶת־הַמִּצְרִ֑י וַיִּירָ֤א מֹשֶׁה֙ וַיֹּאמַ֔ר אָכֵ֖ן נוֹדַ֥ע הַדָּבָֽר׃ 15 וַיִּשְׁמַ֤ע פַּרְעֹה֙ אֶת־הַדָּבָ֣ר הַזֶּ֔ה וַיְבַקֵּ֖שׁ לַהֲרֹ֣ג אֶת־מֹשֶׁ֑ה וַיִּבְרַ֤ח מֹשֶׁה֙ מִפְּנֵ֣י פַרְעֹ֔ה וַיֵּ֥שֶׁב בְּאֶֽרֶץ־מִדְיָ֖ן וַיֵּ֥שֶׁב עַֽל־הַבְּאֵֽר׃

16 וּלְכֹהֵ֥ן מִדְיָ֖ן שֶׁ֣בַע בָּנ֑וֹת וַתָּבֹ֣אנָה וַתִּדְלֶ֗נָה וַתְּמַלֶּ֙אנָה֙ אֶת־הָ֣רְהָטִ֔ים לְהַשְׁק֖וֹת צֹ֥אן אֲבִיהֶֽן׃ 17 וַיָּבֹ֥אוּ הָרֹעִ֖ים וַיְגָרְשׁ֑וּם וַיָּ֤קָם מֹשֶׁה֙ וַיּ֣וֹשִׁעָ֔ן וַיַּ֖שְׁקְ אֶת־צֹאנָֽם׃ 18 וַתָּבֹ֕אנָה אֶל־רְעוּאֵ֖ל אֲבִיהֶ֑ן וַיֹּ֕אמֶר מַדּ֛וּעַ מִהַרְתֶּ֥ן בֹּ֖א הַיּֽוֹם׃ 19 וַתֹּאמַ֕רְןָ אִ֣ישׁ מִצְרִ֔י הִצִּילָ֖נוּ מִיַּ֣ד הָרֹעִ֑ים וְגַם־דָּלֹ֤ה דָלָה֙ לָ֔נוּ וַיַּ֖שְׁקְ אֶת־הַצֹּֽאן׃ 20 וַיֹּ֥אמֶר אֶל־בְּנֹתָ֖יו וְאַיּ֑וֹ לָ֤מָּה זֶּה֙ עֲזַבְתֶּ֣ן אֶת־הָאִ֔ישׁ קִרְאֶ֥ן ל֖וֹ וְיֹ֥אכַל לָֽחֶם׃ 21 וַיּ֥וֹאֶל מֹשֶׁ֖ה לָשֶׁ֣בֶת אֶת־הָאִ֑ישׁ וַיִּתֵּ֛ן אֶת־צִפֹּרָ֥ה בִתּ֖וֹ לְמֹשֶֽׁה׃ 22 וַתֵּ֣לֶד בֵּ֔ן וַיִּקְרָ֥א אֶת־שְׁמ֖וֹ גֵּרְשֹׁ֑ם כִּ֣י אָמַ֔ר גֵּ֣ר הָיִ֔יתִי בְּאֶ֖רֶץ נָכְרִיָּֽה׃ פ

23 וַיְהִי֩ בַיָּמִ֨ים הָֽרַבִּ֜ים הָהֵ֗ם וַיָּ֙מָת֙ מֶ֣לֶךְ מִצְרַ֔יִם וַיֵּאָנְח֧וּ בְנֵֽי־יִשְׂרָאֵ֛ל מִן־הָעֲבֹדָ֖ה וַיִּזְעָ֑קוּ וַתַּ֧עַל שַׁוְעָתָ֛ם אֶל־הָאֱלֹהִ֖ים מִן־הָעֲבֹדָֽה׃ 24 וַיִּשְׁמַ֥ע אֱלֹהִ֖ים אֶת־נַאֲקָתָ֑ם וַיִּזְכֹּ֤ר אֱלֹהִים֙ אֶת־בְּרִית֔וֹ אֶת־אַבְרָהָ֖ם אֶת־יִצְחָ֥ק וְאֶֽת־יַעֲקֹֽב׃ 25 וַיַּ֥רְא אֱלֹהִ֖ים אֶת־בְּנֵ֣י יִשְׂרָאֵ֑ל וַיֵּ֖דַע אֱלֹהִֽים׃ ס

READING 3.2: *Pardes:* A Fourfold Method

Midrash comes from a Hebrew word that means "to interpret, expound, or deduce." It is a method of interpreting the Torah. It is also the name for a large collection of verse-by-verse rabbinic commentary on the Torah. Sandy Eisenberg Sasso describes the methods used by the ancient rabbi to interpret sacred texts:

> The rabbis employed four different methods for interpreting passages.... By examining each of them and applying them to a scriptural verse, we can better appreciate the meaning of midrash. Consider, for instance, these words from the Exodus, chapter two, verse five: "The daughter of Pharaoh came down to bathe in the Nile, while her maidens walked along the Nile. She spied the basket among the reeds and sent her slave girl to fetch it."
>
> The first method of interpretation involves observing the most straightforward meaning of the passage. This is called *peshat,* which is the Hebrew word for plain or simple. It is nothing other than noting the details of the verse—who are the characters, what happens, in what order. In the Exodus passage, we learn that the daughter of Egypt's highest ruler came with her servants to wash herself in the river Nile. She saw a basket floating in the river and sent a servant to bring it to her.
>
> The second level of interpretation looks for connections between one text and another. Sometimes the rabbis see an allegorical meaning in the passage or recognize that the text is hinting at something other than what appears to be its plain meaning. This is call *remez.* In the Exodus verse about Pharaoh's daughter, we notice that the Hebrew word for basket (*teva*) is the same as the Hebrew word for ark in the Noah story of Genesis. There is a connection, then, between the vessel that carried Noah and the one that carried Moses. Even as Noah's "ark" saved humanity from complete destruction, the "ark" that saved Moses made possible the redemption of the people of Israel. The story of saving Israel is related to the story of saving the world. The ark (*teva*) is a symbol of salvation.
>
> The third method of understanding Scripture is called *drash,* or midrash. The word means "to search out," and midrash seeks to derive a homiletical meaning [an understanding related to a sermon or homily] from a passage. It is a way of reading into the text what may not be immediately apparent. In the verse about Pharaoh's daughter, the rabbis wonder why a princess, the daughter of Pharaoh, would need to leave the luxury and comfort of the palace to go down to the Nile to bathe. After all, she could have had her servants bring her the water she needed to wash herself. The midrash says that Pharaoh's daughter went to the Nile to cleanse herself of her father's idolatry.
>
> [T]he rabbis, in interpreting the text in this way, are seeking to fill in what appears to be missing from the Exodus narrative about the character of the Egyptian woman who becomes the instrument for redeeming the people of Israel. Nothing in the passage hints at this, but the rabbis imagine a woman who distinguishes herself from the rest of Egypt's leaders.

The fourth method of interpretation is called *sod*, or secret. It is the mystical understanding of the biblical narrative. A vast literature of mysticism (later known as Kabbalah) developed in Judaism from the time of the destruction of the Second Temple through the present day. Torah was interpreted according to a highly symbolic system that revealed the mysteries of the heavens and of God. The words of Scripture were understood to contain hidden meanings that revealed not just the life of human beings in their search for God, but also the inner nature of the divine.

The mystical, or *sod*, understanding of Pharaoh's daughter is radically different from the other interpretations we have encountered. Pharaoh's daughter symbolizes the *Shekhinah*, God's indwelling presence. When she sees the weeping child who represents Israel, she is roused to compassion.

The passage refers to mystical teachings that see oppression and evil as a result of the imbalance in the universe between absolute justice and compassion. Only when strict judgment and loving-kindness are in harmony is redemption possible. The fourth level of interpretation shows that the passage about Pharaoh's daughter is much more than it seems. It is not just referring to the earthly concerns of redemption from Egyptian bondage but is alluding to heavenly matters, the very inner workings of the divine.

If we take the first letter of each method of interpretation—*peshat, drash, remez,* and *sod*—and add vowels, we form the word *pardes*, which means "orchard." The symbolism is rich: as an orchard provides shade and sweet fruit for those who enter, so it receives the care and nurture of those who come to enjoy its produce. There is mutual relationship and mutual benefit. In the same way, the Torah gives shade and sustenance to those who read it, while those who read and interpret Scripture are like those who tend the orchard, nourishing Torah.[5]

5   Sandy Eisenberg Sasso, *God's Echo: Exploring Scripture with Midrash* (Brewster, MA: Paraclete Press, 2007), 29–32.

READING 3.3: Because They Feared God

"Who were Shiphrah and Puah?" asks Rabbi Jonathan Sacks. After noting that they are sometimes identified as Yocheved and Miriam (Moses's mother and sister), he observes:

> [In] describing them the Torah uses an ambiguous phrase, *hameyaldot ha'ivriyot*, which could mean either "the Hebrew midwives" or "the midwives to the Hebrews." If we follow the second interpretation, they may not have been Hebrews at all, but Egyptians ...
>
> The Torah's ambiguity on this point is deliberate. We do not know to which people Shiphrah and Puah belonged because their particular form of moral courage transcends nationality and race. In essence, they are being asked to commit a "crime against humanity" and they refused to do so.[6]

Rabbi Joseph Telushkin focuses on another sentence in the same story—the words *yirat elohim,* or "fear of God." He notes:

> The Hebrew Bible speaks of two emotions human beings are to feel toward God: love and fear (Deuteronomy 6:5, 6:13, 10:20). Almost all people seem at least faintly uncomfortable with the latter emotion.... Yet in the Torah fear of God is seen as having two positive results:
>
> 1. It *liberates* people from fear of other human beings, and
> 2. It *defends* the weak and the disadvantaged from the powerful.
>
> The first chapter of Exodus tells of Pharaoh's command to Shiphrah and Puah, two midwives, to drown all newborn Jewish male babies in the Nile. The women disobey the edict, and the Bible offers the reason for the *first recorded act of civil disobedience*: "They feared God." In other words, the "fear of God" *liberated* Shiphrah and Puah from the far more natural fear of Pharaoh....
>
> Furthermore, when the Bible appends the phrase "and you shall fear God" to a commandment, it clearly intends this fear to protect society's weakest members, as in:
>
> "You shall honor the old, *and you shall fear God*" (Leviticus 19:32).
>
> "Take no interest [from him, who has become impoverished] *but you shall fear God*" (Leviticus 25:36).
>
> "You shall not rule over [your servant] with rigor, *but you shall fear God*" (Leviticus 25:43); see also "Do not put a stumbling block in front of a blind man, *but you shall fear God*" (Leviticus 19:14).

6   Jonathan Sacks, *Covenant & Conversation: A Weekly Reading of the Jewish Bible* (New Milford, CT: Maggid Books and the Orthodox Union, 2009–2010), 21–22.

Normally, fear of other human beings is sufficient to restrain people from harming them. But in the cases legislated by the Torah, no such fear normally applies. The maltreated servant usually has no one to whom to complain, and it is precisely in this instance that the Bible reminds people to fear God, who is on the side of the weak.

Finally, fear of God means being in awe of Him more than it means being afraid of Him. As the Muslim thinker Al-Qushayri taught: "He who truly fears a thing flees from it, but he who truly fears God, flees unto Him."[7]

Rabbi Harold M. Schulweis is also struck by the phrase "fear God." He writes:

> There is no biblical Hebrew word that translates "conscience." I propose that the biblical term that comes closest to the character and role of conscience is "fear of God" or *yirat elohim*. One of the earliest uses of "fear of God" in the Bible is found in the narrative of the two heroic Egyptian midwives, Shiphrah and Puah, who defied the edict of Pharaoh to kill all Hebrew male infants. By their acts of rescue, the midwives are explicitly said to "fear God" and are therefore rewarded by God, who established a household for them "because the midwives feared God" (Exodus 1:17, 21). The midwives' fear of God superseded their fear of Pharaoh's public edicts.[8]

REFLECTIONS

- What do the comments of the three rabbis add to our understanding of why Shiphrah and Puah defied Pharaoh?
- What do they add to our understanding of the significance of the midwives' decision?
- What do they add to our understanding of what it means to "fear God"?

7   Joseph Telushkin, *Jewish Literacy: The Most Important Things to Know About the Jewish Religion, Its People, and Its History* (New York: William Morrow, 1991), 510–511.
8   Harold M. Schulweis, *Conscience: The Duty to Obey and the Duty to Disobey* (Woodstock, VT: Jewish Lights, 2008), 40.

READING 3.4: A Modern Perspective on Pharaoh's Daughter

Rabbi Jonathan Sacks writes of Pharaoh's daughter:

She is one of the most unexpected heroes of the Hebrew Bible. Without her, Moses might not have lived. The whole story of the exodus would have been different. Yet she was not an Israelite. She had nothing to gain, and everything to lose, by her courage. Yet she seems to have had no doubt, experienced no misgivings, made no hesitation. If it was Pharaoh who afflicted the children of Israel, it was another member of his own family who saved the decisive vestige of hope: Pharaoh's daughter.

Recall the context. Pharaoh had decreed death for every male Israelite child. Yocheved, Amram's wife, had a baby boy. For three months she was able to conceal his existence, but no longer. Fearing his certain death if she kept him, she set him afloat on the Nile in a basket, hoping against hope that someone might see him and take pity on him. This is what follows:

Pharaoh's daughter went to bathe in the Nile while her maids walked along the Nile's edge. She saw the box in the reeds and sent her slave-girl to fetch it. Opening it, she saw the boy. The child began to cry, and she had pity on it. "This is one of the Hebrew boys," she said (2:6).

Note the sequence. First she sees that it is a child and has pity on it. A natural, human, compassionate reaction. Only then does it dawn on her who the child must be. Who else would abandon a child? She remembers her father's decree against the Hebrews. Instantly the situation has changed. To save the baby would mean disobeying the royal command. That would be serious enough for an ordinary Egyptian; doubly so for a member of the royal family.

Nor is she alone when the event happens. Her maids are with her; her slave-girl is standing beside her. She must face the risk that one of them, in a fit of pique, or even mere gossip, will tell someone about it. Rumors flourish in royal courts. Yet she does not shift her ground. She does not tell one of her servants to take the baby and hide it with a family far away. She has the courage of her compassion. She does not flinch. Now something extraordinary happens:

The [child's] sister said to Pharaoh's daughter, "Shall I go and call a Hebrew woman to nurse the child for you?" "Go," replied Pharaoh's daughter. The young girl went and got the child's own mother. "Take this child and nurse it," said Pharaoh's daughter. "I will pay you a fee." The woman took the child and nursed it (2:7–9).

The simplicity with which this is narrated conceals the astonishing nature of this encounter. First, how does a child—not just a child, but a member of a persecuted people—have the audacity to address a princess? There is no elaborate preamble, no "Your royal highness" or any other formality of the kind we are familiar with elsewhere in biblical narrative. They seem to speak as equals.

Equally pointed are the words left unsaid. "You know and I know," Moses' sister implies, "who this child is; it is my baby brother." She proposes a plan brilliant in its simplicity. If the real mother is able to keep the child in her home to nurse him, we both minimize the danger. You will not have to explain to the court how this child has suddenly appeared. We will be spared the risk of bringing him up: we can say the child is not a Hebrew, and that the mother is not the mother but only a nurse. Miriam's ingenuity is matched by Pharaoh's daughter's instant agreement. She knows; she understands; she gives her consent.

Then comes the final surprise:

When the child matured, [his mother] brought him to Pharaoh's daughter. She adopted him as her own son, and named him Moses. "I bore him from the water," she said (2:10).

Pharaoh's daughter did not simply have a moment's compassion. She has not forgotten the child. Nor has the passage of time diminished her sense of responsibility. Not only does she remain committed to his welfare; she adopts the riskiest of strategies. She will adopt him and bring him up as her own son. This is courage of a high order.[9]

---

9   Jonathan Sacks, *Covenant & Conversation: A Weekly Reading of the Jewish Bible* (New Milford, CT: Maggid Books and the Orthodox Union, 2009–2010), 25–27.

The Push to Conform and the Pull of Conscience in Hitler's Europe

This lesson focuses on the role that conscience played in the choices a few people made between 1933 and 1945—the years that Germany under Adolf Hitler and his Nazi Party isolated, humiliated, and ultimately murdered two-thirds of Europe's Jews. Most people in Europe during those years were neither perpetrators nor victims. They were bystanders. They knew something about Hitler's plans for Jews and other minorities but either felt there was nothing that they could do about it or did not want to become "involved." They just wanted to live as "normal" a life as possible. And yet when Jews, "Gypsies," or other members of a society are in danger, is it possible to turn away? A careful look at the choices a few individuals made during those years reveals the power of both the push to conform and the pull of conscience. These individuals are sometimes known as "upstanders"—people who challenge authority on behalf of the weak and the powerless. And yet that label does not quite fit; each is a complicated individual who defies easy classification. The same is true of the people we consider bystanders, victims, and perpetrators.

Essential Questions
- What encourages obedience to authority?
- What prompts people to challenge or defy authority?
- What are the possible consequences of disobedience and resistance?
- What can we learn about a society from its rebels and resisters?

Recommended Resources
- *Pigeon*, video (11 minutes)
- *The Power of Good: The Story of Nicholas Winton*, video (90 minutes; if time is limited, use chapter 10, a 12-minute clip)
- Reading 3.5: Robert Smallbones: A Diplomatic Rescue
- Reading 3.6: Marion Pritchard: A Student's Fateful Decision
- Reading 3.7: Zofia Kossak-Szczucka: "Protest!"
- Reading 3.8: Major Julius Schmahling: A Teacher's Remorse
- Reading 3.9: Quotations on Rescue and Resistance

Optional Resources

- *Obedience,* a documentary that describes the experiment at Yale run by Stanley Milgram, or pages 210–212 in *Facing History and Ourselves: Holocaust and Human Behavior*
- *Facing History and Ourselves: Holocaust and Human Behavior,* 175–76, 235–37, 240–41, 373–76, 382–85 (readings that focus on the decisions made by individuals and groups in Nazi-occupied Europe)
- *The Children of Chabannes,* a documentary about a village in Vichy France where about 400 refugee children were saved from the Holocaust by their teachers and the director of their school
- *The Courage to Care,* a documentary featuring profiles of individuals who helped save Jews in France, the Netherlands, and Poland (note that this is available only in a VHS format)

Activity Ideas

For more information on specific teaching strategies useful in carrying out various activity ideas outlined in this lesson, see the Appendix.

GETTING STARTED

Introduce the lesson by showing *Pigeon,* an 11-minute film based on a true story. The film opens with a man waiting for the train to Grenoble, in France's unoccupied zone. As he checks his forged papers, we sense that this may be his only chance for escape. The man watches as two young boys taunt a small bird on the station platform. He intervenes for the bird's sake and confiscates the boys' slingshot. But in the melee, his passport is stolen.

After students have watched the film, point out that there are two stories in the film. What are they? How do they relate to one another? What might the pigeon represent?

Explain to students that several people in the film might be called "upstanders." They are people whose actions show courage and resilience. Whom do you consider an upstander in this film? What seems to have motivated that upstander or others in the film? In this lesson, students will explore the choices of other upstanders in Nazi-occupied Europe.

An alternative introduction might focus on the Milgram experiment. If students have learned about it as part of a Facing History unit, you may want to review the video (or the reading on pages 210–12 in *Facing History and Ourselves: Holocaust and Human Behavior*). If they have not yet studied the experiment, explain that in the 1960s, Professor Stanley Milgram recruited volunteers to participate in "a study of the effects of punishment on learning." The real point of the experiment was to show how far a person will proceed in a concrete and measurable situation in which he or she is ordered to inflict pain on a protesting victim. At what point will the subject refuse to obey? The volunteers were told to increase the "shock" by 15 volts every time the "learner" (who was actually a member of Milgram's team) gave an incorrect answer. Have the class watch an excerpt from the film or read about the entire experiment on pages 210–12 in

Holocaust and Human Behavior, and then discuss what the results reveal about the power of obedience and conformity. Why do people find it so difficult to say no? What encourages individuals to obey an authority figure? What encourages resistance? These questions lie at the heart of this lesson.

SUMMARIZING CHOICES

This lesson focuses on the tiny minority of individuals who challenged authority in the 1930s and 1940s. The video and each of the first four readings all feature a person who made life-altering choices as the events that we call the Holocaust were unfolding. If time is limited, you may wish to divide students into small groups and assign each group a reading. Then have each group share its findings with the class. The presentations should stress the choice (or choices) that the individual made, why he or she made that choice, and the consequences of that decision. Then, as a class, discuss what these individuals' choices have in common. In what respects is each unique? How did each individual explain and/or justify the choices he or she made?

Nechama Tec, a noted sociologist and a hidden child during the Holocaust, has studied testimonies of many individuals who rescued Jews during the Holocaust. She has found that their choices had little to do with their religion, nationality, social class, level of schooling, or ethnic heritage. Most were independent individuals who refused to follow the crowd. They also had a history of performing good deeds and did not see rescue work as anything out of the ordinary. How do the readings support her findings? How do they challenge those findings?

ANALYZING CHOICES

Choices made by the various individuals highlighted in this lesson can be used to compare and contrast motivations and justifications. They can also be used to highlight the way these individuals inspired others to take part in their efforts to rescue Jews. One way of doing so is to have students comment on one or more of the quotations in Reading 3.9.

MAKING CONNECTIONS

Have students analyze the readings included in this lesson for echoes of the themes and ideas that are central to Exodus 1 and 2. For example, how do the efforts of Pharaoh's daughter inform our understanding of Marion Pritchard's efforts to protect the Jewish family she hid? In what sense was Pritchard's response similar to the way Moses reacted to injustice? What do Robert Smallbones or Nicholas Winton have in common with Shiphrah and Puah? What differences seem most striking? What echoes of the lessons Moses learned from his early choices can we find in the major's story?

Reading 3.7 features Zofia Kossak-Szczucka, a woman who took extraordinary risks to save Jews even though she regarded them as "enemies." Ask students to focus on the conversation Nechama Tec found in one of the woman's novels. Discuss how the word "home" is used in the conversation. Is the author referring to a house, a nation, or a homeland? How does the argument one of the men makes for helping Jews help us understand how Kossak-Szczucka defined Poland's universe of obligation and her own sense of *areyvut*? Do you think she was an upstander? If so, can an upstander be an antisemite? A racist? A bigot? If she is not an upstander, how would you label her and why?

ANALYZING A FILM

The Power of Good: The Story of Nicholas Winton can be used to raise important questions about what it means to be an upstander. The film is 90 minutes long, which may make it difficult to show in many school settings. A number of key themes, however, are highlighted in chapter 10, which is just 12 minutes in length. If you decide to show the 12-minute version, provide students with a context for the story:

In 1938, Nicholas Winton, a 29-year-old stockbroker living in England, was planning to go skiing in Switzerland with a friend at Christmastime. The trip never took place. Winton's friend, who was living in Prague at the time, urged his friend to come to the city instead and see how shamefully Jews were being treated there. He wanted Winton to meet a few of those Jews, particularly the parents of young children. Winton came away from the meeting deeply concerned about what might happen to those children once the Germans took control of the country.

Winton decided to take action. He wrote letters to the leaders of various countries pleading with them to accept Jewish refugees. After the US government denied his request, Winton focused on Britain. He found a number of families there willing to sponsor the children. Winton then worked quickly to get as many of them out of the country as possible. When he realized that time was running out, he began to forge passports and other official documents for the children. The operation continued until World War II began in September 1939. By then, Winton had saved 669 children.

For 50 years, Winton did not tell anyone about the children he saved. In 1988, his wife found a trunk in their attic that contained photographs of the saved children. When she asked Winton about the pictures, he described the children as part of his past, a past that he had never thought to mention.[10]

After watching chapter 10 of the film, share with students the following statement that Winton made in a letter written in 1939. How does it relate to the accounts of the other upstanders highlighted in this lesson?

> [There] is a difference between passive goodness and active goodness which is, in my opinion, the giving of one's time and energy in the alleviation of pain and suffering. It entails going out, finding and helping those in suffering and danger and not merely leading an exemplary life, in the purely passive way of doing no wrong.

ASSESSMENT

Use the written comments students made as part of the various activities in this lesson to evaluate their learning. As an alternative, ask them to write a brief essay explaining how one or more of the rescuers featured in this lesson might have responded to any one of the three quotations highlighted in "Analyzing Choices." Or you might ask students to edit and expand their initial response to the question: What does it mean to be an upstander? The response should reflect an understanding of the readings and discussions included in this unit.

---

10   "The Story," *Nicholas Winton: The Power of Good,* documentary support website, *http://www.powerofgood.net/story.php.*

READING 3.5: Robert Smallbones: A Diplomatic Rescue

On the night of November 9, 1938, the Nazis attacked Jews throughout greater Germany. A thousand synagogues were destroyed and tens of thousands of Jewish homes and businesses were raided. That night the Germans killed at least 90 Jews and shipped 60,000 Jewish men to concentration camps. Robert Smallbones, the British Consul-General in Frankfurt, happened to be in London on government business that day. He later wrote:

> [My grandmother] telephoned me the next morning that hundreds of Jews had besieged the consulate and that she had allowed all who sought refuge to spend the night as best they could in the house. She, [my mother,] and the servants had been up all night supplying them with food and trying to console them. She asked me to do something to help. The Home Office is the department dealing with immigration and I went to see a senior official there who dealt with this question. He had seen in the newspapers what was going on in Germany and I asked him what they proposed doing about it. He replied: "Nothing, What can we do? We cannot let them come in and cause unemployment amongst our own people. Have you got an idea?"[11]

Smallbones did have an idea. He based it on "the fact that under American law quotas for immigrants had been established for every country, according to the number admitted in 1892, which could not be readily expanded to meet this emergency." His idea was that Britain would take in German refugees who were on a waiting list for visas to the United States. After discussing the idea with officials at the Home Office, he wrote:

> It was agreed that under British law and regulations this was possible and I was asked whether I could draw up the details of procedure. I telephoned to Otto Schiff of the Jewish Relief organization and asked him to lunch at the Savoy Hotel with some of his collaborators. We drafted an undertaking to be given by the applicant for the British visa not to seek employment in the United Kingdom and a guarantee to be given by a bank or a responsible person in the United Kingdom that he would not become a charge on public funds. We also worked out the details of the procedure with the American consular authorities in Germany to make sure that the applicant would eventually be admitted to the United States of America. I submitted this at once to the Home Office and was authorized the same afternoon to introduce this system in my district. The Foreign Office was to be asked to send corresponding instructions to the Passport Control Officer at Berlin and to all my colleagues in Germany.[12]

Smallbones returned to Frankfurt that night. The next day, he later noted:

> I went to see the local head of the Gestapo to arrange that Jews would be released from the concentration camps if they produced the promise of a British visa and if they had only been interned because they were Jews and if no charge was to be preferred against them. He said that

11 Robert Smallbones, quoted in pamphlet distributed at the unveiling of the plaque at the Foreign and Commonwealth Office (November 2008), available at *http://www.fco.gov.uk/resources/en/pdf/pdf1/commemorating-diplomats*, 19–20.

12 Ibid., 21.

they could only be released if, in addition, they had all their German emigration papers in order, passports, exit visas, certificates from the inland revenue that they had paid income and other taxes, etc. I replied that this was an impossible condition as they could not themselves attend to these formalities while locked up and as the Jewish lawyers who could act for them were also interned; few Aryan lawyers would risk importuning the authorities on their behalf. We had a fierce argument and I started shouting in the proper German manner....

When I jumped up and said that my proposal to help Germany to be rid of some of their Jews was off, and that I would report by telegram to my Government, the Gestapo bully collapsed and we made an agreement in the sense desired by me. I know of no case in which a promise of a visa given by me did not lead to the immediate release of the interned.[13]

The amount of work Smallbones created for himself and his staff was, in his own words, "formidable." He explained:

I would be personally responsible for the ultimate decision in each case in my district. My American colleague in Frankfurt was not authorized to grant visas and we had to correspond about every applicant with Stuttgart.... I had a relatively large staff and they were hard put to it dealing with the interminable queue besieging us. I usually worked about eighteen hours a day. The longest stretch I remember was from early in the morning until midnight when I fell asleep for a few minutes on my desk.... I went to bed.... After two hours' sleep my conscience pricked me. The feeling was horrible that there were people in concentration camp whom I could get out and that I was comfortable in bed.... I returned to my desk and stayed there until the next midnight. I had a nervous breakdown after a few months.... The last straw that broke my back was the case of a person who died in a concentration camp because one of my staff had failed to get my signature and to dispatch the promise of a visa which was in order.[14]

When Britain declared war on Germany in September 1939, Smallbones and other British diplomats had to return home. Only then did he learn "in confidence and not for publication in the press that some 48,000 persons had entered the United Kingdom under [the Smallbones plan] and that another 50,000 cases were under consideration when war broke out." According to Smallbones, the Home Office "did not want the numbers to be made known, partly because some of the refugees had made themselves very unpopular and partly because the Home Office might be attacked for having admitted such numbers as an administrative measure without the specific sanction of Parliament."[15]

German Jews who benefited from Smallbones's plan never forgot that the consul had helped them escape the Nazis. But the high point of the experience for many was the way he and his colleagues treated them. One woman recalled: "My husband was in the concentration camp, and while I tried to get him out it was too terrible for one even to cry. Then at last I went to the British Consul to see if he could help me. And the first thing they asked me at the consulate was, 'Have you had anything to eat today?' I hadn't of course; I was too worried to think of food. And, before they did anything else, they fed me with coffee and sandwiches, as though I had been a guest. And then I cried."[16]

---

13   Smallbones, 21–22.
14   Ibid., 22–23.
15   Ibid., 23.
16   Ida Cook, *Safe Passage: The Remarkable True Story of Two Sisters Who Rescued Jews from Nazis* (New York: Harlequin, 2008), 166.

READING 3.6: Marion Pritchard: A Student's Fateful Decision

Marion Pritchard lived in the Netherlands during the German occupation of her country in 1940. Soon after the invasion, the Germans began to identify and isolate every Jew in the nation. By 1942, they were deporting Jews. Marion Pritchard was a graduate student during those years. She told an interviewer about the day in 1942 that changed her life:

One morning on my way to school I passed by a small Jewish children's home. The Germans were loading the children, who ranged in age from babies to eight-year-olds, on trucks. They were upset, and crying. When they did not move fast enough the Nazis picked them up, by an arm, a leg, the hair, and threw them into the trucks. To watch grown men treat small children that way—I could not believe my eyes. I found myself literally crying with rage. Two women coming down the street tried to interfere physically. The Germans heaved them into the truck, too. I just sat there on my bicycle, and that was the moment I decided that if there was anything I could do to thwart such atrocities, I would do it.

Some of my friends had similar experiences, and about ten of us, including two Jewish students who decided that they did not want to go into hiding, organized very informally for this purpose. We obtained Aryan identity cards for the Jewish students, who, of course, were taking more of a risk than we were....

We located hiding places, helped people move there, provided food, clothing, and ration cards, and sometimes moral support and relief for the host families. We registered newborn Jewish babies as gentiles (of course there were very few babies during these years) and provided medical care when possible.

Then I was asked by two men I knew well—one of whom had become a lead in the Dutch Resistance Movement—to find a place for a friend of theirs, a man with three small children, aged four, two, and two weeks. I could not find an appropriate place and moved out into part of a large house in the country, about twenty miles east of Amsterdam, that belonged to an elderly lady who was a close friend of my parents. The father, the two boys, and the baby girl moved in and we managed to survive the next two years, until the end of the war. Friends helped take up the floorboards, under the rug, and build a hiding place in case of raids. These did occur with increasing frequency, and one night we had a very narrow escape.

Four Germans accompanied by a Dutch Nazi policeman came and searched the house. They did not find the hiding place, but they had learned from experience that sometimes it paid to go back to a house they had already searched, because by then the hidden Jews might have come out of the hiding place. The baby had started to cry, so I let the children out. Then the Dutch policeman came back alone. I had a small revolver that a friend had given me, but I had never planned to use it. I felt I had no choice except to kill him. I would do it again, under the same circumstances, but it still bothers me, and I still feel that there "should" have been another way. If anybody had really tried to find out how and where he disappeared, they could have, but the general attitude was that there was one traitor less to worry about. A local undertaker helped dispose of the body, he put it in a coffin with a legitimate body in it. I hope that the dead man's family would have approved.

Was I scared? Of course, the answer is "yes." Especially after I had been imprisoned and released. There were times that the fear got the better of me, and I did not do something that I should have. I would rationalize the inaction, feeling it might endanger others, or that I should not run a risk, because what would happen to the three children I was now responsible for, if something happened to me, but I knew I was rationalizing.[17]

---

17   Marion Pritchard, "Marion Pritchard," in *The Courage to Care: Rescuers of Jews during the Holocaust*, eds. Carol Rittner and Sondra Myers (New York: New York University Press, 1986), 29–30.

READING 3.7: Zofia Kossak-Szczucka: "Protest!"

Zofia Kossak-Szczucka was an established author of historical novels, a devout Catholic from a prominent family, and a strong Polish nationalist with very conservative views. She was also known as an Antisemite. And yet in 1942, she wrote an illegal pamphlet entitled "Protest!" It states, in part:

> In the Warsaw ghetto, behind a wall that is cutting them off from the world, several hundred thousand condemned people await death. No hope of survival exists for them, and no help is coming from anywhere. The executioners run through the streets shooting anyone who dares leave the house. They shoot anyone who is near the window. The streets are full of unburied corpses.
>
> The prescribed number of victims is 8,000–10,000 daily. Jewish police must deliver the victims to the hands of the German executioners. If they do not, they themselves perish. Children cannot walk on their own strength and are loaded onto wagons. The process of loading is so brutal that few survive it. Mothers, looking on, become insane. The number of people insane from grief and horror equals the number of people shot to death.
>
> Railroad cars wait on the ramp. The executioners pack the condemned into the wagons, 150 of them in one wagon. On the floor of the wagon lies a thick layer of lime and chloride poured over with water. The door of the wagon gets sealed. Sometimes the wagon moves immediately after loading, sometimes it stays on the siderails a day, two—it doesn't matter to anyone anymore. Of the people crammed so tightly that the dead cannot fall and keep standing arm in arm with the living, of the people slowly dying in the fumes of the lime and chloride, being deprived of air, water, food—no one will remain alive anyway. Whenever, wherever the death-wagons will arrive, they will only contain corpses.
>
> … Just as in the Warsaw ghetto, since six months ago in larger and smaller Polish towns and cities the same is happening. The total number of Jews killed is over one million, and this number is growing daily. All perish: the rich and poor, the old, the women, the men, the youth, the babies. The Catholics dying, with the name of Jesus and Mary, like the Jews: all were guilty of being born as Jews, who were sentenced to annihilation by Hitler.
>
> The world looks upon this murder more horrible than anything that history has ever seen and stays silent. The slaughter of millions of defenseless people is being carried out amid general sinister silence.…
>
> This silence can no longer be tolerated. Whatever the reason for it, it is vile. In the face of murder, it is wrong to remain passive. Whoever is silent witnessing murder becomes a partner to the murder. Whoever does not condemn, consents.

Therefore we—Catholics, Poles—raise our voices. Our feeling toward the Jews has not changed. We continue to deem them political, economic, and ideological enemies of Poland. Moreover, we realize that they hate us more than they hate the Germans and that they make us responsible for this misfortune. Why, and on what basis, remains a mystery of the Jewish soul. Nevertheless this is a decided fact. Awareness of fact, however, does not release us from the duty of damnation of murder.

… We have no means actively to counteract the German murders; we cannot help, nor can we rescue anybody. But we protest from the bottom of our hearts, filled with pity, indignation, and horror. This protest is demanded of us by God, who does not allow us to kill. It is demanded by our Christian conscience. Every being calling itself human has the right to love his fellow man. The blood of the defenseless victims is calling for revenge. Who does not protest with us, is not a Catholic.[18]

Despite her antagonism toward Jews, Kossak-Szczucka helped found Zegota, an underground organization that hid Jews, forged identity papers for them, paid off blackmailers, and provided medical assistance to Jews in hiding. Her underground work eventually led to her arrest; she was held in Auschwitz for a year. After her release, she continued to rescue Jews, particularly Jewish children. Why did she go to such lengths even though she disapproved of Jews? Nechama Tec, a sociologist who was a hidden child during the Holocaust, offers an answer she found in one of the woman's novels. It is a conversation between two friends. Both view Jews with hostility, and yet one is engaged in hiding Jews. The Pole who has no interest in doing so asks his friend why he would risk everything to protect Jews. The friend replies:

Today the Jews face extermination. They are the victims of unjust murderous persecutions. I must save them. "Do unto others what you want others to do unto you." This commandment demands that I use all the means I have to save others, the very same ways that I would use for my own salvation. To be sure, after the war, the situation will be different. The same laws will apply to the Jew and to me. At that point I will tell the Jew: "I had saved you, sheltered you when you were persecuted. To keep you alive I risked my own life and the lives of those who were dear to me. Now nothing threatens you. You have your own friends and in some ways you are better off than I. Now I am depriving you of my home. Go and settle somewhere else. I wish you luck and will be glad to help you. I am not going to hurt you, but in my own home I want to live alone. I have a right to it."[19]

---

18   Zofia Kossak-Szczucka, "The Protest," translated and quoted in Nechama Tec, *When Light Pierced the Darkness: Christian Rescue of Jews in Nazi-Occupied Poland* (New York: Oxford University Press, 1986), 111–112.

19   Zofia Kossak-Szczucka, "Komu Pomagamy?" [Whom do we help?], *Prawda, Pismo Frontu Odrodzenia* (Aug–Sept 1943), 8, translated and quoted in Tec, *When Light Pierced the Darkness*, 108.

READING 3.8: Major Julius Schmahling: A Teacher's Remorse

A village in France known as Le Chambon aided thousands of Jews during the Holocaust. Many scholars have wondered how people there were able to keep so many Jews hidden for so long without the Nazis learning what was actually going on. When Philip Hallie, a professor of philosophy, wrote a book about their efforts, he asked the villagers that very question. Many attributed their safety to "le major." They claimed he was responsible for the anonymous phone calls they received just before a raid.

Hallie discovered that the mysterious major was Julius Schmahling, the Nazi occupation governor of the Haute-Loire district which included Le Chambon. Although the Nazis replaced him in 1943, he stayed on as second-in-command until the war was over. According to Hallie, Schmahling was "no hero, no declared enemy of Nazism or of any other 'ism'—seen from a distance he was just one more dutiful member of the Nazi war machine. But seen up close, and seen from the point of view of the hundreds, possibly thousands of people he protected from the Gestapo and from his own vicious auxiliary troops in the Haute-Loire, he was a good man. He compromised with evil, and helped defenseless people as much as he could."[20] Why did he choose to help when so many others looked the other way?

Hallie cites two incidents in response to that question. The first took place when Schmahling was a young teacher:

> He had prepared a dramatic lesson on the king of beasts, and full of it, and of himself, he walked into the classroom. As he spoke the first words, "The lions," he noticed a little boy in the back of the room who had been sitting dumbly on his wooden bench during the whole term. The boy was waving his hand in the air to catch his teacher's eye. The young teacher kept talking about the great beasts. In a few moments the boy jumped off his bench and called out "Herr Professor, Herr"—Schmahling looked at him in anger—he could not believe that this little dunce was going to interrupt his discourse on lions. Then the boy did something that really amazed the teacher. He called out, without permission, "Yesterday, yes, yesterday I saw a rabbit. Yesterday I really saw a rabbit!"

> Before the words were all out, Schmahling yelled out, "Sit down, you little jackass." The boy sat down and never said a word for the rest of the year.

> In his old age, Schmahling looked back at that moment as the most decisive one in his whole life. Then, while he was crushing the boy with all the power of his German pedagogical authoritarianism, he was destroying something in himself in the very act of destroying the moment of sunlight in that little boy's life. When the class was over he vowed to himself that he would never do such a thing again to a human being. Teaching and living for him, he vowed, would from that moment forward involve making room for each of his students and each of the people he knew outside of the classroom to speak about the rabbits they had seen.

---

20   Philip Hallie, "Major Julius Schmahling," in *The Courage to Care: Rescuers of Jews During the Holocaust,* eds. Carol Rittner and Sondra Myers (New York: New York University Press, 1986), 114.

And he kept his vow. It was as simple as that—and as infinitely complex as keeping such a vow during the German occupation of France.[21]

The other incident took place just after the war ended and Schmahling was brought to trial by the French Resistance:

> As he rolled down the aisle with his sturdy body and in his slightly worn, green-gray, Wehrmacht officer's uniform, he was not a figure of distinction, and he seemed an easy target for all the hatred the French were feeling against the Germans.
>
> But when he was halfway down the aisle everybody in the room, including the toughest chiefs of the Haute-Loire Resistance, stood up and turned to him. As he walked up the aisle, people whispered to him, "Major, do you need more food in jail? Do you need writing materials or books?" As he walked, he smiled, and shook his head gently.
>
> When he came up to the head of the tribunal, the tough old French Resistance chief who was chairman of the [hearing] bowed to him (for he had stood up with all of the others) and made a little speech of gratitude to him on the part of all of the Frenchmen in the Haute-Loire.
>
> Later, in his diary, Schmahling described the meeting as '*fast peinlich*,' almost painful: he was glad for their praise and their affection, but didn't they realize decency is the normal thing to do? Didn't they realize that decency needs no rewards, no recognition, that it is done out of the heart, now, immediately, just in order to satisfy the heart now?[22]

---

21 Hallie, 112–113.
22 Ibid., 112–115.

READING 3.9: Quotations on Rescue and Resistance

"Both evil and goodness evolve. Heroes are not born; their evolution often begins with small steps. People learn by doing, change as a result of their own actions. Very often rescuers agreed to hide a person or family, expecting this to be for a short time. But once people begin to help, their concern for the welfare of those they helped increases. They begin to see themselves as caring people. Some rescuers would take in more people to hide, or if they succeeded to move people to a safer place, they looked for more opportunities to help. What sometimes began as limited commitment often became intense involvement."[23]

—Ervin Staub, a psychologist and a Holocaust survivor who was born in Hungary

"It did not occur to me to do anything other than I did. After what I had seen outside the children's home, I could not have done anything else. I think you have a responsibility to yourself to behave decently. We all have memories of times we should have done something and didn't. And it gets in the way of the rest of your life."[24]

—Marion Pritchard, a psychologist and a rescuer in the Netherlands during the Holocaust

"There were so many people in the village who needed help. How could we refuse them? A person doesn't sit down and say I'm going to this and that. We had no time to think. When a problem came, we had to solve it immediately."[25]

—Magda Trocmé, a French Protestant who rescued hundreds of Jews during the Holocaust in La Chambon

---

23 This statement by Ervin Staub is based on two of his books: *The Roots of Evil: The Origins of Genocide and Other Group Violence* (1989) and *Overcoming Evil: Genocide, Violent Conflict and Terrorism* (2011).

24 Marion Pritchard, "Marion Pritchard," in *The Courage to Care: Rescuers of Jews during the Holocaust,* eds. Carol Rittner and Sonda Myers (New York: New York University Press, 1986), 33.

25 Magda Trocmé, "Magda Trocmé," in *The Courage to Care,* 102.

To Be a Jew in a Time of Genocide

Teaching Focus

Units 1 and 2 consider how a Jewish identity affects the way we see ourselves as well as the way others see us. Unit 3 focuses on the role played by the push to conform and the pull of conscience in ancient Egypt and Nazi-occupied Europe. Unit 4 continues that exploration by examining how all of these factors shaped the responses of the victims of the Holocaust. It focuses in particular on the extraordinary risks taken by Jews to carry out their religious obligations in defiance of the Germans. The unit also examines the determination of Jews in various places to document and record the crimes committed against them. As one resident of the Warsaw ghetto explained, "The record must be hurled like a stone under history's wheel in order to stop it."[1] She and thousands of other Jews across Europe were determined that one day their stories would be known and justice would be served.

The lessons in this unit also reveal why many of the choices open to Jews and other victims of the Holocaust are often referred to as "choice-less choices." Lawrence Langer, a noted Holocaust scholar, defines the term as decisions made in the "absence of humanly significant alternatives"—that is, choices that enable "an individual to make a decision, act on it, and accept the consequences, all within a framework that supports personal integrity and self-esteem."[2]

Lesson 1: Terror and Moral Courage in the "Heart of Darkness"
Lesson 2: Questions and Answers from the Kovno Ghetto

Essential Questions

- What can we learn about human behavior—particularly courage and resistance—from the stories of victims of the Holocaust?
- What particular challenges did Jews with a strong religious identity face?
- To what extent were the choices Jews made during the Holocaust "choice-less choices"?

---

1   Gustawa Jarecka, "The Last Stage of Resettlement Is Death" (late 1942), quoted in "What We Know About Murdered Peoples," *The New Republic* (April 9, 2008), available at *http://www.tnr.com/article/books/what-we-know-about-murdered-peoples*.

2   Lawrence Langer, "The Dilemma of Choice in the Death Camps," *Centerpoint: The Holocaust* 4: 1 (1980): 55, quoted in *The Holocaust: Theoretical Readings*, ed. Neil Levi and Michael Rothberg (New Brunswick, NJ: Rutgers University Press, 2003), 173.

Student Outcomes

Students will . . .

- recognize the dilemmas Jews faced in Nazi-controlled Europe.
- show understanding of the harsh realities of ghetto life.
- develop awareness that "choice-less choices" were often the only options available to many of the victims.

These lessons may be used to extend, reinforce, and enhance concepts developed in:

- Chapters 6 and 7 in *Facing History and Ourselves: Holocaust and Human Behavior*
- Chapters 4, 5, and 6 in *Facing History and Ourselves: Jews of Poland*

Terror and Moral Courage in the "Heart of Darkness"

On September 1, 1939, the German army invaded Poland. Within days, France and Britain declared war on Germany. World War II had begun in Europe. In the weeks before the war officially started, many Jews in Eastern Europe feared that the Nazis would wage two wars. One would be fought publicly on the battlefields of Europe. The other would take place just beyond public view and its victims would not be soldiers but children, women, and men whose only "crime" was that they were Jews. After all, Adolf Hitler had long insisted that another world war would mean the annihilation of Europe's Jews.

A few days before the war began, the Jews of Piotrkow, a town in central Poland, received a letter along with several boxes from the Jewish community in Lipna. In the letter, Jewish officials in Lipna explained that their town was located near the German border, "where the first battles would occur." Aware that "the Germans were fighting against Jewry," they were fearful that their ritual objects would be destroyed. They were therefore sending two crates of "holy vessels" to Piotrkow "where the grasp of the enemy would surely not reach," in the hope that Jews there would protect these objects "until the storm had passed." Rabbi Shimon Huberband, a young scholar who helped open the boxes, wrote:

> The letter and the "holy vessels" terrified us. We sensed the gravity of the situation, and the horror which awaited Jews during the war. And yet, we saw the spiritual strength of Jews as we witnessed an assimilated community in Silesia's overriding concern to save a few religious objects.[3]

On September 2, just one day after the invasion, the Germans dropped the first bombs on the town of Piotrkow. Among those killed in the days that followed were Huberband's wife, son, and father-in-law. By the spring of 1940, he was living in the Warsaw ghetto, where he became involved with Oneg Shabbat, a group that secretly collected diaries, journals, letters, wills, and other evidence of the tragedy that was unfolding in Nazi-occupied Europe. Huberband risked his life repeatedly to gather information for the group. His writings, along with hundreds of other documents, were buried in milk cans and crates that were partly discovered after the war. By then, Huberband and most of his associates had been murdered, including the head of the archive, Emmanuel Ringelbum, a noted historian and teacher.

---

3   Shimon Huberband, *Kiddush Hashem: Jewish Religious and Cultural Life in Poland During the Holocaust*, eds. Jeffrey S. Gurock and Robert S. Hirt, trans. David E. Fishman (Hoboken, NJ: Ktav Publishing, 1987), 5–6.

In this lesson, students examine Huberband's accounts of some of the events that he witnessed and reflect on what these incidents reveal about the role that religion played in way the victims—particularly victims with a strong religious identity—responded to growing evidence of a Holocaust. They also consider the enormous difficulties associated with maintaining a positive religious identity at a time and in a place where that identity was subject to harassment, ridicule, and revile.

Essential Questions
- What can we learn about Rabbi Huberband from his writings?
- What do those writings reveal about the role religion played for many Jews during the Holocaust?
- What does his work add to our understanding of Jewish resistance during the Holocaust?

Recommended Resources
- Reading 4.1: Shimon Huberband: Autobiographical Notes
- Reading 4.2: Jewish Religious Life in Nazi-Occupied Europe: Journey to the *Mikveh*
- Reading 4.3: Jewish Religious Life: Questions of Jewish Law
- Reading 4.4: On the Destruction of East European Jewry: *Kiddush haShem*

Activity Ideas
For information on specific teaching strategies useful in carrying out various activity ideas outlined in this lesson, see the Appendix.

GETTING STARTED
Review with students what it means to have moral courage. What was the connection between conscience and courage in the responses of individuals who rescued Jews during the Holocaust (Unit 3)? What is the connection in the world today? Ask students what they know about the victims of the Holocaust. You may want to have them record their initial responses in their journals. Encourage them to expand, deepen, and revise those responses as the lesson progresses.

ANALYZING PRIMARY SOURCES
Gustawa Jarecka was one of many individuals who reported on events in the Warsaw ghetto. She said of those reports:

> These documents and notes are a remnant resembling a clue in a detective story. I remember from childhood such a novel by Conan Doyle in which the dying victim writes with a faint hand one word on the wall containing the proof of the criminal's guilt. That word, scrawled by the dying man, influenced my imagination in the past…. We are noting the evidence of the crime.[4]

---

4 Gustawa Jarecka, quoted in Samuel D. Kassow, *Who Will Write Our History? Emanuel Ringelblum, the Warsaw Ghetto, and the Oyneg Shabes Archive* (Bloomington, IN: Indiana University Press, 2007), 6–7.

Rabbi Huberband was a colleague of Gustawa Jarecka's, and he too collected evidence of the crime by recording events he actually witnessed (Readings 4.1 and 4.2) or uncovered as a result of interviews with witnesses (Readings 4.3 and 4.4). If you wish to use all four readings and time is limited, you may want to divide the class into groups, with each responsible for one document. Regardless of how the documents are used, remind students to begin by determining the facts presented in the document: What happened? Who was involved? Where did it happen? When did it happen? Why does it matter?

After determining the facts, have students look at the documents with a more critical eye:

- What questions do you have that have not been answered?
- What information is missing?
- From what perspective or perspectives is the story told? What perspectives are missing?
- What can you infer from the documents?
- What conclusions seem most likely?
- What do the documents reveal about the perpetrators, bystanders, and victims?
- What do they add to your understanding of what it meant to be an observant Jew in Nazi-occupied Europe?

MAKING INFERENCES

Remind students that the Nazis insisted that they were not targeting Jews because of their religion but because of their race. Then ask them to find evidence in Reading 4.1 that indicates that religious Jews were subject to particular harassment and humiliation. How do you explain why the Nazis treated religious Jews with such contempt? Why did the Nazis seem to feel that it was not enough to isolate, persecute, and even exterminate Jews, but that it was also necessary to humiliate and ridicule them for being Jews? Their actions sent a message. At whom was that message directed—other perpetrators? Bystanders? Victims?

READERS' THEATER

Rabbi Huberband's clandestine trip to the *mikveh* (Reading 4.2) lends itself to being read aloud. Divide the essay into parts by assigning each student a paragraph to read aloud. Encourage them to use their voices to capture the mood and emotions of the group that made the journey. After completing the reading, ask students what Huberband wants his readers to feel, to understand, and to know as fact. What does he want us to learn from the story? What is the moral or lesson of the story?

BUILDING VOCABULARY

What do the words *Kiddush haShem* literally mean? Assign Reading 4.4 and ask students to explain in their own words how Rabbi Huberband defines the term. What do his examples add to our understanding of the term? Did the Jews he singles out have a meaningful choice, or was *Kiddush haShem* for many of them a "choice-less choice"—a decision made in the "absence of humanly significant alternatives"? That is, were these choices that enabled "an individual to make a decision, act on it, and accept the consequences, all within a framework that supports personal integrity and self-esteem"?

FORMING HYPOTHESES

In Reading 4.4, Huberband presents his readers with a mystery that centers on the behavior of Dr. Gonshar. Why would a man who hid his Jewish identity before the war suddenly accept beatings and even torture rather than deny that he was a Jew? How does Huberband explain Dr. Gonshar's behavior? Have students work with their *chavruta* to develop their own hypotheses. Remind them that a hypothesis is a tentative explanation for an observation, phenomenon, or problem that requires further testing. Encourage partners to share their hypotheses with one another and the class. How might students test their ideas? What insights might psychologists provide? What insights might rabbis and religious leaders have? Why is Huberband reluctant to judge?

ASSESSMENT

To assess understanding of this lesson, provide the following quotation. Ask students to write an essay explaining whether they agree or disagree with Mazor's conclusions. They should not only state an opinion but also provide facts to support that opinion.

Aware that many Jews during the Middle Ages were also forced into ghettos, Michal Mazor, a survivor of the Warsaw ghetto, wrote:

> It takes no great knowledge of Jewish history to note the essential difference between the ghettos of the Middle Ages and those created by the "Master Race" … [T]he former were not completely cut off from the world: Jews could leave them by day; ordinary life took on forms that allowed generations of Jews to live and to succeed one another upholding their distinctive traditions, even creating a civilization. The medieval ghettos still represented a form of life…. In the twentieth century, especially in Warsaw, the ghetto was no longer anything but an organized form of death.[5]

---

5   Michael Mazor, *The Vanished City: Everyday Life in the Warsaw Ghetto*, trans. David Jacobson (New York: Marsilio, 1993), 19.

READING 4.1: Shimon Huberband: Autobiographical Notes

Shimon Huberband lost his family during an air raid in the first days of the German invasion. In the weeks that followed, he kept a notebook in which he recorded events he witnessed in Piotrkow and later Warsaw. Just 10 days after the first bombs fell on Piotrkow in 1939, Huberband wrote:

> On Tuesday, September 12, the seizure of Jews for work intensified.... Broad searches were being carried out for male Jews, who were to be taken to work. During the searches, all their belongings were taken from them....
>
> If a bearded Jew was caught, his life was put in danger. They tore out his beard along with pieces of flesh, or cut it off with a knife and a bayonet. *Mezuzahs* were torn off doorposts and ripped apart. Woe unto the Jew who was found with *tefilin* and religious books! The *tefilin* and books were torn to shreds and burnt. Only Torah scrolls were spared. When a Jew was caught, he was immediately examined to see if he was wearing a *talis koton.** If he was, there was no envying him. He was beaten cruelly and horribly. The same for any Jew caught wearing a Jewish hat. Jews therefore removed their Jewish hats and long coats, shaved their long beards, and kept their religious books and *tefilin* hidden.
>
> The Germans collected *taleysim, talis kotons,* and *kitls.* These holy garments were given to Jews to wash floors, automobiles, and windows. To clean the filthiest of places, Jews were given pages from the Talmud and other religious books.[6]

By 1940, Rabbi Huberband was in Warsaw. On Purim (March 24, 1940), he wrote:

> Despite the fact that public prayer was prohibited, every courtyard had several *minyans* in which the *megilah* was read. Were it possible to read people's minds, one could easily have established that when they stamped out Haman's name, they were thinking about the Haman of our time. There were no jam-filled cakes in the shop windows for *shalach manos.* There were no Purim-*shpilers.*
>
> I went to the home of the [Plaseczno] Rebbe. I saw people exchanging *shalach manos.* The Rebbe sat in his *shtrayml* and silk caftan, and spoke with a few Hasidim about the terrible situation of the Jews. There would be no festive meal and no Hasidic celebration as was the practice every year.
>
> The mood was terrible; the predominant spirit wasn't of Purim, but of Tisha B'av...
>
> It is noteworthy that on this day Poles picked fights with Jews and beat them on various streets of the city. It is believed that this, too, was the work of the Germans, because the attacks were photographed by the Germans. Later on, they would show the world that the Poles were attacking Jews. It is saddening that there are Poles who allow themselves to be used as a tool of the Germans

---

* Literally a "little tallis" worn by observant Jewish boys and men. It consists of a simple rectangle of cloth with a hole for the neck and fringes (*tzitzit*) on the four corners. Sometimes the *talis koton* is simply called *tzitzit.*

---

6   Shimon Huberband, *Kiddush Hashem: Jewish Religious and Cultural Life in Poland During the Holocaust*, eds. Jeffrey S. Gurock and Robert S. Hirt, trans. David E. Fishman (Hoboken, NJ: Ktav Publishing, 1987), 35.

for their own interests. It is even more saddening that there are no Poles to persuade the Jew-beaters to stop their dirty work.[7]

Rabbi Huberband described the first Passover (April 23–30, 1940) in Warsaw after the German occupation:

All winter long, Jews worried about the problem of *matzah*. During the week before Passover it became clear that although the *Kehilah* would not offer *matzah* instead of bread for its ration cards, there would still be *matzah*.

The rabbis permitted the use of flour already found in the market. They made the bakers' ovens kosher for Passover, and *matzahs* were baked. The price was steep, but the Joint Distribution Committee dispensed a huge amount of machine *matzahs* and this kept the cost of *matzahs* in check. The price of a kilogram of *matzah* went from thirteen to fifteen zlotys. Some *shmurah matzah,* supervised from the moment of reaping, was also baked from grain harvested during the summer of 1939 in the presence of Jews.

There were even *matzahs* which were prepared on the eve of the festival, baked by a number of Hasidic rabbis for their own personal use. During the baking, they sang the psalms of *Hallel* as in the good old days.

The peasants brought into town eggs, potatoes, and various vegetables. Everything was relatively expensive, but there were enough potatoes and vegetables to go around. The rich also had fish and meat for Passover.

The rabbis arranged contracts for the sale of *chometz.* Wagons with large kettles of boiling water were led through the courtyards with cries of "We *kasher* everything!" More than usual, one saw little boys running from one Jewish house to the next screaming, "Give me your *chometz* to burn!" But instead of burning the *chometz,* they devoured it themselves.

There was an adequate supply of wine for the four cups, and the display windows of various shops were filled with an assortment of wines which Jews readily purchased….

The Passover of that year was celebrated by Jews in an exalted spirit. These were the honeymoon days of the German attack on Holland and Belgium. The fantastically blown-up reports which circulated among the Jews told of enormous German defeats and casualties, and enormous victories by Holland and Belgium. People said—they shouted—that very soon we would be saved….

Despite the ban on public prayer, people assembled in all the courtyards in which several *minyans* were held. In a whole slew of *minyans,* the congregation made *Kiddush* together. Hasidim gathered after the festival to drink liquor. They also did some singing, but softly. There was no dancing.[8]

---

7   Huberband, 55–56.
8   Ibid., 58–59.

The rumors of Allied victories in Belgium and Holland in 1941 were false. It was the Germans who were victorious. As a result, the war against Jews did not ease in the months that followed; it intensified. On the seventh night of Passover in 1941, Rabbi Huberband and about 200 other Jews were pulled from their homes and herded into a labor camp. He wrote:

> The sun began to set, and night began to fall. One star after another began to pop up in the sky. I recalled that it was now the last night of Passover, and remembered how much joy and spiritual pleasure I used to experience at this moment. I was reminded of this night in the yeshiva, and later on in the rabbi's home, where Hasidim would gather. We would drink, say words of Torah and Hasidic homilies, perform spirited dances, and sing Hasidic tunes. I imagined how Jews were now reciting the *Ma'ariv* prayers with the special festival melody, how they were reciting the *Kiddush*, and how even now, amidst the horrible poverty, where Jews were starving in the streets, everyone would eat *matzah* and not leavened bread. And here there were two hundred Jews in the most terrible of situations, beyond any comparison.

> The hunger was a torture. I always used to fast with great ease, but today's fasting had affected me so badly that I could barely stand on my legs. I guess that my general exhaustion and weariness caused even one day of not eating to have such an effect on me.

> Finally, at 7:30 P.M. lunch was ready. It was not with an easy heart and light mood that I decided to partake of the meal. But I simply felt that this was literally *pikuach nefesh,* a matter of saving my life, and *pikuach nefesh* takes precedence over all else. In any case, finally, after a full twenty-four hours of starving, and after having had the "pleasure" of being seized, and undergone such a difficult and harsh journey, during which we were beaten more than once, we were supposed to receive our first meal in the camp.[9]

After five weeks in the camp, Rabbi Huberband and other survivors were returned to Warsaw. He summarized the results of the forced labor with these words: "five weeks in the camp which accomplished absolutely nothing; fifty-three graves on the hill; fifty men who died in Warsaw; and the rest—physical and emotional invalids for life."[10] The following year on the eve of Shavuot, May 21, 1942, the rabbi and thousands of other Jews were forced from their homes and pushed onto rail-cars bound for Treblinka. Only a handful survived. This time, Huberband was not among the survivors. He was murdered in Treblinka.

---

9   Huberband, 79.
10   Ibid., 101.

READING 4.2: Jewish Religious Life in Nazi-Occupied Europe: Journey to the *Mikveh*

Observant Jews, both men and women, visit a *mikveh* or ritual bath on important occasions to purify themselves. Rabbi Shimon Huberband wrote a description of a very special visit to a *mikveh* just before Yom Kippur in 1940:

> Among all the evil decrees issued by the Kingdom of Wickedness, there was also a decree forbidding Jews to immerse themselves in *mikvehs*. The *mikvehs* were locked up and a notice was hung on their doors that "opening the *mikvehs* or employing it will be punished as sabotage, and will be subject to between ten years in prison or death."
>
> The Rebbe [Rabbi Kalonimus Shapiro] made a decision, an iron-clad decision, that he must immerse himself in the *mikveh* before Yom Kippur. All the arguments put forth by his intimates that this would endanger his life were of no avail. The mere walk to the *mikveh* was dangerous for such a person as the Rebbe. But the Rebbe did not alter his decision, and we made plans to implement it. But how?…
>
> At dawn on the day on which the Thirteen Divine Attributes are recited [Yom Kippur] at exactly 5:00 A.M., the hour when Jews are first permitted to be outdoors, a small group of people headed by the Rebbe assembled and began the dangerous journey to the *mikveh*. It was still dark outside.…
>
> The distance between the Rebbe's home and the *mikveh* was quite long. The wagon which we had ordered did not arrive. By ten minutes past five o'clock, the group was getting nervous because everything had been planned according to the exact minute. We decided to begin walking by foot, in the hope that the wagon would meet us en route.…
>
> Quietly, on our tiptoes, we descended the steps. But then, there was a new, unanticipated problem. The janitor didn't feel like getting up so early to open the gate. He was eager to know why Jews needed to go outside so early. A pretty penny "softened" his heart, and he agreed to let us out of the gate.
>
> With silent footsteps, we walked in pairs, each pair a certain distance between the preceding one. Our hearts beat like hammers. Our eyes strained to look into the depths of the night at each approaching silhouette, to see whether it wasn't one of "them." … Suddenly we heard the ring of an approaching night-trolley. We ran quickly to the station to take the trolley.… But as we drew near we saw it was an Aryan trolley—off limits to Jews.…
>
> We walked from street to street, when suddenly we heard the sound of an approaching automobile. Its headlights cast a blinding light in our eyes. We stood paralyzed in place because in these times it isn't good luck to meet an automobile on the street. In most cases, one is "invited" to a place from which there is no return. There was no gateway in which to hide; the gates were all still locked,

due to the early hour. But we were graced with a stroke of luck. The automobile passed us by and neglected to spot us. Holding our breath, we walked past the more dangerous points and reached the gateway in which the *mikveh* was situated.

The courtyard of the *mikveh* was pitch-black. Mysterious shadows crept about the walls and disappeared into an adjacent cellar. A secret emissary awaited us. Silently, without words, but with a lone wave of his arm, he began to lead us. We descended into a deep, dark cellar. We groped in the darkness. We had instructions to walk straight and then turn left. We reached a chiseled hole in the wall. With great difficulty, we pushed ourselves through the wall. We found ourselves standing on a platform of wood boards, and after a successful jump we entered a corridor which led to the steps of the *mikveh.*

Despite the great danger in which we found ourselves, we were fascinated by the whole event. We imagined vividly the sight of our forefathers in Spain—how they rescued Torah scrolls, how they prayed with a *minyan* in secret cellars, due to fear of the Inquisition. They certainly never imagined that their descendants would find themselves, four hundred years later, in a much worse situation, and that in order to immerse themselves in honor of a festival, they would be forced to follow the same kinds of dangerous procedures. In the *mikveh* we found a sizable number of people who had received secret word that the *mikveh* would be open for an hour. Silently and in great haste, we undressed and immersed ourselves in honor of the festival. A few minutes later, we repeated the same procedure we had used to enter. By the time we reached the courtyard, day was beginning to break, and we could see on the lock and bolt on the entrance gate to the *mikveh* the well-known notice: "Opening the *mikveh* or employing it will be punished as sabotage and will be subject to between ten years in prison and death."[11]

11   Shimon Huberband, *Kiddush Hashem: Jewish Religious and Cultural Life in Poland During the Holocaust,* eds. Jeffrey S. Gurock and Robert S. Hirt, trans. David E. Fishman (Hoboken, NJ: Ktav Publishing, 1987), 199–201.

READING 4.3: Jewish Religious Life: Questions of Jewish Law

During the war, Rabbi Shimon Huberband began work on a book that would trace the history of responsa literature—collections of answers given by rabbis and other authorities to questions as to how the Torah applies to everyday life. These collections are known in Hebrew as *she'elot u'teshuvot* (literally, "questions and answers"). Because both the questions and the answers are deeply rooted in the everyday concerns of Jews, they provide historians with insights into life at a particular time and in a particular place. Most of the work that Huberband did on the book has never been found. We know of it only from references made by Huberband and others. Among those documents is the following account by the rabbi:

> Questions of Jewish law are almost never asked anymore. Firstly, because people tend to behave much more leniently in times of war, and find no need to consult a rabbi. Secondly, there is almost nothing left to ask. There is no ritual slaughter of animals. No chickens and virtually no meat or milk among Jews in the ghetto.
>
> On the other hand, there have arisen specific wartime questions: concerning sitting *shiva* for a deceased or murdered person, regarding burial, *Kaddish,* and *yortsayt.* Should one conduct the Passover Seder when one does not have the four cups of wine or *matzah?* May one drink four cups of wine made from the squeezed juice of unsweetened grapes? Questions were asked regarding sick and weak people as to whether they may eat on Yom Kippur; whether one may violate the Sabbath for the sake of certain sick people; whether they may be fed nonkosher meat, since kosher meat is difficult to acquire and costs much more. A question was asked by a Jew who hid a piece of black bread before Passover, in order to eat it after Passover, and failed to sell the bread to a Gentile for the duration of the festival.
>
> **The Sale of Chometz**
> On the eve of both wartime Passovers, rabbis arranged the sale of *chometz* by means of formal sale contracts, just as they did before the war. On the Passover of 1941, there was a serious problem of finding a Gentile to whom to sell the *chometz,* due to the sealed-off ghetto. After many difficulties a Gentile was found and the *chometz* was sold....[12]
>
> **Observance of the Sabbath and Its Violation**
> The German invasion of Poland occurred in most cities and towns shortly before the High Holidays of the year 5700. Upon entering a city, they would immediately order all stores to remain open on the Sabbath and holidays. In the great majority of cities, the stores were open on Rosh Hashanah and Yom Kippur.
>
> The seizure of Jews for forced labor also took place on the Sabbath and holidays. The Jewish population was thus forced to violate the Sabbath in an additional manner....

---

12 Shimon Huberband, *Kiddush Hashem: Jewish Religious and Cultural Life in Poland During the Holocaust*, eds. Jeffrey S. Gurock and Robert S. Hirt, trans. David E. Fishman (Hoboken, NJ: Ktav Publishing, 1987), 205–206.

When prices began to rise, there began to be shortages of various products which in turn led to further price increases. Many Jews, including the most pious ones, permitted themselves to violate the Sabbath in order to make various purchases, whenever there were items to purchase. This was done for the sake of *pikuach nefesh,* the sustaining of life.

When "they" entered Poland, the *eruvim* in all the cities and towns became invalid. The state of war forced Jews to carry their papers, tools, and other items on the Sabbath, despite the fact that there were no *eruvim.* When the closed ghettos were created, and were surrounded by brick walls on all sides, the ghetto walls formed the most kosher of all possible *eruvim.*

In the cities which were annexed by the German Reich, there is universal forced labor. The whole Jewish populace, both men and women, work seven days a week. In those regions, Jews have simply been forgetting which day is the Sabbath. Women have even stopped lighting candles. In the small towns, one finds one or, at most, two women who light candles. Even in those areas where forced labor is not as severe, there are women who have stopped lighting candles because of the high cost of living.

Since the formation of the ghetto, the famine and poverty among Jews has increased so enormously that one finds on the streets of Warsaw gray-bearded Jews, even wearing traditional Jewish hats, who ask for alms on the Sabbath....

In the ghetto, there are no Gentiles to kindle fires on the Sabbath and [their] absence ... is a serious problem. There is a Jew at 27 Zamenhofa Street who has a Christian maidservant named Sophia Laszicka. This Sophia has worked for him for over thirty years. She raised his children, was present at their weddings, and is closely tied to the family. When the edict creating the ghetto took effect, Miss Laszicka put on the yellow badge; she continues to live in this Jew's home until this very day. This Miss Laszicka alleviates, somewhat, the situation in the ghetto on the Sabbath. On Fridays, people arrange times for her to visit their homes and pay her in advance. All Sabbath long, she walks about the ghetto to kindle fires for the sick. Everywhere, Jews quarrel over her and ask her to kindle their fires.

There are also some Polish smugglers who enter the ghetto on the Sabbath, and take the opportunity to kindle fires for Jews. But one must, in all honesty, state that only a few do so, because it isn't worth their smugglers' while. They have more important business to attend to.

Miss Laszicka and the smugglers are used only to kindle fires for the sick, not to warm people's ovens. There are very few religious Jews who can afford to light their ovens Friday and keep them burning throughout the Sabbath. As a result, most religious Jews must endure freezing-cold temperatures in their homes on the Sabbath.[13]

---

13 Huberband, 207–209.

READING 4.4: On the Destruction of East European Jewry: *Kiddush haShem*

Many Jews in the Warsaw ghetto spoke of *kiddush haShem*—the sanctification of God's name. Rabbi Shimon Huberband tried to clarify what the term actually means:

Kiddush Hashem is performed in three ways: (a) a Jew sacrifices his life when others attempt to make him abandon the Jewish faith, (b) a Jew gives his life to save a fellow Jew, and even more so—to save a group of Jews, (c) a Jew dies while fighting to defend other Jews. Maimonides rules that if a Jew is killed, even without any overt attempt to make him abandon the Jewish faith, but because he is a Jew, he is considered a martyr.… In our current study, we will discuss only the level of *Kiddush Hashem* described in category *b*, for the following reasons:

All of the tens of thousands of Jews who perished at the hands of the evil ones through slaughter, hanging, shooting, burning, and other violent deaths are martyrs, even if they were not forced to deny the Jewish faith. This would be called passive *Kiddush Hashem*. But here we would like to present facts concerning instances of active *Kiddush Hashem*.

Another consideration: Rumors have spread that Jewish "leaders" in a number of cities and towns have issued lists at the demand of the evil ones with the lists of Jews who are to be hanged or shot, and they have justified their actions by saying they were thus saving the entire city or town. We therefore wish to relate some facts about those Jews who gave their lives and refused to issue lists or other hardships for their brethren.…

We also wish to relate a number of facts on how Jews endangered themselves and sacrificed their lives while attempting to save synagogues and Torah scrolls which the evil ones set on fire.…

Bedzin

In September 1939, as soon as the evil ones entered the city of Bedzin, they encircled the Jewish quarter and the synagogue. They set fire to the synagogue and the adjacent houses. When the Jews ran out of their homes, they were shot dead on the spot.

Nevertheless, a group of Jews led by Mr. Shlezinger, his son, and son-in-law, dashed inside the synagogue while the sanctuary was in flames. Despite the blaze on all sides, they reached the holy ark and managed to save two Torah scrolls each, one scroll in each arm. But as they reached the door of the burning synagogue, they were shot dead by the evil ones. They died as martyrs. May their memory be blessed, and may the Lord avenge their blood.…

Miedzyrzecz

In order to save the lives of thirty Jews, the local rabbi, the *dayyan* named Ruskin, and the head of the local yeshiva, Rabbi Dovid Blek, sacrificed their lives.

The evil ones stated that if the above mentioned Jews offered themselves to be killed, the other Jews would be spared. The three did so, but in addition to them, the evil ones killed more than thirty other Jews, including the *dayyan's* wife. This occurred on Shabbos Rosh Chodesh Iyar, April 18, 1942. May the Lord avenge their blood....[14]

Dr. Gonshar of Kozienice

In a separate chapter, Rabbi Huberband wrote of a man known only as Dr. Gonshar. Before the German invasion, he was the deputy mayor of Kozienice. The rabbi writes of him:

By profession he was a veterinarian. He would always speak of Jews with disdain and impudence. When representatives of the *Kehilah* needed to intercede with the authorities on a Jewish matter, they would avoid this "anti-Semite" and attempt to be received by the mayor.

Still, there were rumors that he was—an apostate, and that his wife was Jewish. His appearance strengthened these suspicions but no one thought of investigating the matter.

Till—It was the day after Yom Kippur 5700 (September 23, 1939). The "blackshirts" came into town and seized scores of men for work. Dr. Gonshar was calmly walking down the street when two of "them" went over to him and asked: "*Jude?*" (The Jewish badge was not yet worn at that time.) It did not take a moment for him to give his proud and dignified reply, "*Jude!*"

He was taken along with "other Jews" to the security police who were stationed in a court yard. A Torah scroll was taken and brought directly to Dr. Gonshar. The officer said to him, "You will tear it and burn it." The doctor turned terribly pale and then responded with pride, "No I will not!" He was immediately beaten, murderously and viciously.... "They" assumed that he had died from his wounds but in fact he survived the blows.

After the event, he told his wife that he could no longer remain in Kozienice. He "was ashamed."... On the way out of town, he was halted near the bridge by a guard, and told that if he wished to cross the bridge, he must first repeat ten times, "I am a Jew and a swine." He answered, "I am a Jew, but not a swine." He was bruised and beaten, and then allowed to pass.

When he arrived in Zelechow he poisoned himself. He remained alive for a short time and was taken to Kozienice hospital to be saved. The Jews treated him with great care and attempted to save him. But to no avail—there he breathed his last breath. Before his death, he asked that the confession be recited for him and that he be buried in a Jewish cemetery. Jews carried out his request....

Psychologists and those knowledgeable in the ways of the Jewish soul may, in the future, be interested in this fact. It is unimportant to us now whether Dr. Gonshar lived his life correctly; the way a Jew should live. For now it is important to inscribe in our notebook: The evil ones tortured the Jew Dr. Gonshar, who died as a martyr.[15]

---

14   Shimon Huberband, *Kiddush Hashem: Jewish Religious and Cultural Life in Poland During the Holocaust*, eds. Jeffrey S. Gurock and Robert S. Hirt, trans. David E. Fishman (Hoboken, NJ: Ktav Publishing, 1987), 247–248, 252.
15   Huberband, 260–261.

Questions and Answers from the Kovno Ghetto

Responsa literature is made up of collections of answers given by rabbis and other authorities to questions on how the Torah applies to everyday life at a particular time in history and in a particular place. Because both the questions and the answers are deeply rooted in current events, responsa literature provides historians with insights into everyday life. The questions asked and the answers given during the Holocaust are of particular importance because they reveal much about people's fears and anxieties at a time of unprecedented danger. Only a few collections of *she'elot u'teshuvot* from this time period have survived. The best known was written by Rabbi Ephraim Oshry of Kovno, Lithuania. In the introduction to the English edition of his *Responsa from the Holocaust*, he writes:

> The story is simple. The war came and the ghettoes were created. I was a young rabbi in Kovno of Lithuania whose greats were known throughout the Jewish world. People, the plain people, approached me with their questions. Because life was not normal and there was a war on, they were not always sure what the Torah required of them. Source books were not available, and I could not rule on these questions the way I would have in normal times. My memory had to serve me. But I did note down the questions and my brief rulings on paper torn from cement sacks which I hid in cans that I buried in the ghetto soil to preserve them. If I survived, I'd expand the notes into full-length responses.
>
> I felt that I was not simply burying a diary for the sake of preserving a historical record—although that would have been sufficient. The daily life of the ghetto, the food we ate, the crowded quarters we shared, the rags on our feet, the lice in our skin, the relationships between men and women, the attitudes of German officers—all this was contained within the specifics of the questions; these are the memories they arouse.[16]

Rabbi Oshry answered questions from 1941 through 1945. For Polish Jews, World War II began in September of 1939. The war did not begin for Lithuanian Jews (whose country was occupied by the Soviets) until after the Germans invaded the Soviet Union in June 1941. On June 22, German warplanes carried out the first bombing raids on Lithuanian cities and towns. The German occupation of Lithuania is the context in which Rabbi Oshry answered questions from the "plain people" of Kovno. The ghetto the Germans established just outside the town was home to about 8,000 people before the war. Now more than 35,000 Jews were forced into that space. On July 7, 1941, Abraham Tory, a ghetto inmate and the secretary of the newly formed Jewish Council, wrote:

---

16   Rabbi Ephraim Oshry, "Introduction," in *Responsa from the Holocaust* (New York: Judaica Press, 1983), ix.

A warm and sunny July day. Within just a few weeks the city has lost its usual aspect. Not long ago, a mere fifteen days ago, a storm rolled over the place from west to east, instantly uprooting the foundations of order in the country. The earth shook with the heavy air and artillery bombardments, as if flung by a volcanic eruption.

Two weeks earlier, the Jews of Lithuania were citizens with equal rights. Today—and even as early as ten days ago, two days after the terrible prologue—the Jews have disappeared from the streets and the life of the city. Now they are cooped up in cellars and other hideouts, trembling at every sound from the outside. They fear that death lies in wait for them around every corner.

As early as two weeks ago, bloody battles took place between units of the retreating Red Army and the attacking "brown" German troops assisted by the Lithuanian so-called partisans. The latter fired at the Soviet soldiers from rooftops and from behind the gates of houses. They were assisted by German bombers raining fire and brimstone on the retreating Red Army. The Germans were bent on cutting off the Red Army's retreat to its homeland.

On the same streets and alleys which, just a few days ago, were turned into a bloody battlefield, now a wretched procession takes place: men, women, and children bent under the weight of bundles and parcels. They are in a hurry, fleeing for their lives. On the same streets, Lithuanian partisans, armed to the teeth, march haughtily and brazenly. They appear to think that their time has arrived. They vent the rage that has accumulated in their hearts over the last year of the Soviet rule in their country, and their lust for power, by oppressing the Jews.[17]

Essential Questions
- What do the questions posed to Rabbi Oshry reveal about the challenges of maintaining a religious identity within the ghetto?
- In what respects did ghetto life impact the way in which religious Jews practiced their faith?
- What do Rabbi Oshry's answers add to our understanding of the efforts of many Jews to maintain religious practices during the Holocaust?

Recommended Resources
- "The Hidden History of the Kovno Ghetto," online exhibition, US Holocaust Memorial Museum, *http://www.ushmm.org/museum/exhibit/online/kovno/intro/intro.htm*
- Reading 4.5: Bringing *Tefilin* into a Hospital
- Reading 4.6: Eventual Danger to Life
- Reading 4.7: Critically Ill Patients Fasting on Yom Kippur
- Reading 4.8: Saving Oneself with a Baptismal Certificate
- Reading 4.9: A Man Beaten by the Germans
- Reading 4.10: Reciting *Kaddish* for a Gentile Woman
- Reading 4.11: The Repentant Kapo

---

17   Avraham Tory, *Surviving the Holocaust: The Kovno Ghetto Diary*, trans. Jerzy Michalowicz (Cambridge: Harvard University Press, 1990), 7–8.

Activity Ideas

For information on specific teaching strategies useful in carrying out various activity ideas outlined in this lesson, see the Appendix.

GETTING STARTED

Ask students what they learned from the previous lesson about what it meant to be an observant Jew in Nazi-occupied Europe. What questions do they still have? Discuss where they might go to find answers. Whom might they ask? What questions are unlikely to ever be answered? This lesson explores responsa—answers to the questions Jews have traditionally asked their rabbis about how the Torah applies to their lives. Review Reading 4.3, in which Rabbi Huberband describes the kinds of questions Jews were asking in the Warsaw ghetto. What do you think we can learn from these questions and the rabbis' answers about Jewish life in Nazi-occupied Europe? Have students list their ideas in their journals.

Explain to students that the questions we will be examining were asked in Kovno, Lithuania. Soon after the Germans took control of the country in July 1941, they forcibly moved the Jews of Kovno into Slobodka, a village just outside of the city. They then turned the village into a ghetto and sealed it on August 15, 1941. Unlike the Warsaw ghetto, which was largely emptied and then destroyed in 1942, Jews were imprisoned in the Kovno ghetto throughout the war. Ask students how the questions Jews asked in Kovno in 1941 might differ from those asked in 1943 or in 1945, at the war's end. Have them add their ideas to their journals.

EXPLORING THE HISTORICAL CONTEXT

To understand the context in which Rabbi Oshry responded to questions, have students explore an online exhibition called "The Hidden History of the Kovno Ghetto" (*http://www.ushmm.org/museum/exhibit/online/kovno/intro/intro.htm*). Explain that many Jews in Kovno like Jews in Warsaw, created a secret archive of diaries, letters, drawings, and photographs to document German crimes against their community. As in Warsaw, the idea was to bury these works within the ghetto and dig them up after the war. The online exhibition contains a timeline, photos, documents, and other artifacts from the hidden archive. Ask students to use that information to produce a brief report or drawing about one or two aspects of life in the ghetto. Post their work around the classroom. Set aside fifteen minutes for students to read and/or view one another's work. Then discuss what they learned from the exhibition about life in the Kovno ghetto. Have students apply what they learned about the Kovno ghetto to their reading of Rabbi Oshry's responsa.

ANALYZING RESPONSA

Rabbi Ephraim Oshry was one of the few religious scholars to survive the Holocaust in Lithuania. Throughout the war, he kept notes on the questions Jews asked him and his responses. He later buried those notes for safekeeping and then recovered them when the war ended. The Hebrew edition of Oshry's collection of responsa is called *Mimaamakim*, which means "out of the depths"—an allusion to Psalm 130, King David's plea "from the depths" that God hear his voice and respond to his appeals.

To analyze the questions and the rabbi's responses, have students work with their *chavruta*. Remind the partners to read the question carefully before trying to interpret it. What is the questioner actually asking? How does the question relate to what you learned about the ghetto from the online exhibition? What does the question add to your understanding of conditions in the Kovno ghetto? Would the questioner have consulted the rabbi about this issue before the German invasion? Why or why not? Then ask students to predict how the rabbi will answer the question. Have them record their ideas in their journals. The next step is to have students read the rabbi's response. How does he justify or explain his answer? Would he have answered differently before the German invasion? Why or why not?

CONDUCTING A SILENT CONVERSATION

Divide the class into small groups, with each assigned a single question and answer. Ask the group to read its question and answer silently and then write reactions on a large sheet of paper. Encourage students to ask questions of the text, document what it suggests about life in the ghetto, and/or express agreement or disagreement with the rabbi's response. When each group has completed its silent conversation, have students walk around the room and read how other groups have responded. After they have had time to add their own comments to various responsa, break the silence by having students discuss what they learned from the questions and answers.

ASSESSMENT

Assess what students have learned about the role of religion in the lives of the victims by asking them to respond to the following quotation.

On April 19, 1943, the eve of Hitler's birthday and the first day of Passover, German general Jürgen Stroop arrived in Warsaw with 2,100 soldiers. He planned to present Hitler with a "Jew-free" city for his birthday. Warsaw's Jews fought back. Yitzhak Zuckerman, a leader of the uprising, said of their efforts:

> This was a war of less than a thousand people against a mighty army, and no one doubted how it would turn out. This isn't a subject for study in a military school. Not the weapons, not the operations, not the tactics. If there's a school to study the *human spirit*, then it should be a major subject. The really important things were inherent in the force shown by Jewish youth, after years of degradation, to rise up against their destroyers and determine what death they would choose: Treblinka or Uprising. I don't know if there's a standard to measure *that*.[18]

How might Zuckerman's words apply to the Jews in Warsaw and Kovno who tried to keep their religious practices intact during those same years of degradation? What do their actions teach us about "the human spirit"? What do they teach us about the power of faith?

---

18   Yitzhak Zuckerman, *A Surplus of Memory: Chronicle of the Warsaw Ghetto Uprising*, ed. and trans. Barbara Harshav (Berkeley: University of California Press, 1993), xiii.

READING 4.5: Bringing *Tefilin* into a Hospital

Rabbi Ephraim Oshry wrote:

Question

Among the sufferings imposed on the prisoners of the ghetto, the Germans introduced special horrors for the sick and the weak. Bloodthirsty, they poured down edict after edict upon the head of Jacob; they wanted to see the Jewish people drown in a sea of Jewish blood and tears. And yet, no matter how much suffering they meted out, the fiends always came up with some new scheme to make the Jews suffer even more.

One of their devilish plots was unique. Its ostensible purpose was to give hope to the sick and the weak who had given up on life when they realized that there was no medicine available. The Germans, to confuse the sick even more, allowed them a glimmer of hope. They announced the establishment of a hospital in the Little Ghetto of Kovno. Alongside this small ghetto, there was another, larger ghetto; the two were connected by a wooden bridge. The pleasure this hospital gave the sadistic German enemy is beyond our imagination; simply, though, it was intended to raise the hopes of the weakest Jews by luring them into the German trap and then smashing them.

I was asked to render a halachic decision on the following problem: A boy, whose leg the Germans had amputated, lay in the hospital. Wishing to pray daily to his Creator, he sent a request through the Jewish channels that a pair of *tefilin* be sent into the hospital. A persistent rumor in the ghetto claimed that the Germans burned every patient's personal possessions upon his death or dismissal. Knowing what might happen to the *tefilin*, was it still permissible to send a pair into the hospital?

Response

I ruled that the *tefilin* might be sent to the lad so that he could fulfill the Torah's commandment, in the merit of which G-d would not allow the *tefilin* to be destroyed. The story of the Germans burning personal effects was an unsubstantiated rumor, one of many produced by the fear that reigned in the ghetto. If we had known it to be a fact, I would definitely have forbidden sending him the *tefilin*. But a rumor alone was not enough to deprive that lad from praying with *tefilin*. They were sent through a trustworthy emissary who gave them to the boy secretly, away from German eyes.

I also felt that the *tefilin* would be an inspiration to the boy, a recent *baal teshuvah* who had changed his life around from non-observance to observance; they would make him feel part of the Jewish people. Dr. Davidovitch, who worked in the hospital, testified to the boy's immense joy when he donned the *tefilin* for the first time.

On 3 Tishrey 5702—September 23, 1941—when the accursed Germans destroyed the Little Ghetto, they also burned down this hospital, incinerating the patients, nurses, and doctors inside. Some 60 Jews, including Dr. Davidovitch and the boy to whom the *tefilin* had been sent, were killed in the fire. G-d, avenge their blood!

Wonder of wonders! One of the Jews who had been inside the hospital was miraculously saved, and told us what happened before the incineration. The boy had guarded the *tefilin* literally with his life. When he realized that the hospital would be destroyed together with its patients and its staff, he asked this man to make every effort to hide the *tefilin* so that they would not fall into the hands of the defiling evildoers who would destroy them. The man succeeded in escaping from the hospital trap and showed us the treasure, the boy's *tefilin* that had been saved. May G-d fulfill in our time the verse, "For you, O G-d, have set it afire, and You will restore it through fire."[19]

19   Rabbi Ephraim Oshry, "Responsa 11," in *Responsa from the Holocaust* (New York: Judaica Press, 1983), 20–21.

READING 4.6: Eventual Danger to Life

Rabbi Ephraim Oshry wrote:

Question

Beginning Elul 5701—September 1941—the Jews of Kovno were compelled to work in the airfield next to the city by the Germans who ordered the ghetto Jews were to provide 1,000 men daily. Every one of the slave laborers was allowed one bowl of non-kosher soup as his daily ration plus 100 grams of bread. Many of the laborers understandably refused to defile themselves with this non-kosher soup. But after they grew weak from hunger and from the pressures of hard labor, a number of them came to me in the pre-Yom Kippur days of 5702—late September 1941—and asked if they might be permitted to eat the soup since their lives would ultimately be endangered if they did not eat it.

In brief: Do we look at the present situation, and presently there was no danger to life? Or do we consider that since their lives will eventually be endangered, as a result of malnutrition, they may now eat the non-kosher food to prevent the eventual danger to their lives?

Response

Medical experts maintained that it was impossible for a person to survive with the nutrition then available to the Jews. The laborers' lives were certainly in danger; famine is an extremely agonizing, drawn-out way to die. I ruled that they might eat the soup now because of the eventual danger to their lives. The rabbi of Kovno, the *gaon* Rav Avrohom DovBer Kahana-Shapira, concurred with me.[20]

---

20   Rabbi Ephraim Oshry, "Responsa 12," in *Responsa from the Holocaust* (New York: Judaica Press, 1983), 22.

READING 4.7: Critically Ill Patients Fasting on Yom Kippur

Rabbi Oshry wrote:

Question

On the day before Yom Kippur 5702—September 30, 1941—I was called to Dr. Zakharin, the director of the ghetto hospital. When I got there, he told me that the lives of many of his patients in the hospital would be in danger if they fasted on Yom Kippur.

Despite the doctor's warning, those frail Jews insisted that on that holy day they wished to join all of Jewry in fasting and in praying that G-d show mercy on His people and redeem them from the devouring German enemy. They did not doubt the danger fasting posed to their lives. They knew their weakened condition would grow worse, that the nutrition situation in the hospital was extremely poor, and that the food in the hospital, inadequate at all times, would certainly be insufficient to restore their strength after a fast. The 200 grams of bread and the bit of black horse-bone soup they would get could not possibly provide them with the energy they would need after the fast. Many would grow sicker.

Nevertheless, they insisted that they were relying on G-d to help them survive the fast. The director wanted me, a rabbi, to explain that *Halacha* did not allow a fast at such a time. He also told me that not only religious patients who had always worshiped and served God wanted to fast, but that even people who in their entire lives had never observed Judaism and had not professed any Jewishness wished to fast together with the other patients and the rest of the Jewish people.

I was stunned. In my heart I said "Riboinoi-shel-oilom, look down from Your heavens and see Your Jewish people. Even at such a time of turmoil and anguish Your spirit moves them and they believe firmly that the Eternal One of Jewry will never fail them, that the light of Jewry will never be put out. Even in the face of death they are prepared to sacrifice their lives to sanctify You and to participate as much as they can in the continuity of the Jewish people by keeping Your commandments with all their heart, with all their soul, and with all their being."

I told Dr. Zakharin that I would first clarify to my own satisfaction that *Halacha* did in fact require them not to fast and then do everything in my power to influence them not to endanger their lives by an unnecessary fast.

Response

Since it was the doctor's opinion that if the patients fasted on Yom Kippur they would be endangering their lives, the *Halacha* is incontrovertible: they were forbidden to fast.

Consequently, I spoke to the patients about the great danger involved if they fasted, explaining the seriousness of the ban they would be transgressing. Not only was there no act of righteousness involved, but on the contrary, it was a very great sin to transgress the Torah's commandment which said, "And he shall live by them," not that one should die as the result of fulfilling the commandments. My words, spoken with deep concern, finally got through to the patients and they promised to heed the doctor's instructions.

One patient, however, who had always been non-religious, stubbornly insisted on fasting that year and refused to accept my explanation that in his weak condition it was imperative to eat. Regrettably, the man died on the night after Yom Kippur. The other patients recounted that he had wept throughout the entire day, apparently confessing all the sins of his life in order to die a repentant Jew.[21]

---

21   Rabbi Ephraim Oshry, "Responsa 13," in *Responsa from the Holocaust* (New York: Judaica Press, 1983), 24.

READING 4.8: Saving Oneself with a Baptismal Certificate

Rabbi Oshry wrote:

Question

On the first of Nissan 5702—March 19, 1942—I was asked whether a person might purchase a baptismal certificate which—if he could escape into the forest—would enable him to join the partisans.

Response

A baptismal certificate has only one connotation: the owner of the certificate has, G-d forbid, forsaken his Creator and denied his people, the people G-d chose as His treasure. It is absolutely forbidden for a Jew to use one even though he believes wholeheartedly in the Rock of Israel and its Redeemer. He is commanded to sanctify G-d. I concluded that there was absolutely no way to allow using a baptismal certificate, even if one expected to save his life with it.[22]

---

22 Rabbi Ephraim Oshry, "Responsa 33," in *Responsa from the Holocaust* (New York: Judaica Press, 1983), 64.

READING 4.9: A Man Beaten by the Germans

Rabbi Oshry wrote:

Question

Under the accursed Germans we were nothing more than slaves. Our children were taken from us and killed, leaving us broken and childless. Whatever we had was stolen by a brazen nation that hated the old and took no pity on the young. A yoke of steel was placed around our necks. The soil we had to dig up was like rock. We served our enemy in hunger, in thirst, in cold, and in dirt. We were oppressed, robbed, abandoned by the world. And food—which meant the difference between life and death—was something we were forced to struggle for every day. We received just enough to keep us alive for another day of slave labor. But beyond all the cruelties, an edict was issued which forbade us from leaving our work place in case we considered even looking through garbage heaps for scraps of food.

In the year 5702 (1942), Reb Moshe ben Aryah, who prayed in the *beis hamidrash* where I taught and prayed, the Abba Yechezkel Kloiz in Slobodka, approached me. The man had been beaten so severely that he lost his powers of speech and hearing. Even though the savages had cracked his bones, battered his flesh, and left him unconscious, his intelligence had not been impaired at all. Though totally deaf and [mute], he was still able to communicate in writing.

He posed a serious problem, expressing his anguish at the cruelty done to him for having violated the German edict against leaving his place on the workline. He had not been able to look on and watch his fellow-Jews starving, their flesh turning brown and starting to shrivel and blacken from prolonged hunger. Despite the dangers involved, he had left his work place and gone into the fields during the potato harvest to gather some vegetables that might help his fellow oppressed.

But the accursed evildoers had caught him at his "crime" and, to serve as a warning to other hungry "criminals," they had beaten him so viciously that he became a deaf mute.

Although he gradually learned to live within this new world of total silence, he was profoundly disturbed that he had been robbed of his ability to pray aloud. In addition, since he couldn't recite a blessing to G-d with his own voice, he worried he would not be called up to the Torah any longer. In addition, since a deaf mute cannot be counted in a *minyan*, he was worried whether his disability rendered him a deaf mute by halachic definition. He requested that I find a halachic solution that would allow him to be included in a *minyan* and, even more important, that would allow him to be called up to the Torah.

Response

I ruled that he was certainly to be included in a *minyan*. But including him as one of the allotted number of men called up to the Torah seemed to be impossible. To uplift his shattered spirit, I suggested that he be called to the Torah together with the reader and, while the reader recited the blessings, that he concentrate on each word.

When he read my rulings, his eyes lit up and he wrote, "Rabbi, you have revived me. May G-d console you and grant you life!"[23]

---

23   Rabbi Ephraim Oshry, "Responsa 39," in *Responsa from the Holocaust* (New York: Judaica Press, 1983), 75.

READING 4.10: Reciting *Kaddish* for a Gentile Woman

A short time after the war ended in 1945, Rabbi Oshry wrote:

Question

During the days of affliction, when the accursed Germans mercilessly annihilated young and old, men and women, the Lithuanian gentiles, with whom the Jews had lived for hundreds of years, conspired with the Germans to kill Jews and loot their property. They sought out Jews wherever they were hiding and whenever they caught one immediately handed him over to their German masters who proceeded to torture and kill the Jew.

Despite the violent hatred that the gentiles had for the Jews, a hatred which the Germans fanned into a flame of vengeance, there were unique individuals who were anguished by the cruelty committed against Jews who would not sit by doing nothing. Whatever they did, though, was done at an enormous risk because the Germans immediately shot anyone they suspected of aiding Jews. Nevertheless, such people existed and they saved Jews at whatever cost.

In 1945, shortly after our liberation, Reb Moshe Segal came to me with the following question: He had been saved by a gentile woman who, at enormous risk to herself, had hidden him in her basement, together with ten other Jews, providing them all with food and shelter until the liberation. After the war, when these Jews wanted to repay her in some way for her great compassion, they discovered to their deep sorrow that she had died right after the liberation. The idea took root in their minds to say *Kaddish* for her, and Reb Moshe Segal was chosen for the task. His question was whether it is permissible to say *Kaddish* for a gentile.

Response

Basically, *Kaddish* is a prayer of praise to G-d. When Rabbi Nathan of Babylonia was appointed Exilarch [the head of the Jewish community in exile], the cantor used to add into *Kaddish* the phrase, "In your lifetime and in your days and in the lifetime of our Exilarch and the lifetime of all the Jewish people." Similarly, in the days of Maimonides, they used to add into the *Kaddish*, "In your lifetime and in the lifetime of our master Moshe ben Maimon." In this vein of mentioning others in the *Kaddish*, it is plainly permissible to say *Kaddish* in memory of a gentile woman who saved so many Jews from death. The work *Sefer Chasidim* teaches that it is permissible to ask of G-d to accept favorably the request of a non-Jew who has done favors for Jews. And saving his life is the greatest favor that one can do for a Jew. Not only is it permissible to say *Kaddish* with her in mind, it is clearly a mitzva to do so. May He Who grants bounty to the Jewish people grant bounty to all the generous non-Jews who endangered themselves to save Jews.[24]

---

24   Rabbi Ephraim Oshry, "Responsa 185," in *Responsa from the Holocaust* (New York: Judaica Press, 1983), 165.

READING 4.11: The Repentant Kapo

After the war, Rabbi Oshry wrote:

Question

My soul weeps when I recall how the Germans deceived the Jewish people and blasphemed G-d. As a result of their evil, another evil was born: Jewish Kapos. Serving the Germans, they yelled and beat and informed against their fellow Jews, making their lives miserable.

When the enemy was finally crushed and the day of reckoning came at last, our suffering brothers and sisters within the confines of the ghetto walls burst out into the open spaces and bit by bit began to restore the pieces of their lives. They praised the One Above for finally redeeming His people from their torturers. The houses of worship filled up, and once again the prayers of Jacob and the hum of the Torah could be heard.

That was when I was asked about one of the Jewish policemen. Claiming that he regretted his actions and he had repented fully for his evil deeds, he sought to be appointed a cantor and to lead prayers before Him Who heeds the prayers of the Jewish people. Would this be appropriate?

Response

I ruled that this man was not to be appointed a cantor. All the sources of *Halacha* indicate that a man should not be appointed to any communal position if he has or had a reputation as a sinner. This was certainly true for this man; everyone knew how he had cursed and beaten his fellow Jews. No matter how much penance he might claim to have done, he was not to be appointed to any communal position.[25]

---

25   Rabbi Ephraim Oshry, "Responsa 106," in *Responsa from the Holocaust* (New York: Judaica Press, 1983), 206.

UNIT 5

Zachor and *Tikkun* (Memory and Repair)

Teaching Focus

Every Facing History and Ourselves journey begins and ends with questions of identity and membership. Unit 1 of *Sacred Texts, Modern Questions* engages students in thinking about human behavior and the connections between individuals and the society in which they live. Unit 2 examines questions of membership and belonging in Germany at three critical moments in history. Units 3 and 4 explore the impact of that history on the choices Jews and non-Jews made during the years that resulted in the Holocaust. Unit 5 returns to the opening questions in the context of this history. In reflecting on those events, many have noted the power of memory (*zachor*) to not only shape the present but also to repair (*tikkun*) and build a more just society. On the fortieth anniversary of the Holocaust, Richard von Weizsäcker, then president of West Germany, reminded the German people that guilt, like innocence, is not collective, but personal. He went on to say:

> All of us, whether guilty or not, whether old or young, must accept the past. We are all affected by its consequences and liable for it.… Anyone who closes his eyes to the past is blind to the present. Whoever refuses to remember the inhumanity is prone to new risks of infection.[1]

His words are as true for the victims and their families as they are for the perpetrators and bystanders and their loved ones. A history that has not been confronted is not yet over.

Lesson 1: Confronting the Holocaust
Lesson 2: Beyond Memory
Lesson 3: Choosing to Participate

---

1   Richard von Weizsäcker, "Ceremony Commemorating the 40th Anniversary of the End of the War in Europe and of National Socialist Tyranny" (speech), May 8, 1985, available at *http://www.mediaculture-online.de/fileadmin/bibliothek/weizsaecker_speech_may85/weizsaecker_speech_may85.pdf*. Reprinted in *Bitburg in Moral and Political Perspective,* ed. Geoffrey H. Harman (Bloomington: Indiana University Press, 1986), 265.

Essential Questions

- Why is it important to remember the past?
- How do traditional and modern Jewish sources inform our understanding of our responsibility to others?
- What power do we have to shape our community and society?

Student Outcomes

Students will . . .

- build understanding of the role of memory in shaping our collective and individual identity.
- explore the intersection of memory and history.
- examine civic responsibility from a Jewish perspective.
- explain the roles that an active citizen can play in a democracy.
- assess various strategies that can be used to create change.

These lessons may be used to extend, reinforce, and enhance concepts developed in:

- Chapters 9, 10, and 11 in *Facing History and Ourselves: Holocaust and Human Behavior*
- Chapter 7 in *Facing History and Ourselves: Jews of Poland*

Confronting the Holocaust

Unit 4 focuses on Jews who took extraordinary risks to document and then preserve their history during the Holocaust. Gustawa Jarecka, who reported on events in the Warsaw ghetto, explained the urgency of their efforts:

> The record must be hurled like a stone under history's wheel in order to stop it…. One can lose all hopes except the one—that the suffering and destruction of this war will make sense when they are looked at from a distant, historical perspective. From sufferings, un-paralleled in history, from bloody tears and bloody sweat, a chronicle of days of hell is being composed which will help explain reasons for why people came to think as they did and why regimes arose that caused such suffering.[2]

In this lesson, students examine images and words that raise important questions about the power of history in general and of memory in particular. Much of the lesson focuses on the work of Samuel Bak, a noted artist who writes of himself and his connection to Facing History and Ourselves:

> How did this journey begin? Let me go back to the year when the Nazis seized power—1933. I was born in Vilna, lovingly embraced by a large and happy family. We lived, so it later became apparent, in the wrong place and at the wrong time; because the community to which we belonged was destined for annihilation. I experienced the Ghetto, the labor camp and a hiding place in a Catholic convent. Mother and I survived, and so did my passion for creating images, and not mere images of colors and shapes, but images of the dangerous and troubling realities in which we lived. Realities that my imagination could transform, in accordance with the surging needs of my soul, and thus nourish my art. When I was 12, in a Displaced Persons camp in Germany, Mother made me read *The Forty Days of Musa Dagh* by Franz Werfel, a terrifying book on the massacre of the Armenians in Turkey. According to my mother, every Jewish child had to understand the meaning of the innumerable bloodstains of genocides that blemished the pages of our History books. Unknowingly she prepared me to empathize with the present concerns of Facing History. Little by little, the lost world of European Jewry, the world of murdered children, worlds that we humans perpetually struggled to repair with whatever we could save from the rubble, in short: the world of the "inhuman" human condition, turned out to be the ongoing subject of my paintings.[3]

---

2   Gustawa Jarecka, quoted in Samuel D. Kassow, *Who Will Write Our History? Emanuel Ringelblum, the Warsaw Ghetto, and the Oyneg Shabes Archive* (Bloomington: Indiana University Press, 2007), 6–7.

3   Samuel Bak, "Facing My Own History and My Story with Facing History and Ourselves," in *Illuminations: The Art of Samuel Bak* (Brookline, MA: Facing History and Ourselves National Foundation, 2010), 3.

Essential Questions
- Why is it important to remember the past?
- How does the past shape our identity?
- How do we remember and re-create the past?

Recommended Resources
- Image 5.1: *Creation of War Time* by Samuel Bak
- Image 5.2: *Creation of Adam* by Michelangelo
- Reading 5.1: Faith Despite a Broken World
- Image 5.3: *Pardes III* by Samuel Bak
- Image 5.4: *Shema Yisrael* by Samuel Bak
- Image 5.5: *Tikkun* by Samuel Bak
- Reading 5.2: Interpreting Samuel Bak's Paintings (interpretations of *Pardes III, Shema Yisrael,* and *Tikkun*)

Activity Ideas
For information on specific teaching strategies useful in carrying out various activities outlined in this lesson, see the Appendix.

GETTING STARTED
Remind students of the enormous risks that Rabbi Ephraim Oshry, Rabbi Shimon Huberband, and others took to preserve the history of the Holocaust (Unit 4). They wanted the world to know what had happened to them. Why was it so important to them that we know? To spark a discussion, you may wish to share a few lines from an essay written by James Baldwin in 1965:

> History, as nearly no one seems to know, is not merely something to be read. And it does not refer merely, or even principally, to the past. On the contrary, the great force of history comes from the fact that we carry it within us, are unconsciously controlled by it in many ways, and history is literally present in all that we do. It could scarcely be otherwise, since it is to history that we owe our frames of reference, our identities, and our aspirations.[4]

How does Baldwin view history? How did Jews regard it as the events that we now call the Holocaust unfolded? How do you see it? Explain that in this lesson, we will be looking at history largely from the perspective of a Holocaust survivor, the artist Samuel Bak.

---

4   James Baldwin, "Unnameable Objects, Unspeakable Crimes," originally printed in *The White Problem in America,* editors of *Ebony* (Chicago: Johnson Publishing, 1965), available at *http://blackstate.com/baldwin1.html.*

ANALYZING A PAINTING

The focus of this activity is Image 5.1, *Creation of War Time* by Samuel Bak. Begin by projecting the image on a large screen or making copies for each student. Then take the class through the analysis process step by step:

- Ask students exactly what they see in the painting. List their observations on the board. If students begin to offer interpretations, remind them to hold their ideas for later in the exercise. At this point, they are to focus on what they actually see.
- Use the students' list of observations to begin their interpretation of the painting. For example, what colors does Bak use to paint a particular object or person? Why might he have chosen those colors? How do those colors affect the mood of the painting? Where is the object or person located in the picture? Why might he have painted that person or object there? Why do you think he chose to place certain objects or people in the foreground while others are in the background?
- What does the title of the painting mean? What is the message of the painting? Ask students to write a brief interpretation in their journals.

COMPARING IMAGES

Explain to students that *Creation of War Time* (Image 5.1) was inspired at least in part by Michelangelo's *Creation of Adam* (Image 5.2). Remind them that Michelangelo was an artist who lived in what is now Italy about 500 years ago (1475–1564). His work often features biblical characters and stories. Have students examine the Michelangelo work in much the way they studied Bak's painting. Then ask students to consider the following questions:

- How are the two paintings alike? How do they differ? (Encourage students to look for similarities and differences in terms of the images they feature, the mood they convey, and the positioning of the two main figures.)
- In Michelangelo's painting, there is a very specific figure on the right. Who is that figure? How does Bak show that figure in his painting? Why do you think he chose to draw that image in that particular way? How does that decision affect the message the painting sends?

You may wish to share Professor Lawrence Langer's interpretation of the two works. He writes of Michelangelo's *Creation of Adam*:

> Michelangelo's "Creation of Adam" is charged with tension between human expectation and divine wish. The focal point is the narrow space dividing God's resolute finger from Adam's languid hand, awaiting the spark of vitality that will give it life. The symmetrical skill that separates God in a regal purple cloak from a naked Adam highlights the one-way transmission of energy from omnipotent divine source to inert human dependent.[5]

---

5   Lawrence L. Langer, *In a Different Light: The Book of Genesis in the Art of Samuel Bak* (Boston: Pucker Art Publications, 2001), 6.

Langer writes of Bak's painting:

> "Creation of War Time" repeats the confrontation between Adam and God, but here God is even less defined, a cutout from the empty space that surrounds His image. A helmeted Adam leans upon a landscape in ruins, the tatters of his rainbow-colored garments summoning up memories of an ancient broken promise from biblical times. In the distance rise the familiar ominous pillars of smoke, haunting the foregrounds with their annihilation, while just behind them the curved tops of the Tablets of the Law peek furtively over a low ridge of stone. What fresh covenant will spring from the ravages of war and the Holocaust? The sole sign of renewal is the tree that emerges from the silhouette of God's forearm. But the wary spectator will also note that it is adjacent to His hand, nailed to the wall while blood drips from a different kind of stigmata, leaving us with the disturbing facsimile of a wounded God. Both the painting and its images are inspired by times of violence that form a major legacy to the modern mind. Any renewal or return to creative vigor must be born from arduous passage through Bak's fragmented landscapes of devastation.[6]

Langer asks, "What fresh covenant will spring from the ravages of war and the Holocaust?" To what covenant is Langer referring? How does Samuel Bak seem to answer the question? How would you answer it?

EXAMINING POINTS OF VIEW

Langer asks, "What fresh covenant will spring from the ravages of war and the Holocaust?" Artist Samuel Bak provides one answer. A number of Jewish scholars have also thought deeply about the question. Reading 5.1 includes six responses to the question. (Although the activity will work with fewer quotations, having a variety of quotations seems to spark deeper and more animated discussions.) Tape each response to a large sheet of paper and assign students to work with their *chavruta* on the meaning of one quotation. Allow students 10 minutes to read the passage, silently ask one another clarification questions, and record their own thoughts on its meaning. When the time is up, have students break the silence by discussing their written responses with their *chavruta* and then agree upon a title that summarizes the scholar's perspective. Have them write that title at the bottom of their big paper.

Next, have students reexamine Samuel Bak's *Creation of War Time* (Image 5.1) with their *chavruta*. Ask the partners to interpret the work as if they were the author of the quotation they were assigned. Then discuss the quotations and the interpretations as a class. What do the responses have in common? What differences seem most striking?

A SILENT CONVERSATION

Ask students to examine three other Bak paintings—*Pardes III*, *Shema Yisrael*, and *Tikkun*. Divide the class into groups and have each group study one of the three images and then write an interpretation of that image. (If the members of a group cannot agree on an interpretation, allow for multiple interpretations.) Display the images and the interpretations in the classroom. The **GALLERY WALK** teaching strategy provides a way for the entire class to view all three paintings along with students' interpretations. You may also want to share a scholarly interpretation of each work (Reading 5.2). As a class, discuss what the four paintings reveal about the way Bak views the relationship between past and present.

---

6   Langer, 9, 14.

ASSESSMENT

Have students reread the quotation by James Baldwin. (See "Getting Started.") Based on their analysis of the paintings in this lesson, how do they think Samuel Bak would respond to Baldwin's view of history? How might James Baldwin respond to Bak's paintings? Be sure that students provide reasons and evidence to support their views.

IMAGE 5.1: *Creation of War Time* by Samuel Bak

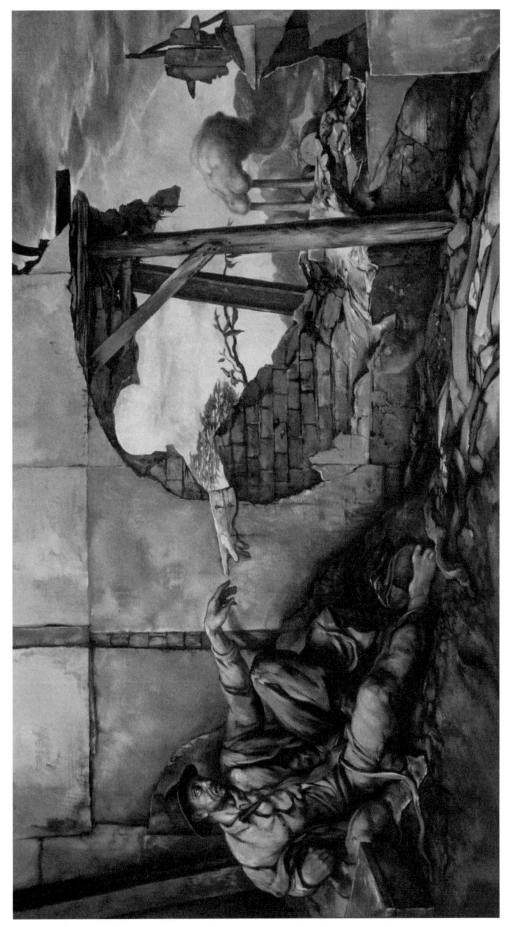

Creation of War Time by Samuel Bak. Image courtesy of Pucker Gallery, *www.puckergallery.com.*

Image courtesy of Erich Lessing/Art Resource, NY.

READING 5.1: Faith Despite a Broken World

Irving Rosenbaum is an Orthodox Jew and the author of *The Holocaust and Halakhah*, a survey of halachic decisions reached during the Holocaust. He writes:

> It has become almost an article of faith that the Holocaust was without precedent in Jewish experience. It was not! ... While much of its technology was novel, the Holocaust simply duplicated on an extensive and enormous scale events which had occurred with melancholy regularity throughout Jewish history.... In the face of events which would make Job's trials seem trivial, Jews retained their confident belief in a just Creator, whose secret purposes they might not fathom ...[7]

Irving Greenberg is an Orthodox rabbi who was born in the United States. He is a theologian and historian who has written books and articles on the ethical implications of the Holocaust. He observes:

> All truths are moment truths.... Pluralism is the living together of absolute truths/faiths/systems that have come to know and accept their own limitations, thus making room for the dignity and truth of the other. This broken truth is the future of truth in a broken world. Rav Nachman of Bratzlav once wrote that there is no heart so whole as a broken heart. After the Shoah, the world will come to know that there is no truth so whole as a broken truth.[8]

Eliezer Berkovits is an Orthodox Jew who served as a rabbi in Germany until 1939. He later worked as a theologian and educator in Britain, Australia, and the United States. He is the author of *Faith after the Holocaust*. He writes:

> The hiding God is present; though man is unaware of him. He is present in his hiddenness. Therefore, God can only hide in this world. But if this world was altogether and radically profane, there would be no place in it for Him to hide. He can only hide in history. Since history is man's responsibility, one would, in fact, expect him to hide, to be silent, while man is about his God-given task. Responsibility requires freedom, but God's convincing presence would undermine the freedom of human decision. God hides in human responsibility and freedom.[9]

Immanuel Jakobovits, who served as Chief Rabbi of the United Hebrew Congregations of the British Commonwealth, was born in Germany but escaped in 1938 just before the war. He has written and spoken on Jewish life after the Holocaust:

> When I am asked, Where was God at Auschwitz? I too have no answer. Perhaps there is none. The real question is: Where was man at Auschwitz? Where was the humanity of a cultured nation mesmerized by a rabble-rouser, to turn into millions of mass-murderers and their accomplices? Where was man when numerous civilized nations remained silent and closed their border to those fleeing from fiendish persecution? Where was man when millions were shipped here in cattle trucks for the crime of being born as Jews?[10]

7   Irving J. Rosenbaum, *The Holocaust and Halakhah* (New York: Ktav Publishing, 1976), 1–2.
8   Irving Greenberg, "Theology after the Shoah: The Transformation of the Core Paradigm," *Modern Judaism* 26, no. 3 (2006).
9   Eliezer Berkovits, *Faith after the Holocaust* (New York: Ktav Publishing, 1973), 63–64.
10   Immanuel Jakobovits, "Where Was Man at Auschwitz?" in *Christian-Jewish Dialogue: A Reader*, ed. Helen Fry (Exeter: University of Exeter Press, 1996), 65–66.

Emil Fackenheim was a German-born philosopher and theologian. Ordained as a Reform rabbi, he tried to place the Holocaust in the context of Judaism:

> The 614th Commandment: Jews are forbidden to hand Hitler posthumous victories. They are commanded to survive as Jews lest the Jewish people perish. They are commanded to remember the victims of Auschwitz lest their memory perish. They are forbidden to despair of man and his world, and to escape either into cynicism or otherworldliness, lest they cooperate in delivering the world over to the forces of Auschwitz. Finally, they are forbidden to despair of the God of Israel, lest Judaism perish.[11]

Historian David Blumenthal is a professor of Judaic Studies and the author of several books on theology after the Holocaust. He writes:

> You must take a stand, if God is integral to who you are.... I reached the conclusion that God is present and responsible even in moments of great evil. God is, indeed, partly responsible for the shoah.... This leaves us with a God who is not perfect, not even always good.... Jewish tradition advocates this position and reaches the conclusion that protest is the only proper response. Not defensiveness. Not denial. But protest—in thought and prayer.[12]

---

11 Emil Fackenheim, "Jewish Faith and the Holocaust," in *The Jewish Thought of Emil Fackenheim: A Reader*, ed. Michael Morgan (Detriot: Wayne State University Press, 1987), 176.
12 David Blumenthal, "Despair and Hope in Post-Shoah Jewish Life," *Bridges: An Interdisciplinary Journal of Theology, Philosophy, History, and Science*, 6: 3/4 (Fall/Winter, 1999).

IMAGE 5.3: *Pardes III* by Samuel Bak

Pardes III by Samuel Bak. Image courtesy of Pucker Gallery, *www.puckergallery.com.*

IMAGE 5.4: *Shema Yisrael* by Samuel Bak

Shema Yisrael by Samuel Bak. Image courtesy of Pucker Gallery, *www.puckergallery.com.*

IMAGE 5.5: *Tikkun* by Samuel Bak

Tikkun by Samuel Bak. Image courtesy of Pucker Gallery, *www.puckergallery.com.*

READING 5.2: Interpreting Samuel Bak's Paintings

Pardes III

Author Ori Soltes writes of the many meanings of the Hebrew word *pardes*:

> Bak's visual vocabulary is both personalized and universal; the distance between those two angles of understanding is bridged by Judaism and, from within Judaism, particularly by the varied threads of the mystical tradition. Repeatedly the number "four" appears, often in the form of four doorways. We are reminded of the four-lettered Name of God, *YHWH*.... We are reminded of the four-fold approach to understanding the Torah, which *is* the *Word* of God and Guide to understanding the Covenant with God—and thus, to leading a *living* life, one within the context of a Covenantal relationship with God.... [Each letter in the word *Pardes*] refers to an approach to interpreting the Torah delineated by the thirteenth-century rabbis. *Pey* ("P") represents *P'shat,* which seeks a literal meaning. *Resh* ("R") stands for *Remez,* which looks for an allegorical meaning. *Dalet* ("D") signifies *D'rash,* which is the method of interpreting by means of *Midrash*—filling in [the gaps] and excavating the text by means of legends; *Samach* ("S") refers to *sod,* the hidden mystical meanings sought beneath the surface of the deepest depths of the texts.
>
> For a people of texts, the continuous cycle of their interpretation and reinterpretation is a synonym for life. For a people whose covenant is with an invisible, intangible God, texts in which that God has spelled out the covenant are the key to the doorways of life. The four doors lie open, each at its own level: there are many paths to the garden within. The garden is the paradise left behind by our aboriginal ancestors after they disobeyed God's commandment and ate from the Tree of Knowledge. Without their disobedience, they would still be there, innocent as children—and we wouldn't *be*.
>
> Thus, the destruction of paradise is the construction of human history—with its magnificent chamber music and its unfathomable ovens. "Paradise" as a word, as text, is derived (by way of Latin and in turn by way of Greek) from Persian. Borrowed into Hebrew, and transformed, it became *pardes,* meaning "garden" or "orchard."... The garden within is the garden of Torah—which *is* the bridge between God and ourselves; it is the creation and creator of our spiritual landscape, the mirror in which God and we see ourselves and each other.[13]

Shema Yisrael

"Hear O Israel" is the literal translation of the title of the painting. Soltes writes of Bak's interpretation of the prayer:

> Bak and the layered memory of Bak appear and re-appear when figures and faces appear in his work. More often the landscapes are devoid of humans, but filled with symbols of the human—and specifically the Jewish—presence. And with reminders of the Divine presence—or the relationship between the human and Divine, in the aftermath of the Holocaust horror which leaves such doubts

---

13   Ori Soltes, *Samuel Bak: The Landscape of Jewish Experience,* ed. Jill K. Richardson (Boston: Pucker Gallery, 1997), 6–9.

in its wake as to God's presence and the relationship with us. "Shema Yisrael" draws its title from the central credo of Judaism, the belief in the One God, its opening words strewn, in convex and concave stone fragments at the base of a small hill. The hill is surrounded by barren, rocky mountains, all bathed in a crepuscular blue light, while the hill itself is crowned by the Tablets of the Law, with only the letters of God's name visible on them (God's presence still apparent, by way of the Divine Name, above the rubble) and bathed in a golden, dawn-like light—as perhaps in the bottom of the hill where the letters lie. In between, smashed fragments of the Tablets tumble over each other, as if a long-gone Moses had been up and down the mountainside a dozen times or more, carving and breaking and recarving.

As if the Covenant has been smashed again and again, even as, one last time, it rises, in the ever-renewing light at the top of the hill. Who broke the Covenant? The God who didn't answer the prayers of those in the gas chambers? The humans who didn't hearken to the words "Hear O Israel…"? The murderers of their fellow humans who ignored the sixth commandment, as they turned the handle to fill the chambers with gas? Embedded in an up-cropping of stone, the number "6" may be discerned, suggesting the fragmentary adherence to the sixth commandment: thou shalt not murder.[14]

Tikkun

The Hebrew word *tikkun* means "repair." Professor Lawrence Langer writes of the painting:

The single painting with the simple title of "Tikkun" is … a tribute to organized confusion rather than clarity. The letters of the word preside, upright and inverted, atop a jumble of accumulated rubble. They take the shape of a mountain peak, framed by a bright but cloud-filled sky. As we gaze on this parody of Mount Sinai where once the divine prescription for human conduct [the Ten Commandments] were presented to Moses, we may recall the shattered tablets that the Lord finally replaced after Moses' intercession for the children of Israel. But when the mutiny of a people is replaced by the murder of innocent victims who require no pardon, even a modern Moses would find little reason to intercede. What then is to be mended, and by whom? Bak's fragile structure is held together only by the strength of artistic form; released from that spell, its components would tumble into the abyss. There is a certain grace to its precarious integrity, but in the absence of spiritual glue to cement the assembly, its unity imparts a successful aesthetic illusion more than a substantive human hope. The articles of domestic use—the broken teapot, the cup and spoon, the cracked vase pierced by the final letter of the word "Tikkun"—seek their own repair. But what of the people who once used them? Implicit in this appeal is the memory of a massive loss; part of its burden is the troublesome question of to whom the obligation to repair should be addressed.[15]

---

14   Soltes, 6.
15   Lawrence L. Langer, *In a Different Light: The Book of Genesis in the Art of Samuel Bak* (Boston: Pucker Art Publications, 2001), 66.

Beyond Memory

The Hebrew root *zachor*, which means "memory" or "remember," appears 169 times in the Bible: "Remember the days of old" (Deuteronomy 32:7), "Remember what Amalek did to you" (Deuteronomy 25:17), etc. And with equal insistence, there is the command not to forget. Moses warned, "Only be careful, and watch yourselves closely so that you do not forget the things your eyes have seen or let them slip from your heart as long as you live. Teach them to your children and to their children after them" (Deuteronomy 4:9). The word *history*, however, does not appear at all. In fact there is no biblical word that translates as "history." In this lesson, students will explore the way history and memory shape not only individual and group identity but also the way nations define their universe of obligation and individuals their sense of *areyvut*.

Essential Questions
- Why is it important to remember the past?
- How does the past shape our identity?
- How does it influence our future?
- How does it affect the way we define our nation's universe of obligation?
- How does the past shape our own sense of *areyvut*?

Recommended Resources
- Reading 5.3: "The Past" by Ha Jin
- *The Difference Between History and Memory*, *http://www.youtube.com/watch?v=gRmG-aRBsPI* (Avraham Infeld addresses a class on the meaning of the word *zachor*. Infeld is the founder of Melitz, a center for informal Jewish education in Israel, and is a past president of Hillel International.)
- Reading 5.4: What It Means to Remember
- Reading 5.5: The Aim of Memory
- Reading 5.6: History and Memory: Two Views
- Reading 5.7: "No Religion Is an Island"

Optional Resources
- *Nobody's Business* (Alan Berliner's 1996 film explores where past meets present, where generations collide, and where the boundaries of family are pushed and pulled, and stretched, torn, and healed. The first 10 minutes of the video raise important questions about memory and history.)

Activity Ideas

For information on specific teaching strategies useful in carrying out various activity ideas outlined in this lesson, see the Appendix.

GETTING STARTED

What do we do with our past? It's a question that Samuel Bak has wrestled with in his work. It also troubles Ha Jin, a poet and novelist who immigrated to the United States from China. Have students read his poem entitled "The Past" (Reading 5.3). What does Ha Jin see as the challenge of memory? Under what conditions does he think that memory holds us back? Under what conditions does it allow us to move forward? Which stanza comes closest to the way you feel about the past?

COMPARING SPEECHES

In the 1980s, Richard von Weizsäcker, then president of West Germany, and Elie Wiesel, a prize-winning author and a Holocaust survivor, each spoke of the importance of remembering the Holocaust. Invite volunteers to read aloud excerpts from the two speeches (Readings 5.4 and 5.5). How do the two speakers distinguish between guilt and responsibility? What does Weizsäcker mean when he says "anyone who closes his eyes to the past is blind to the present"? What are the consequences "of not burdening one's conscience, of shunning responsibility, looking away, keeping mum"? What does Wiesel mean when he says, "We are not responsible for the past, but for the way we remember the past"? Would Weizsäcker agree? Why do both see as the role of young people in the need to remember?

ANALYZING DIFFERING VIEWS

To deepen the conversation around history and memory, have two volunteers read aloud the two quotations in Reading 5.6. How does each distinguish between history and memory? Which seems closest to Weizsäcker's view? Which is closest to Wiesel's view? Which comes closest to the way you distinguish between history and memory? For what reasons?

EXAMINING IDEAS

In Unit 2, students read the following quotation by John Donne:

> No man is an island entire of itself; every man is a piece of the continent, a part of the main; if a clod be washed away by the sea, Europe is the less …[16]

Discuss the meaning of the quotation and then have students work with their *chavruta* on an essay by Rabbi Abraham Joshua Heschel with a similar title: "No Religion Is an Island" (Reading 5.7). What do the two works have in common? How do both help us understand how to bridge the divide between "us" and "them"? What does each add to discussions of history and memory, guilt and responsibility?

ASSESSMENT

To assess learning, have students write a speech describing how history and its memory has shaped their identity and their sense of *areyvut*. How does this history shape the way they see themselves and others? How does it shape the choices they make as Jews? How does it shape the choices they make as citizens?

---

16   John Donne, "Devotion XVII," in *Devotions upon Emergent Occasions* (1624).

READING 5.3: "The Past" by Ha Jin

I have supposed my past is a part of myself.
As my shadow appears whenever I'm in the sun
the past cannot be thrown off and its weight
must be borne, or I will become another man.

But I saw someone wall his past into a garden
whose produce is always in fashion.
If you enter his property without permission
he will welcome you with a watchdog or a gun.

I saw someone set up his past as a harbor.
Wherever it sails, his boat is safe—
if a storm comes, he can always head for home.
His voyage is the adventure of a kite.

I saw someone drop his past like trash.
He buried it and shed it altogether.
He has shown me that without the past
one can also move ahead and get somewhere.

Like a shroud my past surrounds me,
but I will cut it and stitch it,
to make good shoes with it,
shoes that fit my feet.[17]

—Ha Jin

REFLECTIONS

- How does the poem relate to the paintings of Samuel Bak?
- How does the poem relate to the efforts of Rabbi Oshry and other Jews to record their history?
- Which stanza is closest to the way you see the past? Why?

---

17 Ha Jin, "The Past," in *Facing Shadows* (Brooklyn: Hanging Loose Press, 1996), 63.

READING 5.4: What It Means to Remember

In 1985, on the fortieth anniversary of the end of World War II in Europe, Richard von Weizsäcker, then president of West Germany, spoke to the German people about memory:

> Remembering means recalling an occurrence honestly and undistortedly so that it becomes a part of our very beings. This places high demands on our truthfulness....
>
> At the root of the tyranny was Hitler's immeasurable hatred against our Jewish compatriots. Hitler never concealed this hatred from the public, but made the entire nation a tool of it.... Hardly any country has in its history always remained free from blame for war or violence. The genocide of the Jews is, however, unparalleled in history.
>
> The perpetration of this crime was in the hands of a few people. It was concealed from the eyes of the public, but every German was able to experience what his Jewish compatriots had to suffer, ranging from plain apathy and hidden intolerance to outright hatred. Who could remain unsuspecting after the burning of the synagogues, the plundering, the stigmatization with the Star of David, the deprivation of rights, the ceaseless violation of human dignity? Whoever opened his eyes and ears and sought information could not fail to notice that Jews were being deported.... There were many ways of not burdening one's conscience, of shunning responsibility, looking away, keeping mum. When the unspeakable truth of the Holocaust then became known at the end of the war, all too many of us claimed that they had not known anything about it or even suspected anything.
>
> There is no such thing as the guilt or innocence of an entire nation. Guilt is, like innocence, not collective, but personal ... The vast majority of today's population were either children then or had not been born. They cannot profess a guilt of their own for crimes that they did not commit.... But their forefathers have left them a grave legacy. All of us, whether guilty or not, whether old or young, must accept the past. We are all affected by its consequences and liable for it. The young and old generations must and can help each other to understand why it is vital to keep alive the memories. It is not a case of coming to terms with the past. That is not possible. It cannot be subsequently modified or made not to have happened. Anyone who closes his eyes to the past is blind to the present. Whoever refuses to remember the inhumanity is prone to new risks of infection.[18]

REFLECTIONS

- What does Weizsäcker see as the difference between memory and responsibility?
- What is the connection between guilt and responsibility?
- What are links between the past, present, and future?

---

18   Richard von Weizsäcker, "Ceremony Commemorating the 40th Anniversary of the End of the War in Europe and of National Socialist Tyranny" (speech), May 8, 1985, *http://www.mediaculture-online.de/fileadmin/bibliothek/weizsaecker_speech_may85/weizsaecker_speech_may85.pdf*.

READING 5.5: The Aim of Memory

Elie Wiesel, a Holocaust survivor and a recipient of the Nobel Peace Prize, spoke to West Germany's parliament in 1987. He addressed his remarks primarily to young Germans. He told them that he had "neither the desire nor the authority" to judge them for "the unspeakable crimes" committed by Hitler and other Nazi leaders. "But," he added, "we may—and we must—hold [today's generation] responsible, not for the past, but for the way it remembers the past. And for what it does with the past…." He continued:

> To remember is to create links between past and present, between past and future. To remember is to affirm man's faith in humanity and to convey meaning on our fleeting endeavors. The aim of memory is to restore dignity to justice….
>
> Memory means to live in more than one world, to be tolerant and understanding with one another, to accept the mystery inherent in questions and the suspicion linked to answers. Naturally, it can also bring forth tensions and conflicts, but they can then be transformed into culture, art, education, spiritual inquiry, the quest for truth, the quest for justice….
>
> In remembering, you will help your own people to vanquish the ghosts that have been hovering over their history. Remember: a community that does not come to terms with the dead will find that the dead will continue to perturb and traumatize the living. Reconciliation can be achieved through and in memory.[19]

To those who feared that memory perpetuates hatred, Wiesel argued that "memory and hatred are incompatible, for hatred distorts memory. The reverse is true: memory may serve as a powerful remedy against hatred."[20]

REFLECTIONS

- According to Wiesel, what is the aim of memory?
- What does he see as the relationship between memory and responsibility?
- How does he define the connection between past and present?

---

19   Elie Wiesel, "When Memory Brings People Together," in *From the Kingdom of Memory* (New York: Summit Books, 1990), 194–195, 200.
20   Ibid., 201.

READING 5.6: History and Memory: Two Views

"There is a profound difference between history and memory. History is *his* story—an event that happened sometime else to someone else. Memory is *my* story—something that happened to me and is part of who I am. History is information. Memory, by contrast, is part of identity. I can study the history of other peoples, cultures, and civilization. They deepen my knowledge and broaden my horizons. But they do not make a claim on me. They are the past as past. Memory is the past as present, as it lives on in me. Without memory there can be no identity. Alzheimer's disease, the progressive atrophying of memory function, is also the disintegration of personality. As with individuals, so with a nation: it has a continuing identity to the extent that it can remember where it came from and who its ancestors were."[21]

—Rabbi Jonathan Sacks

"History, as nearly no one seems to know, is not merely something to be read. And it does not refer merely, or even principally, to the past. On the contrary, the great force of history comes from the fact that we carry it within us, are unconsciously controlled by it in many ways, and history is literally present in all that we do. It could scarcely be otherwise, since it is to history that we owe our frames of reference, our identities, and our aspirations."[22]

—James Baldwin

21   Jonathan Sacks, *Rabbi Jonathan Sacks's Haggadah* (New York: Continuum, 2006), 29.
22   James Baldwin, "Unnameable Objects, Unspeakable Crimes," originally printed in *The White Problem in America*, editors of *Ebony* (Chicago: Johnson Publishing, 1965), available at *http://blackstate.com/baldwin1.html*.

READING 5.7: "No Religion Is an Island"

Rabbi Abraham Joshua Heschel was a man of great faith and one of the foremost scholars of his time. He began a speech with these words:

> I speak as a member of a congregation whose founder was Abraham, and the name of my rabbi is Moses.

> I speak as a person who was able to leave Warsaw, the city in which I was born, just six weeks before the disaster began. My destination was New York; it would have been Auschwitz or Treblinka. I am a brand plucked from the fire in which my people was burned to death. I am a brand plucked from the fire of an altar of Satan on which millions of human lives were exterminated to evil's greater glory, and on which so much else was consumed: the divine image of so many human beings, many people's faith in the God of justice and compassion, and much of the secret and power of attachment to the Bible bred and cherished in the hearts of men for nearly two thousand years.[23]

Heschel goes on to argue that no individual, no people, no religion in the world today can stand alone. Interdependence is a "basic fact of our situation. Disorder in a small obscure country in any part of the world evokes anxiety in people all over the world." He explains:

> The religions of the world are no more self-sufficient, no more independent, no more isolated than individuals or nations. Energies, experiences, and ideas that come to life outside the boundaries of a particular religion or all religions continue to challenge and to affect every religion.

> Horizons are wider, dangers are greater … *No religion is an island.* We are all involved with one another. Spiritual betrayal on the part of one of us affects the faith of all of us. Views adopted in one community have an impact on other communities. Today religious isolationism is a myth. For all the profound differences in perspective and substance, Judaism is sooner or later affected by the intellectual, moral, and spiritual events within the Christian society, and vice versa….

> The Jewish Diaspora today, almost completely to be found in the Western world, is certainly not immune to the spiritual climate and the state of religious faith in the general society. We do not live in isolation, and the way in which non-Jews either relate or bid defiance to God has a profound impact on the minds and souls of the Jews. Even in the Middle Ages, when most Jews lived in relative isolation, such impact was acknowledged. To quote: "The usage of the Jews is in accordance with that of the non-Jews." Rabbi Joseph Yaabez, a victim of the Spanish Inquisition, in the midst of the Inquisition was able to say that "the Christians believe in Creation, the excellence of the patriarchs, revelation, retribution, and resurrection. Blessed is the Lord, God of Israel, who left this remnant after the destruction of the second Temple. But for these Christian nations we might ourselves become infirm in our faith."

---

23 Abraham Joshua Heschel, *Moral Grandeur and Spiritual Audacity: Essays*, ed. Susannah Heschel (New York: Farrar, Straus & Giroux, 1996), 235.

We are heirs to a long history of mutual contempt among religions and religious dominations, of religious coercion, strife, and persecutions. Even in periods of peace, the relationship that obtains between representatives of different religions is not just reciprocity of ignorance; it is an abyss, a source of detraction and distrust, casting suspicion and undoing efforts of many an honest and noble expression of good will …

On what basis do people of different religious commitments meet one another?

First and foremost, we meet as human beings who have much in common: a heart, a face; a voice; the presence of a soul, fears, hope, the ability to trust, a capacity for compassion and understanding, the kinship of being human. My first task in every encounter is to comprehend the personhood of the human being I face, to sense the kinship of being human, solidarity of being.…

To meet a human being is an opportunity to sense the image of God, the *presence* of God. According to a rabbinical interpretation, the Lord said to Moses: "Wherever you see the trace of man, there I stand before you …"

When engaged in a conversation with a person of a different religious commitment, if I discover that we disagree in matters sacred to us, does the image of God I face disappear? Does God cease to stand before me? Does the difference in commitment destroy the kinship of being human? Does the fact that we differ in our conceptions of God cancel what we have in common: the image of God? …

I suggest that the most significant basis for meeting of men of different religious traditions is the level of fear and trembling, of humility and contrition, where our individual moments of faith are mere waves in the endless ocean of mankind's reaching out for God, where all formations and articulations appear as understatements, where our souls are swept away by the awareness of the urgency of answering God's commandment, while stripped of pretension and conceit we sense the tragic insufficiency of human faith.

What divides us? … We disagree in law and creed, in commitments which lie at the very heart of our religious existence. What unites us? Our being accountable to God, our being objects of God's concern, precious in His eyes. Our conceptions of what ails us may be different, but the anxiety is the same. The language, the imagination, the concentration of our hopes are different, but the embarrassment is the same, and so is the sign, the sorrow, and the necessity to obey.

We may disagree about the ways of achieving fear and trembling, but the fear and trembling are the same. The demands are different, but the conscience is the same, and so is arrogance, iniquity. The proclamations are different, the callousness is the same, and so is the challenge we face in many moments of spiritual agony.

Above all, while dogmas and forms of worship are divergent, God is the same.[24]

---

24 Heschel, 237–240.

Choosing to Participate

In this lesson, students reflect on two concepts introduced and developed in earlier lessons: universe of obligation and *areyvut*. How do the choices we make as individuals and as members of a society affect history? By studying examples of contemporary upstanders and the choices they made, students see how individuals can shape history through their decisions and actions. They will also explore what it means to be a citizen in a democracy and to exercise one's rights and responsibilities.

Essential Questions
- How do traditional and modern Jewish sources inform our understanding of civic responsibility?
- What power do we have to shape our community and society?

Recommended Resources
- Reading 5.8: Rabbinic Quotations
- "Choosing to Participate" (*http://choosingtoparticipate.org/explore/upstanders*): a multifaceted educational and civic initiative that challenges students to think deeply about what democracy means, and what it asks, of every citizen
- "Be the Change: Upstanders for Human Rights" (*www.facinghistory.org/bethechange*): a website that highlights the human rights work of five young Reebok Human Rights Awards recipients from Nigeria, Cambodia, Northern Ireland, the United States, and the Philippines

Activity Ideas

For information on specific teaching strategies useful in carrying out various activities outlined in this lesson, see the Appendix.

GETTING STARTED

Elie Wiesel writes, "The more Jewish the poet the more universal is his message. The more Jewish his soul the more human his concerns. A Jew who does not feel for his fellow Jews, who does not share in their sorrows and joys, cannot feel for other people. And a Jew who is concerned with his fellow Jews is inevitably concerned with the fate of other people as well."[25] What is Wiesel suggesting about the relationship between one's own particular history and the world as a whole? What is he suggesting about the way Jews as a people should define their universe of obligation? What is he suggesting about the way Jews as individuals should define their sense of *areyvut?* What are your views? Explain that this lesson explores the way a number of individuals have defined their obligations to themselves and to others.

EXPANDING WORKING DEFINITIONS

According to Samantha Power, the author of *A Problem from Hell: American and the Age of Genocide,* upstanders are people whose actions reflect courage and resilience, and whose determination to stand up for human rights has influenced subsequent public policy. Have students brainstorm traits that define an upstander. Have them provide examples of upstanders in previous lessons, history class, current events, or from their own lives. What does each add to our understanding of the term?

DEEPENING UNDERSTANDING

To expand on students' understanding of the term *upstander,* introduce the quotations in Reading 5.8. Each is drawn from a rabbinic source. One way to use them is by taping each to a large sheet of paper and posting them around the classroom. Ask students to read each quotation and then stand beside the one that reflects the qualities they think are most important in an upstander. Pair students who have selected the same response and ask them to discuss why they chose this particular quotation. Then have each pair interpret the quotation for the class as a whole.

RESEARCHING UPSTANDERS

Ask students to research the work of young men and women in our own nation and around the world who fit their definition of an upstander. Facing History and Ourselves has two websites that can provide them with a starting point. Each contains stories of young activists who are making a difference in the world today: *http://choosingtoparticipate.org/explore/upstanders* and *wwww.facinghistory.org/bethechange.* Using one or both websites, have students gather information on how these upstanders became involved in their community, what motivated them, and who has helped them make a difference. Students might also be encouraged to identify and interview upstanders in their own community. Have them report their findings in an essay that begins with their definition of the term *upstander* and then uses their research and reasoning to support their ideas. Set aside a day or two for students to formally present their essays to the class.

ASSESSMENT

Use the essays students wrote about upstanders to assess learning.

---

25   Elie Wiesel, *Five Biblical Portraits* (Notre Dame: University of Notre Dame Press, 1981), 151, quoted in Maurice Friedman, *Abraham Joshua Heschel and Elie Wiesel, You Are My Witnesses* (New York: Farrar, Straus & Giroux, 1987), 202.

READING 5.8: Rabbinic Quotation

"When there is no man, you must try to be a man."
—*Ethics of the Fathers* 2:5

בִּמְקוֹם שֶׁאֵין אֲנָשִׁים, הִשְׁתַּדֵּל לִהְיוֹת אִישׁ.

"If I am not [concerned] for me, who will be concerned for me? But, if I am concerned only for me, what am I? If not now, when?" (Hillel the Elder)
—*Ethics of the Fathers* 1:14

אִם אֵין אֲנִי לִי, מִי לִי. וּכְשֶׁאֲנִי לְעַצְמִי, מָה אֲנִי. וְאִם לֹא עַכְשָׁיו, אֵימָתַי.

"Do not separate yourself from the community."
—*Ethics of the Fathers* 2:4

אַל תִּפְרוֹשׁ מִן הַצִּבּוּר.

"It is not up to you to complete the task, but neither can you desist from it." (Rabbi Tarfon)
—*Ethics of the Fathers* 2:16

לֹא עָלֶיךָ הַמְּלָאכָה לִגְמוֹר, וְלֹא אַתָּה בֶּן חוֹרִין לִבָּטֵל מִמֶּנָּה.

"There is no one who does not have his/her hour."
—*Ethics of the Fathers* 4:3

אֵין לְךָ אָדָם שֶׁאֵין לוֹ שָׁעָה וְאֵין לְךָ דָבָר שֶׁאֵין לוֹ מָקוֹם.

APPENDIX

TEACHING STRATEGIES

A reflective classroom is an integral part of a Facing History and Ourselves course. It is a place where students and teachers support one another as they explore important themes in history and think deeply about their meaning, significance, and implications. It is a place where students and teachers show respect for one another, the subject matter, and the learning process. It is a place where questions are encouraged and diverse views are welcomed. Over the years, Facing History teachers have developed a variety of strategies that foster and facilitate reflective learning. These pages contain a few of those strategies. Part 1 focuses primarily on activities that aid students in understanding and interpreting written texts, images, and films. Part 2 provides ideas that promote meaningful discussions. Both sets of activities promote mutual trust and respect. Both are also based on a belief that learning should be a genuine exploration in which ideas build upon each other.

Facing History is committed to learning that is active as well as reflective, collaborative as well as solitary. That view also has an honored place in Jewish education. For generations, many Jewish schools have engaged their students in *chavruta* learning. The term refers to the practice of studying Jewish texts with a partner. In *chavruta* learning, partners interact with the text by puzzling over its meaning word by word, line by line; questioning each other's logic; trying out various interpretations; and expanding on each other's ideas. *Chavruta* learning is rooted in the idea that by working together, students can not only sharpen their reasoning skills and organize their own thinking but can also come to a deeper understanding of the meaning of a text. It is a method that requires trust, honesty, and the capacity to actively listen and respond to ideas that widen one's perspective.

If you or your school promotes *chavruta* learning, you will find that the readings, questions, and activities in *Sacred Texts, Modern Questions* can be used to enhance and reinforce that methodology. If you have never tried *chavruta* learning, you may wish to introduce it to your students by having them work with a partner on the biblical and/or rabbinic texts included in this resource. Some teachers pair students by using various criteria (interest, levels of reasoning ability, and/or knowledge), while others prefer a more random selection process. Still others allow students to choose their own partners.

Whether you use *chavruta* learning or other methods, it is important to contract with students at the beginning of a Facing History and Ourselves course. Students need to know what they will be studying and why this particular content is important. They also need to know what will be expected of them in the course. What are their obligations, responsibilities, and rights? You will want to discuss the importance of a respectful classroom. What behaviors promote reflective learning? What makes learning more difficult? What should students expect of themselves and their classmates?

TABLE OF CONTENTS

PART ONE: Optional Strategies for Reading and Viewing

ANALYZING TEXTS

Rationale

This strategy may be used to enhance students' comprehension and interpretive skills, to develop critical thinking, and to encourage conceptual learning. Many of the readings and images that work particularly well with these strategies are primary sources and interpretations of primary sources.

Procedure

For written texts: Ask students to read, either silently or aloud, a particular passage such as a short reading, a paragraph, a subsection of a longer text, or a brief poem from start to finish without discussion. Encourage them to pay attention to exactly *what* is said in the passage and *how* it is said.

Next have students reread the text. This time, ask them to look for words or phrases that seem important or raise questions about meaning. They might also look for anything that seems to be missing or out of place. Encourage them to record their observations and questions in their journals or on sticky notes attached to the text. Then have students discuss their questions with a partner or others in the class. They might also consult reference books or internet sources. The next step is to have students write a brief summary of the passage in their own words without interpretation. Who was involved? What happened? Where did it happen? When it happen? How did it happen?

The last step in the process is interpretation. What is the main idea of the passage? If you were to write a title for your summary, what would you call it? How do the things you already know about this subject, idea, or topic help you understand the passage? Have students discuss their interpretations with a partner or with the class. They should be prepared to support their views by referring to specifics in the work and what they know about the context in which it was created.

For works of art and other images: Begin by asking students to look carefully at the image. Have them pay particular attention to shapes, colors, textures, and the positioning of people and objects. They should be encouraged to record their observations without trying to interpret the image. Discuss questions students may have about the image.

After students have carefully studied the image, ask them to interpret it. What is the artist (photographer, cartoonist) trying to tell us (i.e., what does the image mean?), and who seems to be the intended audience? In other words, what is the message? Who is the messenger? And who is the audience? Have students discuss their interpretations with a partner or with the class. They should be prepared to support their views by referring to specifics in the work and what they know of the context in which it was created.

For films and film excerpts: Before showing students a film or a portion of a film, provide a context for viewing the work. Make sure students know the title of the film and why you are showing it. If it is an excerpt, try to place it in the context of the film as a whole. As students watch the film, ask them to reserve judgments about the story or individuals in the film until it is over. Then have them use their journals to record what they remember about the film, what images or scenes stood out, and which individuals were memorable and why. Ask students what questions they have about the film. Encourage them to discuss their questions with others in the class. They might also consult books and articles about the historical context of the film. Then ask students to discuss their interpretations with their partner or with the class. They should be prepared to support their views by referring to specifics in the work and what they know of the context in which it was created.

IDENTITY CHARTS

Rationale
An identity chart is a graphic tool that helps students consider the factors that define an individual. It can be used to deepen students' understanding of themselves and other individuals. It can also be adapted to define the characteristics that shape group identity, including national identities. Sharing the charts students create with their peers can build relationships and break down stereotypes.

Procedure
Before creating identity charts, have the class brainstorm the categories we consider in responding to the question "Who am I?"—such as one's role in a family (e.g., daughter, sister, mother), hobbies and interests (e.g., guitar player, football fan), background (e.g., religion, race, nationality, hometown, or place of birth), and physical characteristics. You may wish to model the process by writing your name (or the name of someone students know or have studied) at the center of a sheet of poster paper. Around that name, write the words or phrases that describe the individual.

Ask students to create their own identity chart or one for someone they have recently studied. After sharing their charts with their classmates, have students make a list of the categories they used in creating their chart. Which categories were included on almost every chart? Which appeared on only a few charts? How might the words people used to describe an individual change as he or she learns new things, meets new people, and has new experiences? Reviewing and revising identity charts throughout a unit is one way to help students keep track of their learning.

If you want students to understand how the way others see us differs from the way we see ourselves, you may want to adapt the activity slightly by having students create an identity box. The inside of the box should contain the words and images that represent how one sees oneself. The outside of the box should indicate the words and images that others use to describe that individual.

Activities

Identity and change: After students have created an identity chart, you might ask them to select the five factors they think are most significant in shaping this individual's identity. Which factor or factors are likely to change over time? Which are unlikely to change? Have students explain their choices to a partner.

Identity and context: Some aspects of identity are more significant in one context than another. To help students understand this dynamic, ask them to list a few of the factors that shape their identity at school. How important are these aspects of their identity in other settings, such as home or when hanging out with friends?

JOURNALS IN THE FACING HISTORY CLASSROOM

Rationale

Journals play an important role in every Facing History and Ourselves course. Students use them to connect their personal responses and experiences to the concepts and events they are studying. They provide a safe, accessible space to process ideas, express feelings and uncertainties, formulate questions, and highlight information. And frequent journal writing can help students become more fluent in their writing.

Journals can also be a valuable assessment tool for both student and teacher. They reveal not only what students have learned but also what they are still struggling to understand and how their thinking has evolved over time. Through reading and commenting on journal entries, teachers build relationships with their students.

Procedure

Explain to students that they will be expected to keep a journal throughout the course. It is a place where they can record their responses to various resources and to class discussions. It is also place to raise questions, express feelings, and develop ideas. Some students confuse a classroom journal with a diary (or blog) because both formats allow for open-ended writing. It is important that students understand how the audience and purpose of a classroom journal differs from that of a personal diary. In most classrooms, the audience for journal writing is the author, the teacher, and (at times) fellow students. Therefore, material that may be appropriate for a personal diary is not suitable for a classroom journal. To avoid uncomfortable situations, many teachers remind their students that a teacher is obligated to take certain steps, such as informing a school official if students reveal information about possible harm to themselves or another student. Students should also be made aware of other regulations or guidelines used to determine whether the content of a journal is appropriate in your classroom.

Some teachers try to read students' journals nightly, while others collect journals once a week and read only a page or two—sometimes a page the student selects, and sometimes a page selected by the teacher. Still other teachers never collect journals; instead, they may glance at a page or two during class time or ask students to incorporate quotations and ideas from their journals into collected assignments. Students should also be asked in advance for permission to share any journal entry. Students may also indicate entries that they do not want the teacher or anyone else to read. If journals are to be graded, students should be informed in advance and told what criteria will be used.

Activities

Facing History teachers often use journal writing as an integral part of their classroom. They regard it as an essential tool for achieving a number of important objectives.

Building vocabulary: Journals can be a space for students to build their vocabulary by creating "working definitions" of key concepts. A working definition is one that evolves as students encounter new information and new experiences. Many teachers ask students to set aside a special section of their journal to record, review, expand, and refine their definitions of important terms.

Making connections: Journals provide a space for students to link their reading or viewing to their own lives. Many teachers encourage that process by asking students to respond to a provocative quotation from a reading or film in their journals. They also encourage their students to find a passage or scene that resonates with them and then explain its significance in their journals. For example: Why did you choose this quotation? What feelings does this scene evoke? What questions does it raise?

Brainstorming: Journals can be used to brainstorm. For example, to activate prior knowledge, students might be asked to list in their journals everything they know about a concept or an event. They can then edit, revise, and add to that list as the lesson progresses. As a strategy for reviewing a lesson or unit, have students detail everything they remember about a particular topic.

Free-writing is a form of brainstorming. The teacher asks students to write continuously on a particular topic for a certain amount of time without regard for spelling, style, or grammar. The strategy is sometimes used to collect initial thoughts and ideas on a topic, often as a preliminary to more formal writing. Free-writing can be helpful when students are asked to process particularly difficult material.

Creative writing: Many students enjoy writing poems or short stories that incorporate the themes addressed in a particular lesson. To get started, some students benefit from ideas that structure their writing, such as a specific poem format or an opening line for a short story.

Using drawings, charts, and webs: Students do not have to express their ideas in words. At appropriate times, encourage students to draw their ideas. They can also use symbols, concept maps, Venn diagrams, or other charts to record information.

PART TWO: Optional Strategies for Promoting Discussion

Hannah Arendt, one of the foremost political philosophers of her time, described the activity of thinking as a solitary endeavor—a dialogue with oneself in order to formulate moral principles. But in her view, interpretation and judgment require a dialogue with others. Facing History and Ourselves has found a number of strategies and activities useful in facilitating meaningful discussions. The primary goal of these strategies is to provide a structure for group discussions that not only enables every voice to be heard but also promotes active listening and opportunities to challenge ideas.

BIG PAPER

Rationale
Having a written conversation with their peers gives students an opportunity to focus on the views of others. The activity also creates a visual record of students' thoughts and questions that can be referred to later in the course. The strategy can also help engage students who are reluctant to speak out in class.

Procedure
The "stimulus" for a silent conversation among groups of two or three students can be an open-ended question, a quotation, a brief passage from a historical document, an image, or an excerpt from a novel, a poem, or other text. Each group may respond to a single stimulus or you may prefer to use several, each related to the same theme.

Introduce the activity by explaining that students will be engaging in a silent conversation. Once the activity begins, they may communicate with you or others in their group only in writing. They should speak only when you signal that it is now OK to talk. Allow plenty of time for students to ask questions about the activity to minimize the possibility that they will interrupt the silence later.

Provide each group with a copy of the stimulus taped to a large sheet of poster paper. Make sure that each student has a marker or pen. (Some teachers have each student in a group use a different colored marker, to make it easier to see the back-and-forth flow of the conversation.) Allow at least 15 minutes for the groups to read the text (or look at the image) and then, in silence, comment on it or ask questions of each other about it on the big paper. The written conversation must start with the stimulus but can stray to wherever students take it. Students can draw lines connecting a comment to a particular question or idea. Make sure that students know that more than one of them can write at the same time.

After 15 minutes, have students leave their own big paper and walk around the room silently reading others. Be sure that students bring their marker or pen with them so that they can write comments or questions.

Once students have completed their walk around the classroom, have students return to their own big paper and read comments left by their classmates. Now is the time to break the silence by initiating an open conversation about the stimulus and the way students responded to it. You may also want to debrief the process by asking what students learned from this activity.

Variation

Little Paper: With "Little Paper," the question, image, excerpt, or quotation is placed at the center of an 8½ x 11-inch sheet of paper. Each student in a group of four or five has a different quotation or excerpt. That student begins by "commenting" on his or her "stimulus" on the paper. After a few minutes, the paper is passed to the student on his or her left. This process is repeated until all of the students in the group have had an opportunity to comment on every paper in the group. All of this work is done in silence. Only after students have had a chance to read the comments of their peers on the little paper they had at the beginning of the activity is the silence broken. At this point, have the groups speak to one another about the questions and ideas that emerged from the activity.

Fishbowl

Rationale

Many teachers use the "fishbowl" to help students learn how to contribute to a discussion and actively listen to one. The strategy can help students reflect on what a "productive discussion" is like and provides a structure for discussing controversial or difficult topics. Fishbowls are also helpful in promoting research by raising questions or introducing new ideas that students can explore more deeply on their own.

Procedure

Begin the discussion with a prompt (an open-ended question or quotation). The most effective prompts are those that highlight multiple perspectives and spark a wide variety of opinions. For example, the fishbowl is an excellent strategy to use when discussing a dilemma.

Like many structured conversations, fishbowl discussions require preparation. Give students a few minutes to gather their thoughts on the topic. They should also prepare to be both a speaker and a listener. As speakers, they should be ready to explain their response to the prompt and ask questions of other speakers. As listeners, they need to pay attention to each response. What do the responses have in common? What questions do they raise? Every student should be aware of the guidelines that have been established for a respectful conversation.

Once preparations are complete, have students rearrange the furniture in the classroom by moving about half of the chairs into a circle (the "fishbowl") with enough room outside the circle for the remaining students to sit as they observe the conversation inside the fishbowl. Typically, having 6 to 12 students in the fishbowl allows for a range of perspectives while still giving each student an opportunity to ask questions, present opinions, and share information, while students outside the "bowl" listen carefully to the ideas presented and pay attention to the way the discussion unfolds. Sometimes teachers ask listeners to record specific aspects of the discussion process, such as the number of interruptions, the use of respectful language, or speaking times (e.g., Who speaks most often or least often?).

After ten minutes of discussion, some teachers ask students to reverse roles. At this point, the listeners enter the fishbowl and the speakers become the audience. (If the class is large, you may want students divided into three groups, with each taking its turn in the fishbowl.) Another common format is the "tap" system.

Students outside of the fishbowl gently tap a student on the inside, indicating that it is time to switch roles. After the discussion, ask students to reflect on what they learned from the discussion. How might they improve the discussion next time? Encourage students to also evaluate their own participation as both a listener and speaker. These reflections can be in writing, or can be structured as a small or large group conversation.

Variations

Opposing Positions: If a class is divided on an issue, some teachers use the fishbowl to give each side an opportunity to express its views while the other side listens. After ten minutes, the roles are reversed. The goal of this technique is for each group to gain insights into the perspectives held by the other side. After both sides have shared and listened, encourage each side to ask questions of students on the other side of the issue.

Multiple Perspectives: This technique can help students consider how one's perspective shapes the way one understands an issue or question. Begin by assigning students to small groups and give each an identity (young, old, male, female, industrialist, laborer, peasant, soldier, etc.) or a particular political or philosophical point of view. Then present the entire class with an issue or question for discussion. In responding to that issue or question, each group should represent its assigned perspective. After all of the groups have shared their ideas, encourage each to challenge the views of other groups or find common ground between their group and one or more of the other groups.

GALLERY WALK

Rationale
During a gallery walk, students explore multiple texts or images that have been placed around the classroom. This strategy is a useful way to have students share their work with peers, examine a variety of historical documents related to a single event or issue, or respond to a collection of quotations.

Procedure
Select the texts (such as quotations, images, documents, or student work) to be used for the gallery walk or have students, individually or in small groups, make the choices.

Provide students with instructions for examining the texts before the activity begins. If the objective is to introduce students to new material, you may want them to take informal notes as they move from one set of materials to another. If you would like students to take away particular information, you might create a graphic organizer for them to complete as they view the "exhibit" or compile a list of questions for them to answer based on the texts on display. Some teachers ask students to identify similarities and differences among a collection of texts. Others teachers give students a few minutes to tour the room and then, once seated, ask them to record their impressions.

Jigsaw

Rationale

The jigsaw teaching strategy asks a group of students to become "experts" on a specific text or body of knowledge and then share what they have learned with another group of students. These "learning" groups contain one student from each of the "expert" groups. Students often feel more accountable for learning new material when they are responsible for teaching it to their peers.

Procedure

Select the readings, images, charts, or other materials you want students to explore and then divide the class into groups of 3–5 students. "Expert" groups work best when students have clear expectations about the type of information they are supposed to present to their peers. Therefore, it may be helpful to provide a chart or a series of questions that students answer in their "expert" groups.

To avoid having students present inaccurate or misleading information, teachers may wish to review and approve the content before information is shared with students in the other groups. After expert groups have a solid understanding of the material they will be presenting, assign students to "learning" groups. "Learning" groups typically contain one or two members from each expert group, who take turns presenting information. Often teachers ask students to take notes while the experts present.

After students have heard from all of the experts, give each group an assignment that requires members to synthesize the information that they have shared, such as answering a larger question, comparing and contrasting texts, or generating a plan of action. Or you might ask students to draw from the material they just learned to answer a question about a particular moment in history and how it applies to the world today.

Think, Pair, Share

Rationale

This technique gives students the opportunity to respond thoughtfully to questions by discussing them with a partner before sharing with the larger group. This format helps students build confidence, encourages greater participation, and often results in more thoughtful discussions.

Procedure

Have students reflect on a particular question or write their response in their journals. Next, ask students to discuss their response with a partner. Then have the pair share its conversation with the class as a whole. The "Think-Pair-Share" is particularly appropriate for opening a discussion of a topic new to students, to gauge reactions to a reading or film, to tap prior knowledge, or to gather ideas before students begin a writing assignment.

APPENDIX
GLOSSARY

Alternate spellings of transliterated words appear in parentheses.

areyvut: From the Hebrew term *arev*, meaning "guarantor"; assuming responsibility (economic, social, and/ or emotional) for someone else.

baal teshuvah: Once a name for sinners who repent; now used to describe one who abandons secular ways and embraces Orthodox Judaism.

chavruta (*havruta*)*:* From the Aramaic word for "friendship"; a traditional rabbinic approach to Talmudic study in which a pair of students analyze and discuss a shared text.

chometz (*hametz*)*:* A food or drink that is forbidden on Passover.

dayan: A rabbi who serves as a judge on a religious court.

eruv (*eiruv*)*:* A string or wire encircling a Jewish community within which certain actions forbidden to Orthodox Jews on the Sabbath (such as carrying or pushing a stroller) are permitted. Plural: *eruvim* or *eiruvim*.

giyur: A formal act of conversion by a non-Jew in order be recognized as a full member of the Jewish community.

halachah: The body of Jewish religious laws including biblical and rabbinic laws as well as later customs and traditions.

hallel: From the Hebrew word for "praise"; refers to Psalms 113 through 118, which are sung during Jewish religious services on Passover and many other major Jewish holidays as an expression of joy and thanksgiving.

kasher: To make food kosher—that is, ritually fit for use as required by Jewish law.

kehillah: The Jewish community of a particular place. In Poland and other parts of Eastern Europe, every town had a *kehillah* that collected taxes, maintained institutions required by Jewish law, kept the peace, and administered charities. Today many Jewish communities rely on a *kehillah* to carry out communal work and maintain various charities. Plural: *kehillot*.

kehillah kedoshah: A holy or sacred community. In Eastern Europe, the term was used to describe the Jewish community as a whole because members saw themselves as more than a group bonded together by religion and ethnicity. They believed that they answered to a higher authority.

kiddush: The Hebrew word for "sanctification"; it is also the name of a prayer recited on Shabbat and holidays, usually accompanied by wine, that serves to sanctify the holy day.

kiddush haShem: The Hebrew words literally mean the "sanctification of the Name"; the phrase can describe any action that honors, shows respect for, and glorifies God. It has also come to mean "martyrdom."

kippah (*kipa*): A skull cap or *yarmulke* (a Yiddish word) traditionally worn by Orthodox men to fulfill the religious obligation of keeping one's head covered at all times, and by both men and women in Conservative and Reform congregations primarily during prayer and other religious rituals. Plural: *kippot.*

kitl (*kitel*): A white robe traditionally worn by men on Shabbat and high holidays to mark new beginnings. Some men are buried in a *kitl*, which then functions as a shroud.

matzah *(matza):* Unleavened bread traditionally eaten on Passover.

matzpun: A modern Hebrew word meaning "conscience."

megilah (*megillah*): A scroll containing the Book of Esther, which is read on the holiday of Purim.

mezuzah: Literally "doorpost"; the word has also come to refer to a piece of parchment rolled up in a small container and affixed to the doorframe in Jewish homes to fulfill a biblical *mitzvah* or commandment. The parchment is inscribed with passages from Deuteronomy (6:4–9 and 11:13–21) and marked with the word *Shaddai*, a name of the Almighty.

midrash: From the Hebrew root *d-r-sh*, meaning "examine"; a *midrash* is a story that fills in gaps in the biblical text, supplies missing details, and enlivens the text with personal anecdotes. A *midrash* falls into one of two categories: *midrash halachah* concerns matters of Jewish law and religious practice, and *midrash aggadah* concerns all other matters (including parables and stories that interpret the biblical narrative or explore questions of ethics). Plural: *midrashim.*

mikveh (*mikvah*): A pool of water made up, at least in part, of natural rainwater and built to exact specifications. Immersion in a *mikveh* is meant to purify, renew, or change the status of people such as brides, converts, or scribes.

minyan: A quorum of ten Jewish adults required for public prayers. In Orthodox services, only men are counted toward the *minyan*; in many Conservative and Reform services, both men and women are counted.

oneg shabbat: Literally, "the joy of Shabbat"; traditionally, the phrase refers to an informal gathering of Jews on Shabbat at which refreshments are served. It is also the code name of an underground group of Jews led by historian Dr. Emanuel Ringelblum in the Warsaw Ghetto which secretly chronicled life in the ghetto.

pardes (PaRDeS): The Hebrew word for "orchard"; the acronym refers to four different approaches to biblical text: *peshat* (plain or direct meaning of the text), *remez* (hints for a deeper, allegorical meaning of the text), *drash* (the use of *midrashim* to fill in gaps in the text), and *sod* (secret or mystical meaning given through revelation).

pikuach nefesh: The Jewish principle or law of preserving a human life. *Pikuach nefesh* overrides other religious considerations when the life of a person is in danger.

Purim: A Jewish holiday in early spring marked by readings from the Book of Esther.

Purim shpilers: Participants in the plays, comic acts, and parodies associated with Purim.

sefer hasidim: Literally the "book of the pious"; a book of moral tales, ethical sayings, and essays on religious topics that describe the ideal life of pious German Jews in the 12th and 13th centuries.

shalach manos (*mishloach manot*): Gifts of food and drink sent to friends, family, and acquaintances on Purim. Giving *shalach manos* is a *mitzvah* (a religious obligation) derived from the Book of Esther.

Shechinah (*Shekhinah, Shekina,* or *Schechinah*): Hebrew for "dwelling place"; the term is also used to denote the dwelling or settling presence of God.

shmurah matzah: A *matzah* that has been guarded under special supervision from the time the grain was harvested through the baking process.

shtrayml (*shtreimel*): A fur-trimmed hat worn by married men who are members of some Hasidic groups.

shiva: A week-long period of intense mourning for a parent, sibling, spouse, or child.

talis (*talit*): A prayer shawl. Plural: *talesim* (*tallitot*).

talis koton: Literally, "a small prayer shawl"; the term refers to a rectangular cloth with a hole for the neck and fringes on the four corners known as *tzitzit* that is worn by observant Jewish males.

tefilin: A set of small black boxes containing parchment scrolls with biblical passages written on them. They are an essential part of morning prayer services, and are worn on a daily basis (except Shabbat and festivals) by many Jews.

tikkun olam: Repairing the world, particularly as applied to the pursuit of social justice.

yirat elohim (*yirat shamayim*): Fear or awe of God.

zachor: Remember.

CREDITS

Hebrew texts reprinted from the *JPS Hebrew-English Tanakh: The Holy Scriptures* by permission of the University of Nebraska Press. Copyright 1985, 1999, 2000 by the Jewish Publication Society, Philadelphia.

Reprinted with the permission of Free Press, a Division of Simon & Schuster, Inc., from *HOW TO READ THE BIBLE: A Guide to Scripture, Then and Now* by James Kugel. Copyright © 2007 by James Kugel. All rights reserved.

Reprinted with the permission of Free Press, a Division of Simon & Schuster, Inc., from *A LETTER IN THE SCROLL: Understanding Our Jewish Identity and Exploring the Legacy of the World's Oldest Religion* by Rabbi Jonathan Sacks. Copyright © 2000 by Jonathan Sacks. All rights reserved.

Angela Warnick Buchdahl, "My Personal Story: Kimchee on the Seder Plate." Reprinted with permission from the journal *Sh'ma: A Journal of Jewish Responsibility (shma.com)*, June 2003, as part of a larger conversation on changing Jewish families.

Excerpt by Thomas Friedman was written for *I Am Jewish: Personal Reflections Inspired by the Last Words of Daniel Pearl*, © 2004 by Judea and Ruth Pearl. Reprinted with permission from Jewish Lights Publishing, Woodstock, VT, www.jewishlights.com.

Sarah Greenberg, "Growing Up Jewish," reprinted with permission from *CJ: Voices of Conservative/Masorti Judaism*, a joint publication of United Synagogue of Conservative Judaism, Women's League for Conservative Judaism, and the Federation of Jewish Men's Clubs.

Excerpts from *I Believe In…Christian, Jewish, and Muslim Young People Speak About Their Faith* by Pearl Gaskins reprinted with permission from CRICKET Books, Carus Publishing Company, text © 2004 by Pearl Gaskins.

Excerpt by Kerri Strug was written for *I am Jewish: Personal Reflections Inspired by the Last Words of Daniel Pearl* © 2004 by Judea and Ruth Pearl. Reprinted with permission from Jewish Lights Publishing, Woodstock, VT USA, www.jewishlights.com

James Berry, "What Do We Do With a Variation?" from *When I Dance*. Reprinted with permission from Peters Fraser & Dunlop (www.petersfraserdunlop.com) on behalf of James Berry.

Excerpt from *Civility: Manners, Morals, and the Etiquette of Democracy*, © 1998 Stephen Carter. Reprinted with permission from Basic Books, a member of the Perseus Books Group.

Excerpts from *Jewish Literacy: The Most Important Things to Know About the Jewish Religion, Its People, and Its History* reprinted with permission from author Rabbi Joseph Telushkin.

Jewish Life in Germany: Memoirs from Three Centuries reprinted with permission from Indiana University Press via Copyright Clearance Center.

Hanna Bergas, quoted in *Between Dignity and Despair: Jewish Life in Nazi Germany,* reprinted courtesy of the Leo Baeck Institute and with permission from Oxford University Press, Inc.

Hertha Nathorff, quoted in *Between Dignity and Despair: Jewish Life in Nazi Germany*, reprinted with permission from Oldenbourg Wissenschaftsverlag (Munich © 1987) and Oxford University Press, Inc.

Jonathan Sacks, *Covenant & Conversation: A Weekly Reading of the Jewish Bible.* Reprinted with permission from Maggid Books, a division of Korean Publishers.

Sandy Eisenberg Sasso, *God's Echo: Exploring Scripture with Midrash,* © 2007 by Sandy Eisenberg Sasso. Reprinted with permission from Paraclete Press www.paracletepress.com.

Excerpts from *The Courage to Care: Rescuers of Jews during the Holocaust,* eds. Carol Rittner and Sondra Myers. Reprinted with permission, © 1986 by New York University.

Zofia Kossak-Szczucka, translated and quoted in Nechama Tec, *When Light Pierced the Darkness: Christian Rescue of Jews in Nazi Occupied Poland.* Reprinted with permission from Oxford University Press, Inc.

Shimon Huberband, *Kiddush Hashem: Jewish Religious and Cultural Life in Poland During the Holocaust.* Reprinted with permission by Zborowski Chair, Holocaust Studies, Yeshiva University.

Excerpts from *SURVIVING THE HOLOCAUST: THE KOVNO GHETTO DIARY* by Avraham Tory, edited by Martin Gilbert, translated by Jerry Michalowicz, with textual and historical notes by Dira Porat, pp. 7-8, Cambridge, Mass.: Harvard University Press, Copyright © 1990 by the President and Fellows of Harvard College. Reprinted by permission of the publisher.

Excerpts from *In a Different Light* and *Samual Bak: The Landscape of Jewish Experience* copyright Pucker Gallery Inc, Boston, MA. Reprinted with permission from Pucker Gallery Inc, Boston, MA.

"The Past," in *Facing Shadows*. Reprinted with permission from Hanging Loose Press.

Elie Wiesel, "When Memory Brings People Together" in *From the Kingdom of Memory* Copyright © 1990 by Elirion Associates, Inc. Used by permission of Georges Borchardt, Inc., on behalf of Elie Wiesel.

Excerpts from "No Religion Is an Island" from *MORAL GRANDEUR AND SPIRITUAL AUDACITY* by Abraham Joshua Heschel. Copyright © 1996 Sylvia Heschel. Introduction copyright © 1996 by Susannah Heschel. Reprinted by permission of Farrar, Straus and Giroux, LLC.